Berlin Dance of Death

BERLIN DANCE OF DEATH

by

Helmut Altner

Translated, annotated and illustrated by

Tony Le Tissier

CASEMATE
Havertown, PA

Published by
CASEMATE
2114 Darby Road, Havertown, PA 19083

ISBN 0-9711709-4-0

Printed in the U.S.A.

Contents

List of Maps

Photo Credits

Translator's private collection, except No 5 (RAF Museum, Hendon), Nos 6, 23 and 32 (Heimat Museum, Spandau), and all Falkenhagener Heide pictures (Herr Jürgen Fiehne, Seelow Museum)

Introduction

This is a teenager's vivid account of his experiences as a conscript during the final desperate weeks of the Third Reich, during which he experienced training immediately behind the front line east of Berlin, was caught up in the massive Soviet assault on Berlin from the Oder, retreated successfully, and then took part in the fight for the western suburb of Spandau, where he became one of the only two survivors of his company of 17-year-olds. He later fought in the U-Bahn tunnels and in the battle for the Reichssportfeld. Then, on the morning the city capitulated, he took part in the breakout to the west that turned into a bloodbath for soldiers and civilians alike. Wounded, he was captured near Brandenburg on 3 May 1945.

The detailed description of his experiences makes it still possible today – over fifty years later – to walk in his footsteps. His book, based on notes made in a diary that survived eighteen months of Soviet captivity, was originally published in Offenbach in the spring of 1948 after clearance with the US Military Government and the necessary allocation of paper to print it on.

Helmut Altner's account ties in with events outside his knowledge as a simple soldier, so I have supplemented his text in this revised edition with notes, drawings, appendices and photographs. His regimental command post, for example, was located in an underground factory that had last been used for assembling V-Weapons, but had actually been intended for the production of poison gas and eventually was to be used by the Soviet Army as a secret headquarters in case of nuclear warfare.

Two words or expressions used in the translation will perhaps strike today's reader as rather odd: 'child' as applied to a 17-year-old and 'comrade'. At the time of the Third Reich there was no word for teenager in the German language, and the use of the word 'comrade' has been maintained from the original German text as it had a specific meaning for the German soldier for which I can find no adequate English equivalent.

Tony Le Tissier
Frome
February 2002

CHAPTER I
Called Up

Thursday 29 March 1945

Berlin seems to be falling apart at the seams. The nightly bombing raids have inflicted far greater damage than the official communiques indicate. According to them only a few buildings in Spandau have been destroyed, but the actual situation looks far worse. The U-Bahn is running irregularly, and half hour delays are no exception, while the S-Bahn, with most of the tracks damaged beyond recognition, is almost completely at a standstill.[1]

I am standing hemmed in between thrusting, pushing passengers on an S-Bahn train between Velten and Hennigsdorf. My luggage, which consists of a Persil carton containing something to eat and some underwear, is stuffed somewhere in the carriage's luggage rack.[2] At Hennigsdorf I am forced out unto the platform by the rush and have to use my elbows ruthlessly to get back in to recover my baggage and then jump off the already moving train.

I follow the stream of people down the steps to the station exit, the call-up papers in my pocket already making me feel as if I no longer belong with these people. I make my way to the tram stop from where a tram should take me to where I have to report. The traffic island is already full of people who cram into the tram when it arrives. As everywhere in the Berlin street scene, the field-grey uniform predominates.

After a short while the conductor rings the bell and we move off. I stand on the rear platform and can see the road go by. We leave Hennigsdorf behind us and pass through meadows and woodland to where Route 120 comes to an end and the connecting tram is waiting for us. Soon the first villas in Spandau appear and we can see the consequences of last night's bombing. Ripped apart sections of woodland and shattered venerable old oak trees bear witness to the destructive effectiveness of modern explosives. Then burning houses whisk by, attended to by troops of soldiers and Hitlerjugend armed with fire-extinguishing equipment, while several boys in uniform collect up torn apart pieces of human bodies and a 12-year-old stands by calmly eating his breakfast roll.

1

The tram stops and we have to get off. I take my carton and go on past the wagon. Several metres farther on the overhead cables have been destroyed and are strewn across the road. We will have to wait to see how we can go on.

A few others with Persil cartons have got off the tram with me, and after some hesitant glances, contact is established; we all have the same goal.

With a combined effort we manage to stop a truck, which quickly fills with people converging from all directions, men and women that are clearly moving out of certain areas and others wanting to visit their relatives in the bombed parts of the city to find out if they are still alive. Every vehicle we come across is full of exhausted people. Rumours, every one worse than the other, swirl about us, making us even more unsettled than before.

We rapidly approach the centre of Spandau and here, for the first time, we see the powerful extent of the damage. The empty window frames of a burnt-out factory across the way stare accusingly at the world, fallen beams glowing gently and occasionally flaring up with the breeze, while the owners of a still burning house watch from across the street speechlessly as the fruits of years of hard toil go sky high. Dark figures slink through the destroyed quarter, looking about them furtively like hyenas on the prowl. Berlin, the nerve centre of the Reich, has been turned upside down.

The farther we penetrate this destroyed, burning quarter, the more depressed we get by the atmosphere. Women are crying quietly, stopping people to ask anxiously about certain streets and if many have been killed. They are answered in low voices. One no longer recognises in these faces the heroism mentioned so often by Goebbels in the first years of the war.[3] On the contrary, one sees only a dull, undisguised despair.

We have to leave the truck just before the town hall, where it turns quickly down a side street. We shoulder our cartons and ask our way to the von Seeckt-Kaserne.[4] As we pass Spandau town hall, Civil Defence and Fire Brigade personnel are trying to extinguish the fire in part of the building that is burning like a torch. The streets are strewn with glass splinters and rubble, and people rush by, thoughtlessly trampling the first signs of greenery thrusting through the earth all around them.

The destruction extends as far as the S-Bahn line and then stops abruptly as if drawn with a ruler. On the far side of the line the only reminders of the war are the street barriers and the barracks. At the guardroom of the splendidly built barracks, the conscripts' call-up papers are taken from them and returned stamped with the date and time of arrival. I am a soldier now and there is no turning back.

I go along the smooth asphalt street. Soldiers' voices come quietly from the large blocks on the left, and on the right a platoon marches across the square to the cookhouse. At the far end of this gigantic barracks, complex

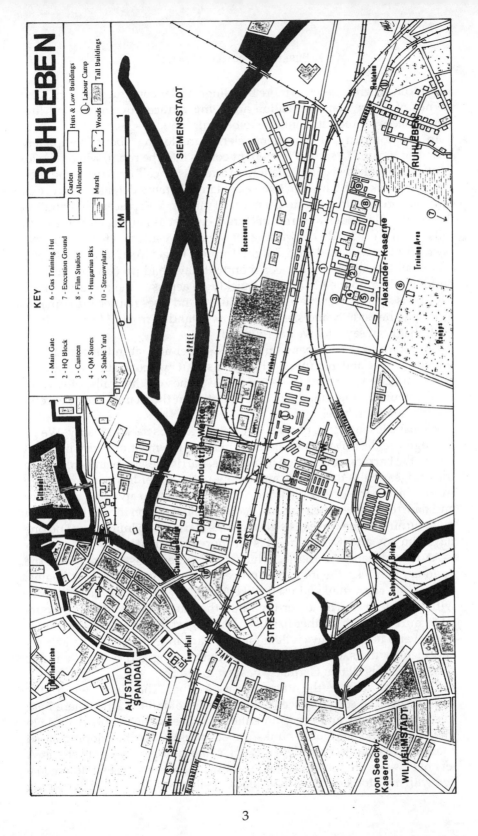

RUHLEBEN

KEY

1 - Main Gate
2 - HQ Block
3 - Canteen
4 - QM Stores
5 - Stable Yard

6 - Gas Training Hut
7 - Execution Ground
8 - Film Studios
9 - Hungarian Bks
10 - Stresowplatz.

☐ Garden Allotments
☐ Huts & Low Buildings
Ⓛ - Labour Camp
Marsh
Woods
Tall Buildings

KM

SIEMENSSTADT

SPREE

Racecourse

Alexander-Kaserne

Training Area

RUHLEBEN

Ragpis

Citadel

Deutsche Industrie Werke

Freiheit

D I W

Charlotten Brücke

Spandau

Schönwalder Brücke

STRESOW

Martinskirche

New Hall

ALTSTADT SPANDAU

HAVEL

Spandau-West

WILHELMSTADT

von Seeckt-Kaserne

3

scaffolding surrounds even more buildings under construction. While the homes of the civilian population are being reduced by smoke and fire, new palaces for recruits continue to be built.

In the company office several clerks are lolling about, completely ignoring me until a second lieutenant comes into the room, when they all contrive to look busy. The subaltern examines my call-up papers and then snarlingly asks me why I am two hours late. Then my details are recorded and I am ordered to report to Grenadier Training & Replacement Battalion 309[5] in the Alexander-Kaserne[6] at Ruhleben. Just as I am leaving, the clerk tells me that my Mother is waiting for me in the canteen. I feel as if I have been hit. Overwhelmed with delight, I almost forget to salute as I dash out.

It is all too much at once. For months I have had no news of her and suddenly I am to see her again. I quickly go across to the canteen, where Mother is sitting at a table eating her lunch and does not see me come in. I go up to her slowly and she looks up as I stand in front of her. 'Mother!' is all that I can say, and we are reunited.

We return to the company building together and sit in the corridor. A whistle blows and recruits dash past us, but we continue talking, the world outside forgotten. There are battle scenes on the walls, of cavalry with colourful, fluttering flags and infantry on the march: how peaceful the war seems in here!

We have lost all sense of time, but a clerk calls us back to reality. We go through the destroyed town quietly, making the most of every moment before the barracks gates close behind me. Barricades are being erected on the bridges across the Havel, and below in the water lies a sunken barge from which bare-legged men and women are busy salvaging preserves and ham to augment their rations. A dead man floats on the slightly raised bow, turning in the waves, his glazed eyes staring into infinity, but no one pays him any attention, for food is far more important.

At the Alexander-Kaserne, which is of older construction than the Spandau barracks, the induction process through various offices begins. Every little clerk thinks himself God Almighty, exercising his authority with a loud voice. The lower the rank, the louder the voice. Two hours later, during which Mother has been waiting, standing in the corridor, it is all over. I have lost my civilian identity card in exchange for a paybook and identity discs. Other new arrivals, both young and old, jostle in the corridor. Is this all that Germany has left to offer?

I climb the stairs to the attic with my Mother. The higher we go, the more dismal the corridors seem. It is bitterly cold in the attic where I am to spend the night, and every time the door opens, the windows rattle in their frames. Some double bunks are scattered about the sloping-sided room with a couple of doorless lockers, some tables and wobbly stools. A few old sweats are sitting at a table talking about the war. I sit down on a bed with my Mother and we look about us silently in the slowly darkening light. Behind us we hear the voices of some soldiers who have lit candles. None of them believe in victory any more, and they say that they will desert as soon as they can.

Mother is desolated by the wretched surroundings, the old sweats' talk, the atmosphere. She turns to me sadly: 'You won't experience much happiness, my boy, but my best wishes go with you all the same.' Then it is time for her to leave, so we go down the stairs slowly and out into the starlit night. The sound of voices comes from the brightly lit barrack-rooms and somewhere a flute is trilling. My worried Mother tells me to look after myself. We look each other in the eyes once more, a final handshake and the outline of her beloved figure fades slowly in the darkness.

Friday 30 March 1945

I am woken up at seven o'clock by the shrill whistle of the orderly sergeant. The morning light is showing through the small windows. At last we new conscripts are issued with the eating utensils and the blankets that we needed so badly the night before, but yesterday the high and mighty quartermaster had had no time for us.

We are given some hot coffee and told to fall in. It occurs to me that today is Good Friday, the weather matching the occasion with a dull, overcast sky.

We newcomers in civilian clothes have to parade on the right flank of the company on the square. A fat sergeant major sorts us out as we stand all mixed up together, 16-year-olds next to 60-year-olds: Germany's last hope!

Our group is assigned to a very young sergeant, who marches us to the medical centre for inoculations. We take off our clothes in the anteroom, which reeks of sweat and leather, and wait freezing for the inoculations to begin. At last we are admitted in threes to the treatment room, where an elderly medical officer with the typical grating tone of a professional soldier looks us over quickly and declares: 'Fit!' In the next room we each get three injections against cholera, typhus and malaria, one in each arm and one in the left nipple. The doctor and medical orderlies work like machines. 'Fit'? injections – stamp in the Pay Book – 'The next – quicker!' They do not see bodies any more, just numbers, flesh destined for slaughter.

I am not affected by these injections and tackle the tasty pea soup at midday with a healthy appetite, but many of the others are, and cannot eat their lunch: all the more for us. They have pains in their arms and are white-faced, their bodies lacking the reserves to take this kind of treatment.

In the afternoon we get our first items of uniform from the

5

quartermaster's stores. The individual items are thrown at us after a quick appraisal of the figure. 'OK? Out!' It is only when we get back to the barrack-room that we can really see the things properly. My jacket is too big and flaps around my body, the sleeves reaching down to my fingertips. On the other hand, the trousers barely reach my knees and the boots pinch. 'OK?' I am not the only one. Most of my comrades look either as if they are scarecrows or wearing their first school uniforms. Only by exchanging items can we gradually achieve some semblance of reasonable dress. Now all but the boots fit me, but two of the boys face the daunting task of returning to the quartermaster's stores to ask for exchanges.

Late afternoon we get an issue of ten cigarettes and some schnapps to celebrate the holiday, the youngsters also getting extra bread and fat with their cold rations. In the evening I go along to the well decorated canteen for a beer. Furtively, I examine an old serviceman sitting at my table with blond hair and a squarish head, obviously a sailor with the blue of the sea mirrored in his eyes, and I get talking to him. He is 58 and comes from Hamburg. His name, Hermann Windhorst, sounds of storms and the sea.

'Retreat' sounds and we have to leave the canteen and go to bed. He is in the same barrack-room as myself, and in the same corner, so it is surprising that I have not seen him before.

I am woken up by noise and swearing during the night. Whistles are shrilling in the building and out on the square as the last notes of the air raid sirens sound. Drunk with sleep I climb into my boots and feel my way through the darkened room down the stairs. One can already hear the sound of engines in the darkness, Mosquitos.[7] Several bombs explode in the city centre and searchlights sweep the skies. Two hours later we return to our beds tired and frozen through.

Saturday 31 March 1945

At breakfast there is sweet milk soup for a change which, tired and hungry, we eat gladly. Further items of equipment are to be issued during the morning, and we are expected to appear in uniform for lunch.

Back in the barrack-room I pack my last items of civilian clothing with a last somewhat painful thought as I close the carton. Farewell civilian life! I am now a soldier. The last barrier has fallen.

Shortly before midday we suddenly have to parade again. Our platoon has to go to Spandau for blood tests. While new arrivals are coming in every day, our platoon is naturally not fully in uniform, so we march separated, ourselves in front, the civilians behind, each with a sergeant as the right marker and Staff Sergeant Becker as the Platoon Commander. It is a lovely sunny day, real spring weather, and the people on the street stop and watch our mixed marching column, some eyeing the youngsters in grey uniform with sad expressions.

Spandau is busy. Anti-tank barriers are being constructed on the Havel bridges[8] ready for closing, and engineers are setting demolition charges. Preparations for defence in the middle of the city, and yet we are being told daily that we are winning?

Several groups are standing in the von Seeckt-Kaserne, waiting like us to be dealt with, while recruits are being put through their paces on the drill square by sergeant majors and sergeants. I recognise several of them from Labour Service.[9]

Now it is our turn. We go in single file past a medical orderly, who pricks us in the forefinger and squeezes out a drop of blood, then a bit farther on we stick our fingers in a jar filled with a light liquid. Afterwards the medical orderly tells each one his blood group. I am A.

We march back in formation to the barracks, where our blood groups are stamped on our identity disks in the armoury. Then it is time for lunch. We stand in a long queue in front of the cookhouse with soldiers coming in from all directions. The Hungarians stationed in the barracks form a separate group. A few soldiers at the back of our queue start a quarrel with them, provoking a heated response from these sons of the Balkans. The result is that they now have to wait until all the Germans have been served. They stand aside angrily with hungry eyes, the remains of a once so proud Hungarian Army who now go about in torn brown uniforms and with dark eyes reflecting their longing for the wide expanse of their homeland. They have no rights and are beaten and kept apart from their German superiors, intimidated and anxious.[10]

In the afternoon the recruits are summoned from their various barrack-rooms. We move together to the medical centre, where we get straw from other barrack-rooms to stuff our palliasses. I have picked out the best sleeping place, protected on three sides with only a small gap giving access to my bed, so that I do not have to be afraid that the orderly sergeant will give me a rough awakening one morning. My upper bunk mate is a Berlin High School boy with whom I share a large locker and the first thing we do is to store our things in it for the present.

After we have been released from duty, I go to the canteen with him, where we meet another of his school friends, and together we raise a few glasses and drink to brotherhood – Heinz Boy my locker mate, Fritz Stroschn, Günther Gremm and myself. With darkness the canteen fills up and the tobacco smoke is thick enough to cut with a knife, so we go outside and arrive just in time for the issue of the evening rations. In our barrack-room ages range from 17 to 35 and the sharing out of rations proceeds with an astonishing lack of friction. Later on we sit and eat our supper by the light of a flickering candle while behind us there is a game of Pontoon being played at the table. A pleasant Organisation Todt[11] man, still in his brown uniform and in civilian life a ship's cook, laughingly loses trick after trick. The banker, a witty railwayman whom we call

Alfons, smilingly gathers in the winnings. But fortune is capricious, and when Stroschn has a try, he wins 30 RM off him in one go. Then this idyll is shattered when someone bursts into the room with the cry 'Orderly sergeant!' and money and cards vanish like lightning.

The candle burns gently. I have lain down on my bed and hear my comrades talking as an indistinct murmuring in my subconscience. No sooner has the barrack-room orderly swept the room and reported to the orderly sergeant than the sirens sound and we have to dive into our things and go down to the shelter together.

There one soldier relates how he was member of a court martial after 20 July 1944 and sentenced 108 soldiers to death. 'All asked to be sent to a Punishment Battalion,' he says, 'hoping to eventually survive that way, but if things went badly they would be shot anyway.'[12]

Bomb explosions sound quite near. When the 'All Clear' sounds the sky is full of light, for some buildings are burning in the east with red-gold smoke far into the night. One can hear sirens howling in the distance as the metropolis breathes out and climbs out of its cellars once more.

Sunday 1 April 1945

Today is Easter Sunday. The weather is misty and it looks like rain. We get a special celebratory sweet soup for breakfast. There is not much food and we are always hungry. It tastes good enough, but the larder is bare.

We are off duty. Stroschn and I sort out our locker, folding and arranging our things in apple pie order with the smaller items stuffed in behind out of sight.

Then the staff sergeant summons us below to make a tour of the barracks. He shows us the rifle ranges in the exercise area next to the buildings, where a Labour Service flak unit has its guns deployed, and the boys of the Home Defence Flak[13] swagger past us in their flashy blue uniforms with white neckerchiefs. Beyond is a tank wreck used as a target for Panzerfausts.[14]

There is a neat group of houses just below the Reichssportfeld escarpment, whose windows glint in the light of the sunshine as it breaks through. People are standing around in their Sunday clothes, their laughter carrying across to us, but there is an unbridgeable gulf between us.

We stop next to a clump of bushes with a few withered pine trees, where three posts have been rammed into the ground. This is the capital's Execution Place No. 5, where deserters, traitors and saboteurs are shot. The wood of the posts is splintered by bullets and dark streams of blood stick to them as if burnt on. The soil is dark red. Human blood![15]

We march back in somewhat thoughtful mood. Some guns are standing rusting in the woods beside the rifle ranges. Why are they not being used? Nobody seems to know.

For lunch there are boiled potatoes, meat and gravy, with pudding to follow. Later the sergeant gives out the cold rations for supper together with a special issue of twenty cigarettes, a quarter litre of schnapps and half a bottle of wine each. Now we can really celebrate Easter.

In the afternoon I lie on my bed and read. Boy has a visitor and with Stroschn we eat the celebration cake that has been brought for him. When she is leaving, his Mother asks us to take care of her son, which we gladly promise, but Boy is embarrassed. In the evening we go to the canteen and discuss our uncertain future with Hermann, who is also there.

Shortly before 'Retreat' the sergeants return drunk to the barracks from the city. Only 'The Scarecrow', whose overlarge uniform flaps around his body, is still sober. His girlfriend came to visit him at midday and he has been otherwise engaged.

Monday 2 April 1945

Easter Monday, the day of peace and spring, has lost its meaning in this murderous world.

In the morning we take our cartons of civilian clothes to the company office to be sent on by post to our next of kin. I go back to the quarter-master's stores once more and press some cigarettes into the hands of the relaxed-looking sergeant major. Now I can sort out a new greatcoat and some good trousers for myself. How the holiday – and some cigarettes – can change the demeanour of some people!

As I am about to return to my barrack-room, a grey-brown column of soldiers wheels into the square singing mournfully. These troops go past singing in brand new uniforms with shiny SS collar patches and white fur hats. These are not German voices, nor is the song German. They are Vlassov Troops – Russians.[16] In their mournful singing, in which the lead singer starts off and the refrain is taken up powerfully by the rest, breathe the vast distances and plains of the Russian landscape. These Russians are officer cadets in the Vlassov Army, an army that hardly exists any more. They have been trained to use German weapons and are just like the Hungarians – cannon-fodder.

At lunchtime, like yesterday, there is food again. The sergeants go out once more on a city pass and 'The Scarecrow' has a visitor again. When we go to collect our cold rations, we catch him in a not quite ready condition for receiving visitors and discreetly withdraw.

Later I lie on my bed and doze. Then Boy, Stroschn and myself go along to the canteen together to write postcards to our Mothers before returning to the barrack-room and trying our luck at cards. By bidding carefully I win RM 30. Today's issue of alcohol helps the congenial atmosphere, which is peaceful. We three friends play another game of Skat together, and later Staff Sergeant Becker comes along and joins in. Boy and myself are the barrack-room orderlies, so shortly before ten we chase everyone to bed and sweep out. The staff sergeant inspects the room and we are dismissed, switch off the lights and are soon fast asleep.

Tuesday 3 April 1945

Today our training is to begin. The day hardly starts well, for Sergeant Rytn has a hangover and is in a bad mood. After we have drawn our morning coffee, he marches us ten times round the barrack block with our steaming mess tins singing the same song over and over again.

The other companies are already falling in outside their barrack blocks, and we are cold with anger. Just because this youngster, no older than ourselves, wears a sergeant's insignia on his collar, we are entirely at his mercy. One could cry with mortification.

We have no time left for breakfast. We swallow down our cold coffee and fall in again. Then we have to collect equipment from the armoury – ammunition pouches with ten rounds, gas masks and gas capes. The sirens go off while these items are being issued and we go to the bunkers. We can see the first Mosquitos flying east like flies in the sky. When the 'All Clear' sounds the sun is shining brightly on the earth and a few giant mushrooms of smoke are rising above the city centre.

Staff Sergeant Becker has the youngsters fall in. The others can go back to barracks with the sergeants. It seems that something special has been lined up for us.

As we march off toward the ranges, Staff Sergeant Becker explains to us that an execution is to take place today and we have to watch. He adds with a smile that our company commander, Lieutenant Stichler, has given the order for this in order to strengthen our nerves.

A small grey van with barred windows is standing under the trees next to the ranges. We stand on the edge of the woods and keeep quiet. The door of the van opens. Three men in green denims are sitting along one side, a grey-haired civilian, the padre, and an SS staff sergeant on the other. When one of the prisoners gets out, we can see that he is wearing handcuffs. Behind him is the SS staff sergeant with a pistol. The prisoner says something to him with a smile and gets slowly back into the van.

The waiting gradually makes us nervous, and the chatting has stopped. Two SS men, former comrades, appear and shake the prisoners by the hand once more. Then they vanish between the trees. It all seems unreal to me – the woods, the birds singing, the sun in a cobalt blue sky. And we have to wait to see how men are murdered, the spectacle diminished as if it were nothing more than a play at an annual fair.

Our staff sergeant speaks with the SS escort. He tells us that this morning one of the prisoners tried to escape during his medical examination and was knocked down in the doctor's waiting room. All prisoners have to be declared medically fit before they are shot. What a mockery of humanity! One has to be physically fit in order to be shot!

The hastily assembled firing squad, formed from all the companies, marches up from the barracks. The task is not liked and everyone tries to avoid it. Only one tall, freckled soldier has volunteered.

We wait for the Judge-Advocate officer to appear. An open-sided truck comes round the corner carrying the three coffins, whose black polish gleams in the sun. We watch the prisoners, who are paying no attention to their surroundings but hanging on the lips of the padre as if they were already in another, better world.

At last the vehicle appears with the doctor, the Judge-Advocate officer and a clerk. The officer jumps down lightly, the sun reflected on his gleaming, patent leather jackboots. He casually touches a finger to his cap and looks briefly at the van, then beckons the clerk and walks to the execution place.

The occupants of the van climb out. With the padre praying beside them they slowly go towards the firing squad. They are all wearing handcuffs. Loud commands ring out over the area. The firing squad has taken up position and the three open sides of the square are covered by two men to prevent an escape. Quietly, as if not to disturb anyone, the staff sergeant gives us his orders and we move up to the execution place. We take position to the right of the firing squad with the smaller ones in front so that everyone can see. A few officers' wives stand around chatting: 'An exciting show, isn't it Mrs Lieutenant?'

The prisoners shake the padre's hand for the last time. He raises his hands in blessing and draws back. The Judge-Advocate officer stands in front of the the posts with his clerk and leafs through his papers with the prisoners standing in front of him. The three men's fate will be determined in the next few seconds. They can still be reprieved even with the execution posts staring them in the face.

The silence is uncanny. Everyone watches the group of men, hardly daring to breathe. Even the women have gone quiet and hang on the lips of the Judge-Advocate officer. He clears his throat and the words drop one by one into the silence: 'Sentenced to death by shooting. The appeal for clemency has been rejected.'

The words hang in the air for several seconds. The condemned men have hung their heads. The youngest is 18, the others not much older. The officer withdraws and the clerk vanishes into the crowd. Three soldiers step forward and release the handcuffs. The denim jackets are removed and they place themselves at the posts, two pale-skinned, well-developed youngsters with blue eyes, the third a smaller, frailer lad. They are fastened to the posts with leather straps, their chests trembling under their thin shirts. Once more they look at the bright sunny day. Their children's eyes take in the beauty of the morning as a memory to take with them to the other world.

11

The firing squad takes aim. 'Goodbye, comrades!' a high-pitched voice calls out and then the officer's shining dirk drops. 'Fire!' Suddenly all the posts are empty and blood runs from the wood as if it itself has been killed. The doctor checks the shot men. The little one raises himself once more and blood flows from his mouth. The doctor puts his pistol to his temple and presses the trigger. The shot sounds muffled.

Sharp orders ring out and the firing squad withdraws. I have a bitter taste in my mouth and, as we march back, we all look unnaturally pale.

A truck overtakes us by the barrack gate with its cargo of three coffins.

Back in our barrack-room we move around in silence. The older men bombard us with questions but get no answers, and at noon we are unable to eat anything. But the Judge-Advocate officer sits in the dining room with his cheeks stuffed full, cracking jokes.

The lieutenant arrives after lunch. Some of the men are to be sworn in and tomorrow they are off to the front, but none are from our barrack-room and they are all older men. The dining room is decorated with the Reichs War Flag on the wall and two machine guns set in front of it. The persons concerned undergo a big kit check prior to be sworn in.

I go to the canteen with Boy and buy two pounds of salted herrings, and then we drink of litre of beer to give the fish something to swim in. We have to get sozzled to forget what has happened. When we get back the swearing-in ceremony is already over and addresses are being exchanged. Friendships had been made, but now everything is being torn apart again. Such is the lot of a soldier!

At night I lie sleepless on my bed. The moon hangs like a yellow disk in the sky. I see the youngsters at the posts in front of me, how their chests rise and fall, how their eyes seek the blue of the skies. And their end. Will it happen to me too? Should I weaken, I would prefer death from an honourable bullet.

Gradually the day dawns and I fall into a light semi-sleep. The duty NCO's whistle blows and I get up still tired.

Wednesday 4 April 1945

This morning everything has to be at the double. The sergeants go through the barrack-rooms urging haste. We get our breakfast soup and quickly get it down. Then at 0800 hours the older ones fall in in front of the building. We go through their ranks once more and shake the hands of this one and that. Many have their cartons of civilian clothes with them. Are they taking them off to the front? The staff sergeant comes along and we pull back. The sergeants then go through the ranks checking that their equipment is correctly fastened. Then Lieutenant Stichler arrives and Staff Sergeant Becker makes his report. The company commander makes his farewell and announces their destination: Frankfurt on the Oder. These recruits are being sent into the front line to be trained in accordance with a Führer-Order.

Orders are given. We step back and escort them as far as the barrack gate. The sun breaks through as the Russians march in singing for their training. Life goes on.

We return to our barrack-rooms, but on the way a young SS staff sergeant, whose cap is not worn regulation straight, chases us several times round the barracks. We then sit about in our barrack-rooms until about 1000 hours. A group of comrades gather round the table in our room and play cards until Staff Sergeant Becker disturbs our peace. We have to have our hair cut, but Stroschn and Boy decide to try and dodge this. I have the matchstick length of the Labour Service, but who knows when I will get another opportunity.

I put on my cap and go to the battalion headquarters, where the barber has his place in an undamaged part of the burnt-out building. I am already sitting down in front of the mirror with an apron over me when two quartermasters come in and I have to get up again and let their lordships, who receive an immediate greeting, take my place. Recruits fall into the lowest category and have to wait their turn. When I eventually emerge, it is with a real Prussian haircut.

Before lunch we receive orders to clean out a barrack-room in the East Block, whose occupants were sent off to the front several days ago leaving behind torn palliasses, upturned broken lockers and strewn bedding. The room is full of dust and we hurry to get out of the dirt. From time to time a sergeant sticks his head through the door and barks out orders. We pay no attention until he is reinforced by two other sergeants and stands in the room screaming at us. We stand to attention and listen quietly, each one thinking: 'Go to hell!', but adopting expressions of eager attention to duty mixed with a modicum of contriteness, until he runs out of steam. Then the three of them vanish together leaving behind in a corner several palliasses that they have ripped apart so that a cloud of dust creeps slowly through the room.

These 'indispensable' shirkers are all the same. The louder the mouth, the more essential they become for the barrack square, something of which they are fully aware. In the barracks there are more 'indispensables', clerks, orderlies, instructors and storemen rather than simple soldiers, all clinging to their roles like drowning men to the last straw, terrified of being sent to the front. Sometimes I would like to punch them in the face.

After a short lunch of dried vegetables, we have to clean out the filthy dining room, where potato peelings have been lying about for days, while in the kitchen the fat cook munches a meat ball with the fat running down his cheeks, making our mouths water.

By the time we have finished, the guard is being mounted. The

13

Hungarians come in for a meal and shyly make way for us, but their eyes glimmer with anger, their officers only holding them back with difficulty. Poor chaps, but watch out when that volcano erupts!

Then our platoon parades for duty with gas masks and capes. We are down to 100 men now, eighty having left, but new ones are arriving all the time. A 58-year-old arrived today with one leg shorter than the other but still declared 'fit for duty'.

New filters for our gas masks are issued by the armoury. We have already been given new eye pieces, every item being entered in our pay books, and now we only lack weapons.

We then go to the gas chamber, which is situated outside the barrack area under some trees, and Staff Sergeant Becker releases some training gas in the chamber for us to test out our new filters. We enter the chamber in groups. Light enters the smoke-filled room through a window. The comrades go around like primeval animals, like circus ponies. We have to bend our knees, hop, turn and jump. The air soon runs out under our masks and the eye pieces mist up. My skull pounds like a drum. Then we slow down and do breathing exercises through the mask. Unscrew the filter, hold it up, screw it on again. Finally we sing, the sound muffled as from the grave.

We stumble out again with our lungs wheezing and rip our masks off. Boy has to hand his in, as it does not fit. Gradually we regain our breath, sitting on tree stumps and enjoying the sounds of nature. A bird is singing somewhere and the hum of the metropolis can be heard in the distance.

Finally the last ones come out. Even 'The Scarecrow' and Sergeant Rytn have taken part. When the latter removes his mask, his blond hair flutters in the wind and for a moment he looks the large child he is, but he soon resumes his duty expression. How status and some symbol of rank can change us Germans, then all the rest become puppets and must dance to our tune.

In the evening I break my spoon, and the supply clerk gives me another one in exchange for my cigarette ration. Then Boy, Stroschn, Windhurst and myself play rummy in the canteen before going to bed.

An air raid wakes us up again. A window in the battalion headquarters shines brightly in the night. Searchlight fingers reach up into the sky, Mosquitos hum, and multi-coloured Christmas trees swing about as explosions shatter the earth. The flak fires with heavy thuds, sending their shells high into the night. When we return to our beds, red flickering fires are lightening the sky above the city centre.

Thursday 5 April 1945

After reveille the staff sergeant bursts into our room. Ten men are detailed for bomb damage clearance, but I am not one of them. During the morning the rest of us are marched to the officers' mess for a lecture. A brand new second lieutenant, fresh from officer training school, talks about soldierly duty and obedience. I imagine this boy without his uniform. Snoring comes from a corner where Alfons has fallen asleep. We are visibly bored. Milkface has us stand up and pay attention. He stands right in front of me, the first fluff just showing on his upper lip, and can be no more than 19. After an hour he dismisses us and goes into the officers' kitchen, from where gentle odours tempt our nostrils. Apparently our superiors get roast meat, while we only have dried vegetables.

Then we loll about our barrack-room. We have to exchange all our unsuitable items and are glad to get rid of them. Boy and myself look through the window and see two lads from the Home Defence Flak going past behind a civilian, an old man with a limp, presumably wounded in the First World War, the oafs imitating him, laughing and joking. We go down to the square and give them a piece of our minds, and when they get cheeky they get a punch on the chin and slink away like whipped puppies.

A group of chattering women with headscarves and shopping bags come from battalion headquarters, several of them with pistol belts fastened over their aprons, some SS officers walking along with them. These are Berlin housewives who are getting five hours' shooting instruction per week in response to an appeal put out by Goebbels.

Steel helmets are issued after lunch. We are to be sworn in today, so three comrades go off to decorate the dining-room. We clean and polish our equipment, and parade at five o'clock. The staff sergeant goes through the ranks. Everyone looks the same under the steel helmets. It is the universal face of 1945, the face of youth.

We take up position in the dining room. The Reichs War Flag and the Party Flag with the swastika are hung on the panelled walls, symbols of the unity of the armed forces and the Party? Opposite there is a poor oil painting of Hitler and two machine guns on the floor with their barrels pointed towards us. An officer enters and the staff sergeant makes his report. The young second lieutenant speaks about the flag, the Führer and obedience until death. I am not with it; to me it is all like the stage of a theatre, myself a stand-in in a sad scene. He reads out the form of the oath in a dull voice and we repeat it slowly after him 'With God's help!' The hands return to our trouser seams. I see red before my eyes and would like to punch him in the face. We then have to sign our names in a big book to say that we have sworn the oath.

Friday 6 April 1945

This morning the lieutenant informs us that we will be leaving for the front early tomorrow morning. Since the swearing-in ceremony we are called 'Grenadiers'.

We begin slowly packing our things together in the barrack-room. Our peaceful time in barracks has come to an end. The staff sergeant expresses his regret that we should be leaving so early tomorrow, as another fifteen men are to be shot, ten of them from the 20 July plot.

During the morning we work on our kit until it is spotless, for the battalion commander will be taking the kit inspection. After lunch we hand in our cutlery to the supply clerk, then go back to playing cards in the barrack-room with Alfons, the former railwayman, and Erich, the ship's cook, now 'Grenadiers Müller and Schulze', names symbolising our future.

Then we have to parade outside on the big barrack square in front of the war memorial. We stand well apart with our kit spread out on the ground in front of us. The battalion commander takes over the parade. 'At ease!' he croaks, then Staff Sergeant Becker reads out the individual items from a paybook. We have to hold up each item as the major passes through the ranks. If something is not to his satisfaction, we have to go through the whole thing again. Finally he wants to see if we are wearing the first issue set of underwear. Wegner and Ebel have to change clothes on the square after first running ten times round it in their second set. After nearly two hours of this, the major is getting hungry. In a bombastic speech he tells us it is an honour to die for Hitler so young, and about the man-eating Bolsheviks, and then extracts a 'Sieg Heil' from us before disappearing in the direction of the officers' mess.

In the evening a fat paymaster, another 'indispensable' whose home comforts clearly show, hands out our pay. Each of us is given three RM10 notes of freshly printed 'Himmler Money'.[17]

Then we all get together in the canteen. Windhorst has heard that we are leaving in the morning and has come to join us. We talk about our future prospects. In the Armed Forces Report there is mention of fighting in the west near Nuremberg and Hannover. Peace reigns behind the lines again, but there the war rages with undiminished ferocity, daily crushing new lives between its millstones, while the leadership speaks of miracle weapons in order to whip up the suffering people into the utmost destructive nonsense. After us the deluge! That is the slogan, and the youth believe in Hitler as if he were the Messiah. Me too!

The sirens break us up. In the shelter a mouth-organ plays softly while outside the flak thunders and the earth shudders from its wounds, and the bombers' engines roar in unison as they bring death and destruction to the stricken city.

Saturday 7 April 1945

Sergeant Rytn goes through the barrack-room waking us up. Once more, and for the last time, we stretch out in our beds and then dash for the washroom. Rations for the journey, consisting of bread, sausage, butter and cigarettes, are available in the duty NCO's room, but there is hardly any space for them left in our packs, so we decide to eat immediately anything we cannot pack, and we all chew away with our mouths full.

The clock's minute hand moves remorselessly on, the last minutes stretching like rubber. I quickly repack again, underclothes, writing materials and a small photograph album, all that remains of my civilian existence. It is a wonder that we have been left this much, a hitch in the drive for conformity. What did the major say yesterday? 'Thoughts of home are sentiments unworthy of a young soldier!'

Staff Sergeant Becker calls from the square. We take our things and go slowly down the stairs. The sergeants go through the ranks again. There a strap is not right, here a belt not straight. In the background are the comrades staying behind. Alfons is cracking jokes: 'See you in the mass grave!' 'We'll keep a window seat for you!' comes back. A pity that the older ones are remaining here, for their experience could be useful in holding back the impetuous enthusiasm of us youngsters.

The lieutenant comes on the parade ground. 'Attention!' He quietly accepts the staff sergeant's report, then says goodbye. A sergeant, our escorting NCO, steps forward and we march off.

The platoons are emerging from the East Block, coffee carriers are hurrying across the square, the Hungarians are marching singing to the ranges, and the fat sergeant major is detailing fatigues outside the convalescent company block. Windhorst salutes with a nod. The barrack gates swing open and we leave our comrades behind. The Russians march past singing mournfully. The barracks are behind us as the bright sun breaks out.

A new phase of our lives is about to begin.

NOTES

1. The Western Allied bombing of Berlin reached its peak in early 1945, and on 28 March 1945 the American 8th Army Air Force based in England sent 383 B-17s of the 2nd Air Division to attack Spandau and nearby Falkenhagen with 1,038 tons of bombs. Spandau, an old garrison town and ordnance industry centre, had been incorporated into Greater Berlin in 1920. The U-Bahn is Berlin's underground railway system and the S-Bahn its city railway system.

2. The Persil carton was favoured by conscripts as it could then be used to post their civilian clothing back home after they had been been issued with their uniforms.

3. Although better known as the Minister of Public Enlightenment and Propaganda, Goebbels was also the original Gauleiter of Berlin and was also Reichs Defence Commissar for Wehrkreis III (Berlin) with plenipotentiary powers in the organisation of the defence of the capital.

4. The von Seeckt-Kaserne had originally been built in 1935–6 for the Reichswehr behind the older Schmidt-Knobelsdorf-Kaserne, with which it

connected. From 1939 until 1945 the von Seeckt-Kaserne accommodated the 218th Infantry Replacement Regiment. (Infanterie-Ersatz-Regiment 218.) From 1945 to 1994, as Wavell Barracks, it then housed a succession of British infantry battalions.

5. 309th Grenadier Training & Replacement Battalion (*Grenadier Ausbildungs- und Ersatz Bataillon 309*) was intended to train and provide replacements for the 309th 'Berlin' Infantry Division, which had been formed from miscellaneous Berlin-based units on 1 February 1945, and was deployed on the Eastern Front near Letschin as part of the 9th Army's CIst Corps.

6. Alexander-Kaserne was originally built in 1875 next to the Ruhleben ranges for the Military School of Musketry (*Militär-Schieß-Schule*). It was occupied throughout World War II by the 397th Infantry Replacement Regiment (*Infanterie-Ersatz-Regiment 397*), but by this stage provided basic training for all sorts of troops. It is now the Berlin Police training school.

7. The intruder bomber version of the famous British aircraft, which was fast enough to fly without a fighter escort, and yet carried a bombload of 4,000 lbs, almost equivalent to the average load of a Flying Fortress at this extreme range.

8. See map. The Dischinger Bridge had not yet been built.

9. Six months' service with the Reichsarbeitsdienst was a statutory preliminary to military service for German youth and included generous amounts of drill, marching and discipline in its programme. Towards the end of the war the RAD armed some of its units for the field as part of the stop-gap measures being introduced.

10. These ragged remnants of a once proud army were now regarded with contempt and suspicion. As members of the Axis, the Hungarians had participated in the invasions of Yugoslavia and the Soviet Union in 1941, but when their country's Regent, Admiral Horthy, tried to negotiate a separate peace with the Allies in October 1944, Hitler forced him to abdicate and then had him interned in Germany.

11. The Organisation Todt was the official construction engineering organisation for military projects.

12. Both the Soviet and German forces had such punishment units for employment on suicidal missions. The failure of the 20 July 1944 plot against Hitler's life by Colonel Claus Graf Schenk von Stauffenberg led to a massive witch-hunt by the Gestapo and the death of thousands.

13. The Home Defence also included Luftwaffe anti-aircraft artillery manned by teenage schoolboys and polytechnic students, all compulsory members of the Hitler Youth, who were expected to continue their studies as well as man the guns, in order to save adult manpower for front line duty.

14. The Panzerfaust was a cheaply produced, hand-held anti-tank weapon of considerable effectiveness at short range.

15. See Appendix I.

16. Having been captured in May 1942, Lieutenant General AA Vlassov was eventually allowed to raise an anti-Stalinist Russian Liberation Army (ROA) from prisoners-of-war and slave-labourers. Although coming under Himmler's aegis, they refused to wear Nazi insignia. Two Divisions were finally formed for the Eastern Front. The fate of the survivors was to be handed over to the Soviet authorities in accordance with the Yalta agreements and most, including Vlassov, were executed.

17. Reichsführer-SS and Chief of the German Police Heinrich Himmler was also Minister of the Interior and, since the abortive 20 July 1944 plot, both an Army

Group Commander and Commander of the Home or Reserve Army, the latter appointment covering such important areas as all recruitment, training, development and allocation of equipment, as well as pay.

CHAPTER II
Off to the Front

We are marching along to Ruhleben U-Bahn station and ever since the barracks gates closed behind us, hopefully for ever, I feel as if I have been set free. The trees along the road are covered in greenery, and the buds seem ready to burst open. We are heading into an unknown future.

Volkssturm[1] with reluctant expressions are working on the construction of a barricade near the underpass. They have already ripped up the pavement and driven iron girders into the earth, and Reichsbahn[2] goods wagons have been filled with stones ready to be pushed across the road should the need arise.

At the U-Bahn station we go through the barriers up to the sun-drenched platforms[3], the escorting NCO remaining below to get our movement order stamped. The train's departure time approaches. 'All aboard!' We all pile into the carriages the way we did as civilians in the old days when there was no time to spare. As soldiers we should have waited, but the civilian in us is still not dead.

The doors close and we are off. As we start to move, I can see the escorting NCO running up the steps, gaping in astonishment after the departing train. On our way we discuss among ourselves what we should do about him. He has all our papers, including our paybooks, in his possession.

The carriage gradually fills up, mainly with women going shopping in the city. We get out at the Kaiserdamm and make ourselves at home on the platform. The trains roll up, stop and roll on again to vanish as small spots in the distance.

There are some magazines displayed outside a newspaper stand, and the front page of the *Illustrierte Beobachter* shows a smiling SS officer wearing the Oak Leaves to the Iron Cross.[4]

At last the escorting NCO turns up on one of the trains. He approaches us angrily but calms down when he sees that we are all here. We take the next train to the Zoo, where we leave the U-Bahn and climb up to the S-Bahn station above, the traffic surging round us. The women and girls strolling along the streets have discarded their warm clothes for spring outfits. The ruins of the Memorial Church[5] lie in the morning sunshine on the left. The Memorial Church, Kurfürstendamm, all are well-known names, favourite parts of Berlin that only a short time ago we were able to look at as free citizens. What a world divides them from us now when we can only catch a fleeting glimpse of them. A tram stops, cars race by. Bustle, business – the tempo of a big city!

We get up to the S-Bahn platform just as the Erkner train pulls out of the station, and now we will have to wait another twenty minutes for the next one. We put our packs down and wander up and down the platform, where SS officers with immaculate creases, in leather coats with fur collars and wearing light belts with pistol holsters, are casually smoking their cigarettes, their pig leather suitcases at their feet. Political leaders in their yellow uniforms are wearing Volkssturm armbands, and a fat man with a briefcase and wearing a swastika armband on his overcoat is blowing his cigar smoke into the air appreciatively. Girls in transparently light spring dresses, careworn women, bleary-eyed workers, and hungry children are standing around; the many faces of Berlin.

At last the name Erkner comes up on the board and the train rolls in already overfull. We push and shove to get in. The stations go by like a film strip – Friedrichstrasse with the burnt-out dome of the Wintergarten on the right, and across a desert of ruins; the Schiffbauerdamm, the Admiralspalast, and Alexanderplatz with the Berolina statue, and the Hertie and Awag department stores.

The big city's sea of houses thins out and the countryside begins to fly by – Karlshorst, Rummelsberg, allotments with people working in their gardens, a farmer ploughing. The trees and bushes are freshly decked in greenery and the jubilant birds climb high into the blue sky.

The S-Bahn ends at Erkner and we will have to go on from there by suburban train, the next leaving in three hours' time.

The platforms are full of activity with officers and soldiers of all arms of the services, even sailors fighting on the Oder[6], waiting for their connections. There are posters everywhere warning the troops that desertion means facing court martial. There are also some women on their way to barter in the villages for food for their hungry children, and refugees from Frankfurt on the Oder wanting to go back to rescue more of their things, all sitting on baskets and sacks, while SS[7] and military police check passes.

We get our paybooks and are allowed to leave the station. I leave my pack and haversack on the platform.

There are some ruined houses in front of the station and the remains of a bombed-out factory. Erkner, once a blooming suburb with hidden beauties, was transformed overnight by a sea of fire, the Kugel-Fischer ball bearing factory having brought death and destruction to this place.

There are no pubs open in Erkner. They are all filled with refugees and bombed-out residents eking out their sad existence with the remains of their belongings.

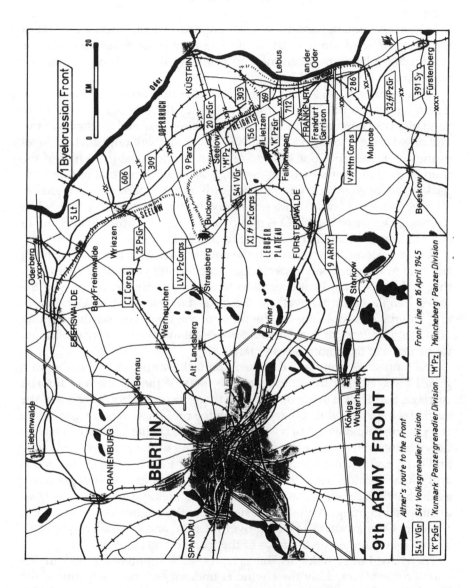

9th ARMY FRONT

1 Byelorussian Front

KM

BERLIN

SPANDAU

ORANIENBURG

Liebenwalde

Oderberg

EBERSWALDE

Bad/Freienwalde

Bernau

Wriezen

5 Lt

606

309

SEELOW

Buckow

Werneuchen

Alt Landsberg

Strausberg

C I Corps

LV I Pz Corps

25 PzGr

9 Para

20 PzGr

Seelow

M'Pz

541 VGr

303

156

169

712

ODERBRUCH

Oder

KÜSTRIN

Lebus

an der Oder

FRANKFURT

Frankfurt Garrison

'K' PzGr

Lietzen

HEIGHTS

Falkenhagen

FÜRSTENWALDE

LEBUSER PLATEAU

X I SS Pz Corps

Erkner

9 ARMY

Starkow

Königs Wusterhausen

V SS Mtn Corps

Mulrose

286

32 Pz Gr

391 Sy

Fürstenberg

Beeskow

Altner's route to the Front

Front Line on 16 April 1945

541 VGr   541 Volksgrenadier Division

'K' PzGr   'Kurmark' Panzergrenadier Division

M'Pz   'Müncheberg' Panzer Division

23

I walk slowly through the place past burnt-out weekend allotments and small family houses standing accusingly in the greenery of their gardens. I am frequently accosted about my age, and a young girl even offers me her brother's civilian clothes and to hide me, but I lack the courage to accept.

In front of the station there is a small grassed-in area, where I spread out my greatcoat and stretch out on it. The now quite warm sunshine is comforting. I lie there dreaming and thinking of the future. A comrade wakes me. It is time to go!

There is no way of getting through on the platform. The trains from Berlin have been discharging more people at the station, most of them civilians. The train comes in and is immediately stormed by the civilians, and now I can get to my pack, which is still lying there undisturbed. Most of the comrades from our group are there. SS clear the front half of the train of civilians so that we can get on. I take a window seat and put my pack in the luggage rack. Once all the soldiers are aboard, the civilians are allowed back on and stand gratefully in the corridors, packed like sardines. Our escorting NCO is nervous as Wegner is still missing, but at last he storms aboard just before the train leaves.

We chug along slowly through the countryside with the heath coming right up to the tracks on either side. Trenches and barbed wire fences in this undisturbed landscape serve to remind us of the seriousness of the times. People stand like walls at the little stations, trying to get aboard, and clumps of people are on the roofs of the carriages, on the running boards and buffers, and in the brakemen's cabins. Some are even clinging to the pipes of the engine's water tanks.

The train stops from time to time. Air attack alarm! Soldiers of the train guard are watching the skies from the roofs of the engine and the last carriage. Suddenly a bugle blows. Low flying aircraft! People fly out of the carriages in panic, while others jump off the roof on to those below. There is a roaring sound as the first of them reach the shelter of the woods. I lie down between the rails listening to the tacking of the machine guns over and over, and when all is quiet again, I get up. People lying in the woods and ditches timidly raise their heads and slowly begin to breathe freely again, but then comes the sound of aircraft engines and everyone vanishes again like lightning. White steam rises from the engine like candles. But these are German aircraft passing over the train and gradually the people return, fear stamped on the faces of the women and children.

There are bullet holes in the carriage and splintered wood in the compartment. Incredibly the engine is undamaged, nor have any of the people been hit. Only a few women have been hurt in the panic, and a 12-year-old has had her ribs crushed.

The carriage fills up again and the train slowly rolls on, the German planes criss-crossing overhead. I stand at the window and look out. The oncoming train is on the other track, its engine riddled with bullet holes, and soldiers are bandaging the wounded. Some women stop our train and the wounded are put into our luggage van. The others follow the rails on foot to the next station.

At last we roll into Fürstenwalde, which is a hive of activity. The majority of the people on the platforms are soldiers in field grey. Posters in glaring red warn of low flying aircraft. We form up and change over to the Seelower station, the station for the Oderbruch Railway.[8] The next train leaves at 2000 hours.

We put down our packs and go into the town, where Stroschn, Boy and myself have lunch at the Station Hotel, our uniforms looking shabby in such elegant surroundings. Afterwards we take a stroll. There are signs indicating the various units and branches of the armed services on every tree. Cars and motorcycles race past and tanks rattle through the once quiet streets, for Fürstenwalde has become a military nodal point, being only thirty kilometres from the front and thirty from Berlin.[9]

We wander slowly through the town, using up the last of our ration coupons in various shops, being attended to politely and being given something extra in each one. The shopping housewives willingly make room for us ahead of them and ask our ages, only to shake their heads. I buy some bread, butter, oatmeal and sugar.

We look in the shop windows on the high street. There is a special SS imprint in a bookshop. 'Happy Youth' stands in large letters above a picture of a Hitler Youth carrying a large kettle drum. This annoys me. Yes, that was indeed my 'happy youth', marching behind such a drum and such a drummer. Our youth was as dull as the thud of the drum from the day we started school right up to now. Will it always be like this?

We stand on the market square in front of the pretty town hall, which has little houses gathered round it like chicks around a mother hen. The pretentious stone building with swastika insignia housing the Nazi Party offices looks out of place in this town. Nearby is a sign saying 'Autobahn 4.5 Kilometres'. The racing vehicles, the marching columns, the soldiers and officers of all arms of the services, and the sentries and patrols have robbed this little town of its normal peaceful existence.

We slowly make our way back to the station, the traffic that broke into this town overnight flowing around us. I spread out my greatcoat on the platform, put my pack under my head and go to sleep. When I wake again it is afternoon. A short train rumbles by carrying flak wagons destined for Frankfurt on the Oder. I have something to eat and then stroll along the platform with Stroschn. Two girls are standing at the fence, pretty things. One look and we have hit it off. Two sisters, blond with blue eyes, beckon us. Soon we are chatting eagerly as we go along the street with them. We have another three hours before the train leaves.

The girls live near the station. One is 17, the other 18, Ilona and Gisela.

We stop in front of a house near the edge of town and the girls invite us in for a glass of wine. Pictures of their parents hang in the dining room. Their father is a colonel in the Luftwaffe, a professor of philosophy in civilian life. Their mother has gone to Berlin and will not be back until evening.

We let the wine slip slowly over our tongues. Ilona goes into the next room and Stroschn follows her, closing the door gently behind him.

I am alone with Gisela. Streaks of sunlight strike the table. I look at Gisela and she looks openly back at me. Her eyes shine like the deep blue of a clear mountain lake. I take her hand, which she willingly accepts. Her breast heaves, she leans on my shoulder and closes her eyes.

When we wake from our state of euphoria it is nearly seven o'clock. Giesela lies next to me smiling, little dimples showing on either side of her mouth, a mischievous look in her eyes.

At seven a gentle knocking sounds through the room, like bells calling us back to duty. We look each other once more in the eyes as I impress her image on my mind yet again, her blue eyes, gold-blond hair, quivering nostrils and glistening, curved mouth, so that I can recall her before my eyes in the darkest hours and relive these memories.

We all leave the house together and make our way to the station. The escorting NCO gives orders that we are not to leave the station again, so we lift the girls over the fence. Our train draws in slowly. We put our packs aboard and get off again. Time passes all too quickly.

A train from Frankfurt pulls in on the next platform. Men and women get out loaded down with rucksacks and small carts full of potatoes. Mothers have made the exhausting journey to get food for their hungry children and housewives for their hard-working, careworn husbands. Suddenly the railway police come along and snatch the stuff off several crying women, confiscating the potatoes. Immediately everyone tries to escape. The SS, who have sealed the exits, push together the people trying to flee, forcing them back; young boys who could themselves be the sons of these mothers, children reacting like puppets who would even kill their own parents.

Gisela is leaning against me, her eyes full of tears. 'That happens every day,' she says. 'Last week they shot a woman who protested at having to give up her potatoes. Her two children had to be handed over to the police.' Having to watch this struggle fills us with rage. We clench our hands in our pockets with powerless anger.

Then suddenly something happens that no one would have believed possible. Men, fathers of families, break through the walls of discipline that here only signify misery and disgrace. To a man, the soldiers who had been sitting in our train waiting to go to the front, climb out and intervene, making a threatening wall between the people and the SS. The confiscated items are calmly taken from the SS and given back to the people. Their weapons are held ready in their hands and they would not be reluctant to use them. We escort the people to their train and wait until it vanishes over the horizon before going slowly back to our train, thinking of those people travelling back to the metropolis with nourishment for their children and husbands.

The time for departure has long gone. We stand at the window talking to Ilona and Gisela. Then the engine is hooked on and the time to leave has come at last. The station master gives the signal. A warm handshake, a last meeting of the eyes and we glide slowly out of the station. Two light spots remain on the platform and melt away in the distance.

A short dream is past and grey reality takes over. Outside the landscape with its woods and fields flies by and the first stars appear in a clear sky. Imperceptibly we come on to the Lebuser Plateau with its rich meadows and pastures, stopping at every little station for soldiers to get on and off noisily. Then the engine sets off again puffing and wheezing. It is quiet in our compartment. Occasionally the pinpoint of a cigarette glows ghostily and from the next compartment come the snores of a tired sleeper.

The landing lights of an airfield[10] glow in the distance, and from time to time the sky in the east is illuminated by flares. We are getting closer to the battle front.

Suddenly the train stops on the open track. The train guard goes through the carriages warning caution. The engine damps down and the train then moves on slowly and carefully. Everyone is asleep. The front rumbles in the distance.

We wake with a start. Everyone out! Drunk with sleep we stumble out into the cold night. I am freezing. The skies have drawn over and it is a star-dark night. The escorting NCO is called off somewhere. At last, still half asleep, I find the group to which I belong. The light of a torch shows the name 'Falkenhagen' on the station signboard.

We march off. Fortunately we are all present. Guns and supply columns rattle through the village streets as we wait at a crossroads for the escorting NCO, who has gone to see the village commandant. Dispatch riders with dimmed headlights force us off the road. The moon breaks through the blanket of clouds and its weak light gives us a glimpse of the sleeping village.

The NCO returns. The village commandant has ordered us to continue on our way forward under cover of darkness. We set off again. It is midnight as our march to the front begins.

NOTES

1. The Volkssturm were raised on 18 October 1944 under Party auspices as a form of Home Guard from able-bodied men between 16 and 60 years of age not already committed to military service. Despite wearing a Wehrmacht armband, they were mainly reliant on Party resources for rations, arms and

equipment, some even lacking any kind of uniform, and varied considerably in their effectiveness.

2. The state railway.
3. The Ruhleben U-Bahn terminus stands on a ramp high above street level.
4. The Iron Cross was awarded in sequence for acts of bravery of Iron Cross Second Class, Iron Cross First Class, Knights' Cross of the Iron Cross, then with oak leaves, with swords and, finally, with swords and diamonds.
5. Kaiser-Wilhelm-Gendänkniskirche.
6. Sailors had been drafted to the 20th Panzergrenadier Division at Seelow for training as infantry.
7. The Allgemeine-SS employed here in a police-type role should not be confused with the combatant Waffen-SS.
8. This railway ran over the Lebuser Hochfläche (Plateau) and the Seelow Heights to serve the communities in the Oderbruch valley west of the Oder river.
9. At this time General Busse's 9th Army Headquarters were located just south of the town in Bad Saarow.
10. Neuendorf-im-Sande.

CHAPTER III

Recruit at the Front

Sunday 8 April 1945

We leave the village heading north. A light shows here and there behind the windows of the houses – military billets. Occasionally a face drunk with sleep appears at a window to peer wearily at our column.

My pack is heavy and the cold cuts into my face. There is busy traffic along the road to the front. Shadowy, unlighted wagons and supply columns appear out of the dark and rattle past, their drivers casually whipping up their exhausted nags.[1] From time to time the dimmed headlights of a car appear like a ghost from around a bend in the road and cut through the darkness, leaving it to fall even heavier over our eyes afterwards.

We march past the meadows, and the wooden gates of pastures, so beloved by the cows in daytime, gleam faintly in the moonlight. Now the woods begin and it is much darker. The presence of the man in front can only be sensed.

Sometimes the cloud cover is torn apart and the moon shines down on the earth. At the road junctions signs advise the location of individual units. We leave the main road and turn right into a narrow road running through the woods. The escorting NCO orders a short rest.

I remove my pack and lean against a tree. About twelve kilometres away dozens of flares shimmer in the heavens, pouring their light over the front line. As soon as a flare goes out, another shoots up to replace it. Occasionally a dull rifle shot or the bellow of a machine gun shatters the silence of the night.

We have to move on. We advance slowly, often stopping and waiting for the already well spread out column to close up. On the right a small pond glimmers in the light of the stars and the moon when it breaks through the cloud cover. There is not much farther to go. A strong wind blows the scraps of cloud apart and gives the moon free passage.

Suddenly we come to a well tarred road. A light gate appears out of the darkness and a sentry's torch flashes. We have reached our destination, a V-Weapons assembly plant.[2]

We march past massive workshops that rise out of the dark like threatening giants and stop in front of one of them, the command post of our regimental commander.[3] The escorting NCO reports our arrival and receives further orders.

I lean back on my pack and look to the east. There are only ten kilometres to the front, which is coming relentlessly nearer. Farther north and south, the front seems to run in a curve based on the key points of Küstrin and Frankfurt.[4]

The NCO returns and reads out our names by the light of a torch. Two men are missing. At last we move off into the workshop in single file. We feel our way in the dark through several passages and doorways, banging our helmets and mess tins with a clatter. I miss a turn on some cellar steps and run into a wall, but feel no pain; I am too tired. A weak light appears from somewhere. We are in a cellar.

A sergeant shows us our sleeping places in a long passage with boxes on either side like a stable. I stumble over some boards and throw my pack on to the straw. Hand and rifle grenades are lying about on the ground. I slowly pull off my boots from my aching feet, which are swollen because the quartermaster insisted that the boots fitted.

There is a tap under the stairs and I wash off the coarse dust of the day by the light of a torch, the ice cold water driving away my fatigue for a moment. Meanwhile it has turned one o'clock. The comrades have laid themselves down and are eating. I too take some refreshment and munch away. The march has made us hungry.

In the boxes across the passage are some soldiers who have been relieved from the front, or what is left of them. They say that only seventy-three remain out of 800, and they are all happy to have come out of that mess intact.

We are woken up at eight o'clock by a sergeant, a typical rear area type, and a real one because he is the rations NCO for the regiment. The older ones ignore him, so he turns his lust for power upon us. We are not to eat but must first clean the hundred-metre passage of straw and sand. Every corner has to be rinsed with water, which then runs into the boxes and wets the straw. Finally we have to wipe the floor dry with cloths. A right pig-headed Prussian, this slave-driver orders me to deal with the corners that have not yet been cleaned.

I slip away and go outside where the weather is beautiful. The sun is driving away the cool of the night and shines in the early morning mist. The main road goes past the workshops, and dispatch riders on motorcycles and horses raise clouds of dust that sink slowly back to the ground, while horse-drawn carts drive past with food and ammunition to supply the troops.

The sergeant appears in the doorway, so I go behind the workshops and help with chopping wood for the regimental commander's kitchen. Boy and Stroschn are also there. Then we fade into the background and tour the deserted workshops and factory streets. Camouflaged entrances lead to the underground workshops, whose open doors are an invitation to share their secrets. V-Weapons are no longer being assembled here, for the workers have become soldiers, and boxes of ammunition and Panzerfausts lie next to the gleaming bodies of the flying bombs, while cobwebs and dust lie fingerthick on the workbenches.

We then return to the cellar to eat our breakfast in peace. In the adjacent boxes the front soldiers are making up for nights without sleep, trying to forget the horrors they have seen.

In front of the workshop, the sergeant is exercising his authority over our comrades, mainly the older ones. They have to sweep the whole width of the main road with large brooms, even though every vehicle passing through raises clouds of dust and cancels out their efforts. But orders are orders, even when they are as stupid as this.

The sun slowly climbs higher. It is nearly noon on Sunday. We sit on the grass under the scraggy trees on the mound behind the workshops and abandon ourselves to our thoughts. The sergeant finds us and drives us back to work.

We have to load wagons coming from the front with ammunition and supplies. The inevitable Panzerfausts, which according to Goebbels any newborn child can use, are packed in with them. The horses pull away their heavy loads and new wagons constantly arrive to be loaded. We have already eaten all our transit rations and are now loading food on the wagons with our stomachs grumbling.

The escorting NCO arrives at about noon. We have to parade at the east gate with all our equipment. Greatcoats and blankets are quickly strapped on and we stamp out of the cellar. A corporal falls us in and counts us. We are all present as the two men who were missing last night have caught up with us.

The NCO arrives with the regimental commander and two officers from his staff. The corporal makes his report and the regimental commander stands us at ease. He asks each one his name, home town and background. When he discovers that none of us is older than 17, he says delightedly: 'The 1928 intake is Germany's last hope. Your Führer is relying on you!' Then he says a few words, remarking that the Führer has sent his youths into the trenches so that they can learn about the sacrifices to be made at the front. The Knights' Cross swings gently at the colonel's throat and its Oak Leaves glisten in the sun.

The old ones fall out, the officers leave for their mess and the escorting NCO gives: 'Right turn!' We march off to the front.

We leave the factory complex by the east gate. The tarmac has come to an end and the wheels of the supply wagons and tank tracks have cut deep furrows in the roadway. Giant tanks have been driven into the woods on either side of the road. I am astonished at their number, more than one would expect. But their appearance is deceptive. They lie still, lack of fuel preventing their use in combat, and their black-uniformed tank troops are now deployed in the trenches as infantry.

Some barrack huts have been erected under the trees and are occupied by Waffen-SS. A soldier can only get back as far as here if he is not to be snapped up by the military police, for this is the rear boundary for front combatants, where the military police reign, casting a ring of fear and horror in the hearts of the men at the front.

They tease the dogs that they take over the fields at night in the hunt for anyone who can no longer take the horrors of war. They stretch out lazily in their chairs, turning their placid faces to the sun, as if they had not already seen enough misery.

We pass some German Red Cross barrack huts in which a field hospital has been set up, reeking of blood and carbolic. Wounded soldiers with emaciated faces are lying out in the sunshine, while amputees attempt to walk again.

We leave the main road to the right, enter a wood and then go across meadows and fields with the sun burning the landscape. My pack seems to get heavier with every step, my throat burns and my stomach is demanding its rights. The red of a church tower gleams in the distance.

Our goal lies unexpectedly before us. The land dips down and drops into Lietzen, a typical village with fat, majestic cattle and lively, rosy piglets romping in the village street – a peaceful idyl behind the lines.

We ask for the battalion command post in the village and have to drag our weary bones back two kilometres, since it turns out to be in the last house of the village on the Fürstenwalde road. A supply column, whose weary nags hang their heads, takes us along. We have enough time for a rest at the command post, where we lie down in the roadside ditches and close our eyes.

After a good hour we are sent off to the command post of the company to which we have been allocated. We have to march the whole way back to where the post lies at the far end of the village, which is occupied by troops of all arms of the service. A platoon has fallen in for its rations, and the bells of the village church are summoning people to prayer.

We turn left and march past the railway station. No trains have used it for some considerable time and weeds are growing between the rails. A lorry set on the rails goes by hooting its horn.

The company command post is in a little farm not far from the railway station. The escorting NCO reports our arrival and then heads back to regimental headquarters.

We lie down on the railway embankment and sunbathe. A young second lieutenant, the company commander, has us fallen in and we are divided up into sections according to age and size. Practically everyone

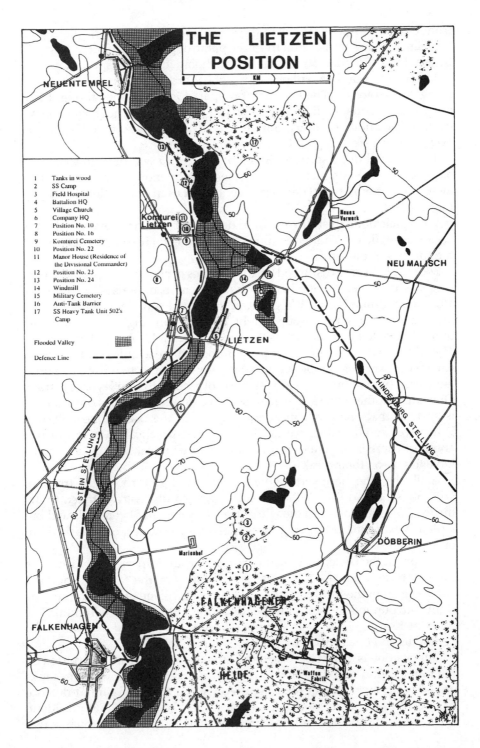

THE LIETZEN POSITION

1	Tanks in wood
2	SS Camp
3	Field Hospital
4	Battalion HQ
5	Village Church
6	Company HQ
7	Position No. 10
8	Position No. 16
9	Komturei Cemetery
10	Position No. 22
11	Manor House (Residence of the Divisional Commander)
12	Position No. 23
13	Position No. 24
14	Windmill
15	Military Cemetery
16	Anti-Tank Barrier
17	SS Heavy Tank Unit 502's Camp

Flooded Valley

Defence Line

NEUENTEMPEL

Komturei Lietzen

Neues Vorwerk

NEU MALISCH

LIETZEN

STEIN STELLUNG

HINDENBURG STELLUNG

Marienhof

DÖBBERIN

FALKENHAGENER

FALKENHAGEN

HEIDE

V-Waffen Fabrik

33

from our old barrack-room is in the same section, and we are allocated a sergeant who has transferred from the paratroops to the infantry[5], a small, pleasant East Prussian and a man with whom we can communicate.

Meanwhile a cauldron of pea soup, whose aroma tempts our nostrils, is being cooked for us. They were not prepared for us as they thought that our transit rations would have covered us until this evening, so we have been spared another administrative error. The soup is soon ready and we each receive a steaming ladleful in our mess tins.

Then we fall in by sections. Some of our group will have to sleep in a barn next to the command post as there is not enough accommodation available. We move off. There are seventeen of us in our section, including the sergeant.

We march along the railway line and then turn off on to a path that leads across dusty fields. Young seedlings are pushing their soft greenery out of the furrows in the fields.

Soon we see some disturbed earth and piles of shovelled up sand where dugouts have been scooped out of the earth. In front of us is Position No. 16, our accommodation. We go carefully down some cut-out steps, the loose sand moving under our weight, and enter in single file. It is so low that we have to bend our heads. The room is terribly small, like a toybox. There is a small, clear area near the entrance where a table and two small, collapsible benches can be set up when required, and two rows of bunks have been built along the rear wall and covered with thin layers of straw. One after another enters, lays his pack on a bunk and comes out again. It is so tight that one can only manoeuvre with the use of one's elbows. When we are all inside, we lie like sardines, practically on top of one another. There is not enough room for all of us to eat at once, and some have to stay on their bunks.

While the others are sorting themselves out, I go through the trenches with Stroschn and Boy. Villagers and Hitler Youths were detailed to dig the local fortifications and the whole trench system has been built without a plan. Next to the completed parts there are whole sections marked out only a spade deep.

In front of the trenches, which face east, the land drops gently from the railway line to the flooded meadows below. On the far side the land climbs again in the form of some low hills. The village of Lietzen is on the right, surrounded by fields, and ends at the hill with the windmill. The roofs of Komturei Lietzen[6] shimmer on the far left. The terrain is flat behind us and one can see woods in the far distance.

Our position is meant to be designed for an anti-tank role, supported by the hilly ground and the flooded meadows, but I wonder whether tanks would really turn off the road here. We are on the third line of defence from the front, and our position is named after the last German President. The land is undulating and obscures the view of the front, which is two

34

kilometres away.[7] The old windmill is the only prominent landmark. Left of the village and its windmill, one can see a military cemetery on the side of a hill, its crosses looking like bald trees, where some rolled up bundles are being thrown off a wagon.

Wegner and Blaczeck have found a potato store and returned with a sackful. We pile a few bricks together and collect some wood. The sergeant has a big pot and soon a brisk fire is crackling under it.

It gradually gets dark. A fireplace has also been set up at the adjacent dugout and the figures there appear shadowy in its glow. Engine noises come from the distance, then several Me 109s[8] roar over us heading for the front. Several seconds later a barrier appears in the sky, which seems to be on fire, as streams of light Russian flak rush up solidly, making an impregnable net.[9] Heavy calibre weapons add to the din. The aircraft return low over the trees, streaking back and disappearing behind us. Silence gradually returns.

We take the pot and put out the fire. Back in the dugout we get practically a mess tinful each. Several are on their bunks and eat lying down.

A candle flickers on the lintel over the entrance. Guard duty is being detailed and I get the ten-to-midnight shift with Boy. The sergeant talks about the front, and tells us that prisoners are talking of a major offensive being imminent. We have landed in a fine mess.

I slowly prepare for guard duty, but Boy can stay in bed as one on duty is enough. I take the sergeant's weapon, a No. 42 rifle, with which I am totally unfamiliar, never having held one in my hands before, and would be absolutely useless if anything should happen.

I go out into the starry night, climbing the steps slowly. A fresh wind is blowing over the fields and makes me shiver. I make my rounds between the trenches and the dugout, and time drags. The light goes out in the dugout and I can hear muffled snores.

Verey lights go up quite close in front of me. I want to throw myself down as it is so bright, but I have to look out. When the verey light suddenly goes out one becomes night blind and has to become used to the darkness again.

It is quiet at the front. No shot disturbs the stillness of the night.

Time creeps by slowly, the minutes seeming like hours. Occasionally one of the sleepers emerges from the dugout and asks the time, then quickly returns to the warmth below.

An aircraft sweeps across the lines and flies into the German hinterland, its engine sounding like a sewing machine.[10]

Midnight. I go slowly down the steps and wake my relief. He gets up reluctantly from his bunk. I remove my greatcoat and crawl into my bunk, having to push my neighbour back into his space before I can lie down. I am dog tired and my eyes close immediately.

NOTES

1. The majority of German military transport continued to be horse-drawn throughout World War II. By this stage of the war there was no motor fuel to spare for supply tasks anyway.
2. See Appendix II. The V-Weapons (*Vorgeltungswaffen* = reprisal weapons), consisting of flying-bombs and long-range rockets, were expected to turn the tide of war in Germany's favour. Flying-bombs were last reported in use near Stettin against the 2nd Byelorussian Front offensive a few days later.
3. The 1314th Grenadier (Field Training) Regiment is believed to have been the unit concerned. Instead of reinforcing their parent formation, the 309th (Berlin) Infantry Division, these conscripts had been sent to help make up the 156th Field Training Division, which had been formed from a miscellany of military, Customs, Forestry Department, Police and Fire Brigade sponsored units on 12 March 1945, and allocated to the 9th Army on the Eastern Front. This formation was sub-divided into the 1313th, 1314th and 1315th Grenadier (Field Training) Regiments, and was redesignated the 156th Infantry Division on 15 April 1945.
4. Both these towns had been declared fortresses, but Küstrin had fallen on 28 March 1945.
5. The paratroops were part of the Luftwaffe, but had in fact been used almost exclusively as normal ground troops ever since the costly invasion of Crete in May 1941. This sergeant may have been an exceptional case.
6. Komturei Lietzen had been founded by the Knights Templar as a caravan-serai on the route to the east and was now a large manor farm.
7. The Hindenburg Line was actually the third defensive strip. Each consisted of a series of trenches and defensive positions, the first being down in the Oderbruch some eleven kilometres away, and the second on the Seelow Heights some eight kilometres away, so considerably farther than Altner thought. Both these strips would have been out of sight, with a hundred-foot(thirty-metre) drop from the Heights to the Oderbruch.
8. The Me 109 (officially Bf 109) was a highly successful single-engined Messerschmitt fighter, of which several versions were built, ending with the Me 109K with a top speed of 452 mph (725 kph).
9. The Soviets had built up a formidable anti-aircraft artillery defence in the Oderbruch, consisting of the twenty-nine regiments and twenty-two independent battalions of Marshal Zhukov's 1st Byelorussian Front, plus twelve divisions of the Stavka Reserve.
10. The Po-2 as described here was armoured against infantry fire and was used extensively for night bombing behind enemy lines. Many of the crews were female. The observer would drop clusters of handgrenades or light bombs in WWI style. It had a top speed of 81 mph (129 kph), a load of 250 kilos and a range of 250 miles (400 km). Its nickname 'Sewing Machine' came from the distinctive sound of the engine.

CHAPTER IV
Training in the Trenches

Monday 9 April 1945

We are woken up at six o'clock. I take my washbag and go down to the flooded meadows with Boy. We put our stuff down and then wade out a few paces into the ice-cold water, wearing only our PT shorts. There is a light ground mist over the meadows and the clear, ice-cold water drives all tiredness out of our bodies. We quickly run back to the dugout, where one could cut the air with a knife, and go in. Most of our comrades have got dressed and are standing about freezing, unwashed and uncombed.

A little later while the dugout is being tidied up, I go along with Poziemba to the command post to collect hot coffee in our mess tins. Then we have our breakfast outside in the open air. I sit on a pile of sand with Boy and Stroschn to eat as the sun breaks out behind the windmill opposite.

We have no electric light in the dugout, nor do we have a stove. We will have to look for some cable and fitting for an electric light, as we only have a few candles left. I volunteer to find the cable.

Meanwhile the time is passing and we have to go to the command post, where the whole company gradually assembles. The second lieutenant has us counted, then divides us into eight sections of ten men each for training, and we move off by sections to the meadows where the training is to begin.

Little attention is paid to theory – we only have to learn about the weapons in a practical sense. First the No. 42 rifle is explained to us and dismantled. Each one of us then has to either reassemble or dismantle it. After an hour the sections change over and we go to a sergeant who dismantles a No. 42 machine gun and explains its parts. After another hour we come to the Panzerfaust.

We then have a short break, whereupon the staff sergeant orders our favourite pastime, footdrill. We fall in as a platoon and do drill. The water is soon running in our boots in the wet meadows. We wheel in formation and practise turns, order following order in quick succession. When wheeling, the outer wing has to double to keep in line, causing the water to splash knee-high. The staff sergeant is not satisfied and makes us go farther into the meadows where the water is already a hand's breadth deep. Suddenly he shouts: 'Lie down!' We hesitate and then lie down in the cold water. 'Stand up! Double!' We get up again and continue to double. 'Lie down!' We have no time to think any more, letting ourselves drop into the water, which splashes up high. 'Crawl!' 'Turn on your belt buckles!' We turn round and round, slipping deeper into the water. The staff sergeant has lit a cigarette and stands smiling beside the solemn-faced sergeant. We are exhausted and panting for breath.

Stand up, lie down, double, crawl! We cannot think any more. We are like engines responding to the slightest touch of the gear lever, mere marionettes, but orders are orders. Meanwhile the arrival of the company commander passes unnoticed, and a storm breaks over the head of the nonplussed staff sergeant. In his shock he forgets to order us to stand up. We remain lying quietly and stick our noses even deeper into the muck.

We then return at the double by sections to our dugouts. Our wet uniforms are hung up on trees to dry, and we move about despondently in our training denims, trying to get warm. Did we actually expect that everything except footdrill would be taught at the front? The training programme still sticks to the schedule used in peacetime, but our section leader is against such practices and says that the staff sergeant, who comes from the military police, is always like this.

We march to the kitchen at the command post with our mess tins for lunch and get a ladleful of hot bean soup that restores our spirits, but unfortunately not enough to satisfy our hunger.

During the lunchbreak I go over to the Komturei with Czech to see if we can find some cable. A signals company has been billeted among the houses still occupied by civilians. We exchange some cigarettes for a short reel of cable and then pinch another big reel from their radio truck. That should keep them guessing! We then wander slowly through the Komturei, where some civilians call out to us and give us bread and dripping. Surprised, we thank them. Despite the nearness of the front, these people are still living in their homes, hanging on to their last bits of land, and the old folk sit in the sun in front of their houses while children play noisily in the roadway and vanish whenever a vehicle comes screeching up from the causeway. The farmers go about their work calmly, tending their fields, and only occasionally one of them looks to the east as if to check how long the front will hold.

We make our way back past the old cemetery, in the middle of which a trench has been dug. Bits of bone lie in the excavated sand, and weeds and rubbish have accumulated within the compound, in which the hump of a freshly dug grave stands out.

At three o'clock the section is called back to duty, but fortunately I have been given the cushy job of laying the electricity cable. The two pieces joined together just reach from the supply pole to the dugout. I fasten it securely in the dugout with a roll of plaster and then dig the cable a few centimetres in. I will look for a bulb and light fitting later.

The second lieutenant comes along and looks inside the dugout. He asks me what I think of the war, and I tell him that Hitler will soon have everything in order again. Then I sit on top of the dugout and watch the activity in the fields. Now and then a loud command carries across to me. The engines of several aircraft roar in the distance as I sit and dream.

The section comes back across the fields at six o'clock, after which there is an hour devoted to platoon chores and weapon cleaning, but we only have two rifles for cleaning. I clean my still damp uniform and slip shivering into the trousers. Comrades carry in some bricks and mortar and start building a stove.

I finish getting dressed, get the sergeant's permission and head for the village for a bulb and light fitting, taking a short cut across the fields, where there is a narrow path of sand and gravel through the water, partly flooded. In the centre the pressure has caused the dam to crumble away, and as I jump across, my boots are soaked through again, but I have saved half an hour by taking this short cut.

The village street is busy with traffic as the farmers return from the fields with their yokes of oxen. As they receive their orders, a platoon of artillery recruits billeted in the village is surrounded by a crowd of curious children, who then play soldiers until some wounded men with blood-soaked bandages come through on their way back from the front, and the children hang back shyly. Goebbels' propaganda slogans are painted in bright white paint on the walls of buildings alongside advertisements for unbreakable security glass.

I get a roll of insulating tape from the village store. On the house next door hangs the sign 'District Leader's Command Post'. Two political types are sitting at a table inside with a bottle, while two soldiers stand in the yard flirting with girls. I chat up a young village beauty, who finds me a light bulb and also presses some cigarettes into my hand.

I think of Gisela. Inwardly I regret seducing her, but the war has swept away all barriers and I am still so young!

I then go back along the back of the farmyards. The cattle are lowing and rattling their chains, and the village church bell is ringing its reminder that it is evening.

They are already eating their supper in the dugout. Boy has saved my cold rations for me, consisting of half a loaf of bread, butter, sausage and fifteen cigarettes. There is also half a bottle of wine per head: Frontline Ration No.1. I exchange my cigarettes for another bottle of wine to make *Glühwein* on the already completed stove.

It is comfortable in the dugout with the stove roaring away and the comrades lying chatting on their bunks. I fix a temporary connection and soon the bulb is shedding its light.

The sergeant returns from the command post. He has several Panzer-fausts and boxes of ammunition with him and is leaving tomorrow for Frankfurt with our predecessors. He says that the Russians are already in Vienna, the Americans have taken Hannover and Göttingen, and are also fighting in the Thüringer Forest.

The comrades talk about the war. Bayer complains that he has rheumatism in his right leg, and says that he will be unable to take part in the victory march through the Brandenburg Gate as he cannot do the goose-step. Stroschn wonders how he can still believe in victory. The stove roars away. The sergeant's things lie on the table. The guard duties are detailed, the light turned off and the sentry climbs out.

Tuesday 10 April 1945

Our training schedule gets under way again in the morning with the machine gun. Our former section leader leaves with the company that occupied our positions before us. Unfortunately, the second lieutenant, who was a reasonable chap, also leaves with the staff sergeant. From battalion we receive Second Lieutenant Fricke as our company commander. He wears an eyepatch and has the Iron Cross First Class. We are now divided into sections of ten men each and at last we will have some room in our dugout. Our sergeant is called Helmut von Lentzke and he seems a decent fellow.

The comrades who have been allocated to another section take their things and leave. We then go on practising loading the machine gun in the trenches as German bombers fly over to the east at a great height with their roaring engines. We still have aircraft, which gives us new hope! A thought goes through my head; they are destroying German towns, killing German people too! But only for a moment, for hope prevails. The Russian flak opens up hesitantly.

We gradually begin to learn all about the weapons and to master them, and all without any boring theory. Our armourer hands out two egg grenades each to attach to our belts, but they don't have any fuses. We go to lunch with our new sergeant, who is certainly no soldier. With his slender, aristocratic head he looks more like a scholar.

We lie in the trenches in the afternoon and practise target identification. I am not with it. The spring sunshine could be better used, but because we are soldiers we have to fight for our people and country – what country? Today the area between the Oder and Elbe rivers is all that is left of it.

When we return to the command post in the evening, our old colleagues from the barracks are sitting on the railway embankment waiting for allocation. It is a happy reunion. Alfons and Erich are as indestructible as ever with their quips. Sergeant Eckert has also come from Ruhleben with them and is detailed as supply NCO. We sit down with our comrades and hear what they have to say. They left on Monday and on Sunday had to witness the execution of another fifteen. They were shot in groups of three with the next batch having to put the dead in their coffins, the last three being left to the recruits. 'To accustom you to death!' as the Judge-Advocate officer said. A truck then removed the fifteen coffins.

Later the rations are handed out together with twenty cigarettes each, razor blades and writing paper. I give away my razor blades as I have no use for them. Some of our comrades have to sleep in the hay at the command post that night. We get an additional four men allocated to us, so that we are no fewer than we were before.

In the dugout they tell us that there has been another big air attack on Berlin and that the barracks are now practically empty. Even the Hungarians and the Russians have been sent into action. Now schoolboys from 12 years old upwards are receiving weapons training daily. The Jungvolk[1] have set up tank-hunting units and have been armed with old French and Belgian rifles. Many girls have volunteered for the front, even 14-year-olds.

I have sentry duty again tonight. The sergeant gives the order for 'Lights out!' I put on my greatcoat and turn off the light, then climb slowly up the steps into the cold, clear night. At 1130 I go back into the dugout and close the door. I can hear the gentle breathing of the sleepers. Someone is snoring. I sit down beside the stove and doze. I wake up with a jerk when one of the comrades gets up to relieve himself. One-thirty. I quickly turn on the light and wake my relief.

Wednesday 11 April 1945

We are woken at dawn by artillery fire. Mushrooms of smoke are rising behind the Komturei, which I find disturbing.

A runner arrives after breakfast. We are to report to the command post with all our equipment. Grumbling we collect up our things and pack them in the open air. We hardly have a chance to settle down before we have to move on again. I take my light bulb with me and Wegner rips out the stovepipe. Now we can go.

At the command post we are paraded according to height. The company has grown to 150 men. A rumour goes through the ranks that we are returning to Berlin, so when the second lieutenant appears, we all await his instructions with keen anticipation, only to be disappointed. Instead of going back, we are going forward! We are assigned to new positions. Ours is Position No. 22 and Sergeant von Lentzke stays with us, while a section of the older comrades takes over our former position.

We march along the railway embankment to our new location. A vehicle goes by on the rails carrying officers and propelled by two soldiers. Flour is being loaded at the Komturei's little station, and a field kitchen stands steaming behind the houses.

41

Our new position is in the eastern part of the Komturei. Where the land dips below the smithy, trenches and dugouts have been built in the fields. The trenches run down a bit and under the boundary wall to the road. The clayey soil in the bottom of the trenches is full of mud and water. There is a latrine next to the wall. Our dugout is in the middle of the trenches, its top flush with the meadow and well camouflaged. Inside it is quite roomy with places for twenty-five men, the furnishings consisting of a table and a stove without a stovepipe. I quickly take over the upper bunk near the door for myself, thus acquiring a favourable spot. Steel helmets and gas masks are hung outside so as not to clutter up the dugout.

Then I go and explore the Komturei with Boy. We need a stovepipe as ours is too short. Just behind our position a field hospital has been set up in a house. Opposite is the smithy where there is the sound of loud hammering. There is also a pump from which we can draw water. There are big barns and cowstalls in the Komturei, many of them new. A building similar to a large manor with a broad driveway serves as the divisional commander's residence, and a new kitchen has been installed there in the cellars. A few miserable cats live with the farm labourers.

A coach drawn by four horses drives past. We come to attention and salute. The general, who is wearing a monocle, thanks us casually. He then calls us over to him as he gets stiff-legged out of his coach. In a grating voice he asks us why we did not salute him properly. We tell him that we have not learnt how to. When he hears that we are from the 1928 intake, he tells us that we are Germany's last hope and must be prepared to stem the Bolshevik onslaught with our bodies. 'Yes, sir!' is our reply. Then he goes off. And we carry on slowly. Cows are standing in their stalls waiting to be milked, and rosy, fat sows grunt around the dungheap behind the stalls with their piglets. There is a large weathered structure with the date 1530 that is used for storing corn. It used to be the manor church but no services have been held here since the 1920s.[2]

A cauldron full of potatoes stands on the trench parapet just in front of our dugout and we haul it inside with the help of some of our comrades. While we have been away the dugout has been cleaned out so that everything is now spick and span.

The sergeant goes through the trenches with us, detailing the individual positions we will have to man if things get serious. My place is at the roadway. We still have no weapons, only two grenades without any fuses.

We have to go to the command post for lunch. The distance is much greater than before and we will have no opportunity to return during the lunchbreak. Stroschn stays behind with Wegner to cook the potatoes.

A fresh wind has blown through the command post. Erich, the former ship's cook, has taken over the kitchen and concocted a magnificent lunch for us. He says that there is a whole piglet in the soup, and the few globules of fat and pieces of meat swimming around in it are convincing enough.

In the afternoon we have more training on the rifle and machine gun in the fields. The procedures have now become ingrained in us. At about five o'clock we return to the dugout for an hour of fatigues and weapon cleaning. I press to clean the sergeant's weapon and then wash my socks and darn a hole the size of a fist in my stockings. Because I am wearing boots, nobody sees this. Then I get two bowls and heat up some water in them on the stove, and Stroschn and myself have a thorough wash. This is essential, as we are not able to take our clothes off at night.

In the evening we eat most of the boiled potatoes. I mash mine and add some salt. Now one just needs some roast goose to go with them. Sulvatern, who brought his civilian clothing with him from the barracks, has bartered some of them. He shares out bacon fat and dripping, and returns in the dark with a bucketful of milk still warm from the cow. He says that I should exchange my watch, I could get a lot for it.

Later on I write to Gisela and my mother. I will send the letters off in the morning. Then we talk about the spring offensive, which is going to change everything in our favour. The sergeant remains silent, saying nothing, then suddenly bursts out: 'Do you really believe that we can still win?' We believe it. Even I still believe it. Stroschn makes a sceptical grimace and grins.

We do not go to sleep until late. When the light goes out the stove is still burning and throws light across the room. A comfortable warmth fills the dugout. I whisper quietly with Boy until I fall asleep. Outside we can hear an aircraft, its engines buzzing like a hornet.

Thursday 12 April 1945

I am woken up at five as I have the last spell of guard duty with Boy. I quickly slip on my boots and greatcoat and go out into the fresh morning, hanging on my gas mask and putting on my ice-cold steel helmet. I have grabbed Reinhold's rifle, which is almost as tall as I am.

We slowly make our rounds as the last stars shimmer in the sky. We go along the fence and then up to the roadway. A Volkssturm man with an Italian rifle is standing guard on the bridge. He has three bullets. A few trees stand in the water alongside the road, their branches burnt by gunfire and thrusting protestingly into the sky. Up ahead some wagons appear out of the morning mist with a 15-year-old boy in SS uniform leading the horses. He is from Lietzen and was pressed into uniform along with his 60-year-old father. The latter was killed yesterday by a shot through the head, but his mother knows nothing about it yet.

The hours goes by slowly. At six we wake up the sergeant, who then drives out the tired sleepers. We have a quick wash under the pump and are ready for the day. I go with Boy to the kitchen at the divisional head-quarters to collect coffee, saving a long walk to the company command post.

The latest Armed Services Report is hanging in the kitchen. 'Königsberg Fortress was handed over to the Russians by General of Infantry Lasch. Despite this, parts of the loyal garrison have continued to resist. For handing over to the enemy, General of Infantry Lasch has been condemned to death by hanging. His family has been arrested. Fighting on the western front in Nuremberg.'

At eight o'clock we go to the company command post. According to the schedule we are due an hour's lecture period. The second lieutenant tells us of a new wonder weapon that will shortly be arriving at the front in thousands. Rifles that can shoot around corners! At first we laugh and then become serious. Could this be the first of the new wonders? After the lecture the second lieutenant announces that a new decoration has been approved for shooting down low-flying aircraft.

Positions No. 23 and 24 are often disturbed by enemy artillery fire, but otherwise have a peaceful existence, even allowing time for fishing in the small lakes as if it were high summer. Between them and the front there is a small wood. It is rumoured that there is in fact no front there at all, for Russian voices are heard in the wood at night. These positions have only two rifles each.

Later we go shooting. Cardboard targets have been set up on the opposite bank of the flooded fields for us to fire live ammunition at. I keep firing too short, the bullets hitting the water. Perhaps the rifle is also to blame.

We have boiled potatoes for lunch with gravy, meat and vegetables. The cook is doing his best to keep us happy. At the same time we collect our cold rations and once more there are extras – cigarettes, wine, shaving soap, writing paper and patent trouser buttons. I really need those as I have six buttons missing, and they are very practical, as they do not need sewing on.

During the afternoon we go through our trenches with the sergeant. In the event of an attack, we have to defend the road. The sergeant says that we must be familiar with our trench system and the positions he has delegated to us, even in our sleep.

We finish early and go back to cooking potatoes. In the evening the sergeant tells us that Roosevelt is dead and we discuss the consequences of his death at length, and whether America will now end the war. One of the main enemy leaders is dead. Is this an incentive for us, a good omen?

We go on chatting. Hans complains as usual about his rheumatism and being unable to take part in the victory parade through the Brandenburg Gate. We discuss when the big offensive that Hitler has forecast will take place. Once the front has been breached we will advance quickly, for the Russians are also stretched to the limit.

I have guard duty from ten to twelve with Boy again and we make ourselves ready shortly beforehand. The sergeants orders: 'Lights out!' and the comrades get into their bunks. We put out the light, grab the rifles and stamp out into the darkness.

We slowly make our rounds through the Komturei. A light is burning in the field hospital, throwing a bluish glow over the yard. We go up to the road. Far behind us in the west clusters of searchlight beams show up against a reddened sky, and green and red light signals swing about. Berlin is having another air raid.

We have been standing on the road for minutes, hours? We both jump at the roar of a tank engine and the rattle of tracks approaching. Russians? We quickly dive behind the wall and listen. A colossus goes past us, the giant gun barrel betraying a 'Tiger'.[3] We come forward slowly, still suspicious. The tank stops and a man gets out and directs it close to the wall.

Then we talk with the tank crew, who say that over there the Russians can be seen making massive preparations for an attack. Hundreds of German tanks are hidden in woods ready to counter-attack. There are also Seydlitz-Troops in our sector of the front, wearing German uniforms with all their decorations and red armbands. Germans against Germans![4]

It is nearly midnight. We go back to the dugout and sit on the bench outside. I go in to wake the reliefs so that they have time to get ready. Then we wait.

An aircraft flies in front of the Russian lines with a clattering engine like a giant bird of prey about to pounce on its victim, the engine making a noise like a sewing machine and disturbing the quiet of the night for miles around. It is an old-fashioned Russian double-decker which extinguishes every glimmer of light with a well-aimed discharge of bombs. It is also used as an artillery spotter, and is called 'The Bird of Death'.[5]

At last the relief arrives. We hand over our weapons and climb down into the dugout, quickly hanging up our steel helmets and gas masks on their hooks and pushing into the warm room. Greatcoats and boots are rapidly removed and we fall on our bunks.

Friday 13 April 1945

The day begins as usual. Fatigue is partly removed with fresh water from the pump, and when the section marches off at seven-thirty, I stay behind with Boy as we have to remain on guard duty today. I look after the potatoes while Heinz sees to the fire.

The dairy maids are busy milking the cows in their stalls – splendid animals with fat thighs. I pluck up courage and ask for some milk, and they jokingly fill my mess tin full.

We then tidy up the dugout and set up a new stovepipe that Wegner has organised. Then I sit in the sun and write to Gisela. The morning passes slowly. We add to the potatoes on the stove several times, for we will be really hungry tonight.

At noon the comrades return bringing our lunch with them. This afternoon we have training in the trenches again.

A runner appears at two o'clock. Back to the command post in full marching order immediately. Our respite was only a short one. We stuff our pockets with potatoes and I unscrew the light bulb from its fitting. Wegner pulls out the stovepipe and we are off.

The whole company assembles at the command post. Our positions are going to be taken over by other troops. We will have to wait and see where we are to be accommodated. This turns out to be the hayloft, which has a rotten ladder leading up to it. Boy, Stroschn and I take the best places. There is enough hay and so it is bearable. I spread out my greatcoat and sit down to eat. When the cold rations are issued no one can be trusted to share them out fairly, for the sergeant has always done this until now. Finally Poziemba steps forward and shares them out. To prevent any argument, one of us draws a portion and then asks who is to get it, so it is done as fairly as possible. It seems to me that my share is a bit smaller, but: 'Tough luck!'

Wegner comes along at five and says that there is a film in the village this evening, starting at eight. All those who want to go set off at seven. There are about twenty of us who want to see the film. We split up in front of the church, and Stroschn, Boy and myself stroll down the village street together. Some girls giggle behind us and I start blushing.

At seven-thirty, as the church bell announces evening, we go to the pub where the film is to be shown. Only those who have tickets can go in and only the artillery recruits have tickets. I go cheekily up to the sergeant at the entrance and tell him that I had already been inside and handed over my ticket, which is in fact a beermat. Before he can do anything about it, I am inside the hall. I still have the red piping of the artillery on my greatcoat shoulderstraps, so it is just as well that I have not removed them.

The hall is already almost full. I sit down behind a table to make sure that I can stay there. Stroschn gets in somehow and sits down beside me. The faces of our comrades appear in the doorway looking dejected. A sergeant goes through the rows looking at shoulderstraps and Stroschn vanishes under the table. The others are allowed in shortly before the film begins and rush to find empty places. A sheet is stretched on the wall opposite the stage and we are ready to begin, but first a plate is passed round through the rows for the RM1 entrance fee. We both pass the plate on without putting anything in it. We are not going to pay for the artillery!

The atmosphere in the hall is like Christmas. What film is being shown? Will we be able to see it without interruption? At last the lights go out in the hall and the beam of the projector cuts through the darkness. The film is called 'Wiener Blut' and, despite our circumstances, grips us. Not a sound disturbs the showing of this old film with its immortal Strauss waltzes completely captivating us.

When the lights come on again, the illusion of peace suggested by the film is shattered. Our breath taken away, we leave the hall and march back under a heaven shining with stars and spanning the world.

We carefully climb up the ladder and clamber over the sleepers to reach our places. I lie down on the straw and pull my greatcoat over me. The film runs past my eyes all over again. The starry sky shows through gaps in the roof. Worn out, I close my eyes.

Saturday 14 April 1945

When I wake up, I am lost. I want to climb out of my bunk to the left until I realise where I am. The morning light is coming through a half-open door. I get up slowly and carefully pick my way over the feet of my comrades and climb down the rotten ladder balancing my washing kit. There is a big wooden barrel at the pump in the yard. I fill it up slowly and quickly undress and jump in before I can regret it, the ice-cold water removing all the dross from the body. Then a quick rub down and some breathing exercises, and back into my uniform.

I climb up again and lie down on my greatcoat. I quietly chew the remains of my bread as things slowly come to life in the command post, the cook clattering about with pots and pans. At six o'clock the sergeant comes along and gets us out of the straw.

At eight o'clock we fall in in front of the command post, where bit by bit the whole company is assembled. We then go back to the fields to do some more rifle practice.

We are already having a break when the second lieutenant appears with a captain, whose arm is covered with tank-destroyer badges. The captain stands on the embankment and chats quietly with the second lieutenant, then he begins to address us: 'Hitler has ordered the establishment of a tank-hunting division to consist only of the latest intakes. Whoever volunteers will get a special armband.' In glowing terms he describes to us how the men of his division ride their bicycles behind the Russian lines and destroy dozens of Russian tanks with their Panzerfausts. For every tank destroyed there is a tank-destroyer badge and for every four the Knights' Cross. He goes on and on.[6]

When he is finished, he calls for volunteers. Everyone climbs the embankment, all that is except for Stroschn and eight men who remain below. When he starts collecting names another few vanish. I already have doubts myself but am too cowardly to draw back. But it does not matter, the second lieutenant has only to look at us and I lose my courage.

When the captain disappears the rifle practice resumes. Later we make our way back to our accommodation. Then with Boy and Stroschn I go to the station where two locomotives are shunting a 305mm railway gun about. The gun barrel has been lowered and covered with a camouflage net. Two crew and ammunition wagons are standing on the parallel track.[7]

We have to take over a new location in the afternoon. Our section is split up and I am detailed with Wegner to a section of the older men. Fortunately our sergeant is von Lentzke. Our new location is Position No. 10, which is right on the road between the village and the station. There is no straw available and we have to sleep on bare boards. The dugouts have neither doors nor windows, and are built into the embankment, so we find a large board to fix provisionally across the entrance. Later we place our kit on the bunks and return to the command post. Once we think that we have everything we need, we head back. Hopefully we will not have to stay long with the older men, for that would not be very agreeable.

In the evening there is a big row over the sharing out of rations. We youngsters get the smallest portions and also the first shift of guard duty. As we get ourselves ready in the narrow space, grabbing our greatcoats, belts and steel helmets, my egg grenades roll out on the floor, causing a rapid exit by some scared men, who return grumbling after a while. I stuff my grenades into my greatcoat pockets and go outside.

The trenches are not yet finished. We go from the dugout to the railway and back. A light is burning in the gun crews' wagon and a radio is playing. It is bitterly cold. We get out cigarettes and smoke cautiously. The guards on the dugout opposite give us the time. It is midnight.

We go back to the dugout and prop the rifles against the wall. There is a horrible smell like a stable in the narrow room. It reeks of food, sweat and leather.

We try to wake up our reliefs without success. Let them sleep. Drunk with sleep, we climb into our bunks. My place is occupied, so I force my way in between two sleepers, who pull aside grumpily, put my pack under my head and fall asleep.

Sunday 15 April 1945

When we are woken up there is a thunderstorm raging overhead. It is cloudy and misty, and there is still morning mist covering the fields. It is Sunday again.

We do not have any water and stand around unwashed and half asleep, but hot coffee wakes me up a bit. We sit down on the roadside and look at the village. The sun breaks through the fog and shines on the bright tiles of the roofs. Then it starts to rain. Buckets are rattling in the cattlesheds and snatches of conversation can be heard. The first churchgoers appear on the village street, and the church bells urge them on. Peace only four kilometres from the front. At any moment the flames of war could descend on this village, but everyone is going about their work quietly and without haste. The farmer ploughs his field, the housewives attend to their yards, and in the evening they all meet up for a chat on the village street. The farmers are making their way to church quietly and with dignity. War and peace, life and death, in such close proximity!

During the morning we have to peel potatoes in the command post yard, and later I chop wood. Tessmann pulls a piglet out of the stall and vanishes with it into the garden, later returning with it slaughtered for the kitchen.

From the village comes the sound of bells signalling the end of the church service. The second lieutenant comes along and helps us with the potato peeling. He says that our offensive is due to start within the next few days in time for Hitler's birthday[8] The general has telephoned to say that he has received a telegram from Hitler announcing the arrival of 500 tanks and 1,000 long-barrelled guns.[9] Also trenches have to be prepared for some special divisions that are on their way to reinforce us with new weapons! We look at each other. We have hope once more. The second lieutenant goes on to say that the British have offered peace. The guns in the west will be silenced and we will then combine against the Bolsheviks.

We go down to the fields at eleven o'clock. Only a few remain behind on kitchen fatigues. We lie down on the edge of the fields and practise firing the Panzerfaust until the break. Then we lie in the sun.

Mushrooms of smoke rise from behind the Komturei. Ivan is laying down a barrage. The older men from Position No.24 are missing. A runner goes off and returns shortly before midday carrying a pack. They bring in a dead man, who was sitting near the dugout when the firing started and has been riddled through with splinters. Our first fatal casualty! Sixty years old and with a wife and two daughters at home. He will not see or take part in the big change in our favour.

We disperse and sit on the railway embankment. The second lieutenant sends the section with its dead man off to the cemetery. We have fallen silent.

Lunch, good as it is, simply does not taste right. Erich keeps offering second helpings, but only Sorgatz, who eats anything and everything, does not hold back and has three helpings. He has a rubber stomach – the more he eats the bigger he gets. When he is finished, he takes another mess tinful, just in case.

The meal is over when a runner arrives from battalion. We have to start work on the trenches for the reinforcements due to arrive tonight. We march through the village and past the cemetery, and then wheel off to the left. Because of the danger from low-flying aircraft, we move across the fields in single file and well spread out until we reach the trenches, where hand tools, picks and shovels are lying scattered around. We are divided up and I am in the group tasked with deepening the trenches, while others work on the dugouts. There is plenty of flying activity and we often have to stick our noses into the sand.

Later on I go with Boy, Stroschn and Sergeant Weerts over the fields and green meadows to a distant barn to collect straw. Lively little piglets, only two weeks old, are playing on the dungheap, jumping about like puppies, and when I try to catch one and put it under my arm, it makes a fearful screeching. The farmer, who is returning from a walk in his fields in his Sunday suit, gives us straw and we then go back heavily laden. A plane crosses over high up, its engine humming monotonously, its silver surfaces gleaming in the sun.

The walls of the dugout are already complete and it is being covered with sand. We lay our straw down inside and return to our work.

At six o'clock we gather up the tools and go back to the command post. Then we put on our packs and fall in. The armourer hands out fuses for our grenades and we march off.

We march through the village to the windmill, where we are to stay until the morning, when we will return to the forward positions. We lay our kit down in the big barn and are then divided up again. I go to No. 3 Section with Boy and Stroschn under Sergeant Weerts. Later we get some straw from a farmer and make our encampment in the barn.

A flak platoon is accommodated in the windmill. I go up the stairs of the windmill with Stroschn and look out to the east. The land beyond a hill is pitted with craters – the front. In the middle of the craters are the trenches, German and Russian. A staff sergeant lends us his binoculars. He says that those are the Russian lines and that there are also Seydlitz-Troops in German uniforms fighting against us. Dejected, we go back down the stairs.

A wagon brings us our evening rations, on which I fall hungrily. Later it gradually gets dark and I burrow into the straw. Tonight I have guard duty with Boy from midnight until one.

I am woken up in the night. I quickly slip on my boots and don my greatcoat. Then we go out. It is bitterly cold and we put up the collars of our greatcoats and stamp around. There is a clear sky above us. A friendly moon lights up the world with its gentle glow. We run round the windmill to warm ourselves up. A door grates somewhere. The front is quiet as if asleep. Not even a verey light in the sky. At one o'clock Boy wakes our relief and we quickly slip into the barn. I pull the boots off my feet and lay them down. The straw is nice and warm.

NOTES

1. The junior division of the Hitler Youth for 10–14-year-olds.
2. This property has been returned to its pre-war owners, the von Hardenberg

family, and the manor house, whose basic structure comes from the west side of the original caravanserai, has been beautifully restored, as has the church. Many old structures and those of the collective farm of the post-war years have been cleared away, but the property still boasts the oldest barn in Germany.

3. The 'Tiger' (PzKfw VI) weighed 54 tons and had a maximum speed of 23 mph (37 kph). It was armed with an 88 mm gun and two MG 34 machine guns. This tank probably belonged to the SS Heavy Tank Battalion 502, which was in reserve in the woods across the lake immediately east of the Komturei.

4. 'Seydlitz-Troops' was the name applied by the German regime to auxiliaries raised by the Soviets from German prisoners-of-war to fight the Nazi regime after General Seydlitz, scion of a distinguished military family, who had been appointed President of the 'League of German Officers' by the Soviets in 1943, following the establishment of the 'National Committee for Free Germany' in Moscow a year earlier. General Seydlitz, who was condemned to death in his absence, was in fact totally against this use of German prisoners-of-war in combat and was exonerated after the war. The East German government, which was proud of the propaganda activities of this organisation, made no reference to combat activity and no record can be found in its military archives, but sufficient evidence exists to prove that Seydlitz-Troops were used in combat in this last phase of the war. (See article 'Deutsche gegen Deutsche' in *Militär Geschichte*, Volume 4, 1995.)

5. The Po-2 again.

6. There was a Tank-Destroyer Division nearby astride the Seelow–Müncheberg highway, consisting of the *'Dorn'* and *'Pirat'* Jagd-Panzer Brigades, and the equivalent of a third anti-tank brigade, all under the command of HQ 541st Volksgrenadier Division. The captain described here was probably Gerhard Konopka, born 27 March 1911, of the *'Grossdeutschland'* Grenadier Regiment, who had been decorated with the Knights' Cross on 29 August 1943.

7. This was one of the three guns of the 8th Battery, 100th Railway Artillery Regiment. The other two guns were located at Seelow and Müncheberg. All were to be destroyed by air attack on 16 April 1945.

8. 20 April.

9. At a conference in the Führerbunker on 6 April, Göring, Himmler and Dönitz had promised Hitler reinforcements for the Eastern Front in the form of 100,000 airmen, 25,000 SS and 12,000 sailors. However, this grandiose gesture only produced some 30,000 men, none of whom were equipped or trained for the role expected of them, and 9th Army were only able to find 1,000 rifles to share out among them. At the same time Hitler continued to play a game of bluff with his field commanders, promising them non-existent 'wonder weapons', guns and tanks, for which in any case no fuel was available.

CHAPTER V

The Storm Breaks

Monday 16 April 1945

We are woken in the middle of the night by the sudden shaking and shuddering of the earth beneath us. We are under heavy fire. We grab our things. I quickly pull on my boots, take my greatcoat and pack under my arm, and stumble out into the night. The earth is quaking and the night is full of lightning and roaring. Heavy shells are passing over us and we can see each other's tired faces whenever an explosion bursts and a flash of light hangs briefly in the night.

The sergeants are quite nervous. At last the staff sergeant appears and takes us to the trenches behind the windmill. I look at the time; it is four o'clock. The Russian offensive has begun.[1]

The thundering of the guns has turned into a single roar and the air is full of howls, whistles and a quivering and buzzing. Heavy bangs come from behind us between the lesser explosions, sounding like railway wagons shunting into each other. A vast red wall of fire rises up into the sky in front of us, clouds of smoke rising with it. The shapes of bombers appear like giant birds in the black clouds. Fountains of dirt and iron erupt. We duck deeper in our trenches. From behind us comes a rolling and whistling. Lietzen is being bombed and columns of fire are rising up in their gruesome beauty with trees and the roofs of houses whirling through the air.

We are in a vast cauldron. In front of us, around us and behind us is an enveloping hell as the Russians drum on our trenches. The explosions go on and on. Our ears have long since been deafened. Hardly anyone speaks. Only when a fountain of dirt and steel erupts close by does an angry word escape that one can read from their lips.

Burning barns and villages stand out in the distance like torches in the night, and refugees are coming back dragging their belongings in prams and handcarts, or on their backs. A woman in a dressing gown that flaps in the wind stumbles past with her hair loosened, her eyes a complete blank. She has a coffee mill in her hand which she keeps turning endlessly. Her mouth moves but makes no sound.

Ammunition and supply carts surprised by the attack are racing back along the road, the drivers wildly whipping their nags while shells howl into the banks and explode. Refugees hurry by like creatures of the underworld – women, children and old men surprised in their sleep, some only half-dressed. In their faces is despair and deadly fear. Crying children holding their mothers' hands look out at the world's destruction with shocked eyes.

The shelling stops abruptly. Our ears are deafened and our abused eardrums have to accustom themselves to the silence. Gradually one discerns heavy, flaring infantry fire. Shots whip by, machine gun salvoes chase burst after burst in the night, but we still have no weapons.

The staff sergeant takes the company back under cover of the breaking dawn to collect weapons from the command post. I stay behind with Bayer to look after our things. The trench walls have partially collapsed and there is sand all over our packs. The veil of night that lay protectively over the shattered earth slowly lifts. A black wall stands in front of us. Shreds of dense smoke chase across the sky. The first wounded are making their way back.

My whole body is shaking. My consciousness was switched off during that hour of horror for, like an animal in danger, the body automatically shuts down, the senses unable to take in all that is going on. But now it is quiet and more horrors are yet to come. One dare not think back.

The company returns in a long line, all having been issued with rifles. They go past the windmill and press on. Bayer and myself are released and go back through the village to the command post.

Lietzen is no longer recognisable. Destruction has descended on the village like a hurricane and houses are burning on both sides of the street. The farmers are removing cattle from their stalls and and roping them together, driving them away apprehensively. Smouldering timbers lie in the village pond with ducks swimming around. Bellowing cows run through the village as refugees hasten by. A foreign worker carries a sack of sugar on his back. Crying children are running about looking for their parents. A little girl cries over her doll. The village church is on fire.

The command post has run out of weapons, so we have to go back to our trenches in the Hindenburg Line. Reinicke, Berger, Bittrich, Grigat, Helios and Bayer's stepbrother are here too. There were not enough weapons to go round. Later we are joined by Paulat, Solga, Staub and Steinseufzer, making twelve of us from our barrack-room in Ruhleben, all 17 years old.

We are restless and pale, and yet composed. Death stands at our elbow.

The sun has driven the last shadows of night away and dispenses its beaming rays. Low-flying aircraft streak over the lines rattling their cannon, allowing no respite.

The second lieutenant comes through the trenches and asks if we are scared. Not scared, but with a tight feeling in our stomachs. I then go back to the command post with Bayer again. The sergeant there has now got some Italian submachine guns. I have never handled one of these things before, but I tell him that I know how to use it. I leave with two submachine guns with some magazines and a few rounds of ammunition. Bayer has got a submachine gun and a No. 42 rifle. As I go back across the fields I try to find out how it works. It refuses to function, the rounds keep sticking and then suddenly it goes off, and now I am more careful with it.

While I am passing under some old trees there is a sudden roar quite close as if a coal bucket were hurtling through the air. The railway gun has opened fire and thunders out every six minutes, hurling shells at the enemy.

The sun lies over the fields. I take the narrow path across where the water is spilling over the sand. Suddenly a low-flying aircraft appears over the hill and I stand still, unable to move, ready to take whatever comes, but it passes over and I slowly climb up to the village. The fields are damp and sand clings to my boots. I stop at a latrine and sit comfortably on the pole. Boy and Bayer come by and wait for me, then we go on together.

Fire has destroyed the houses. Here and there flames flicker in the ruins while cattle bellow in the undamaged sheds. A farmer is driving a foal ahead of him at the village entrance. 'Get on with you, Satan!' The animal looks at us in astonishment and then gallops away whinnying.

As I go along I try to find out how my weapon works, but it still refuses to function. However, I have time.

The firing has gradually died down at the front. Then the guns begin to thunder again and lay a barrage over us. We continue going forward as the shells explode. Wounded are coming toward us. The windmill stands in the sunlight on our left, and the miller's truck is driving off to the rear fully laden. On our right the sandy slope of the cemetery rises up the hillside. The crosses shimmer in the sunshine like ebony. There is still plenty of room available there.

The trenches lie behind the cemetery.[2] This is the second line of defence, where the enemy are expected to be caught and held, and a platoon of the older men is deployed here under Staff Sergeant Köster. The anti-tank barrier leaves only a narrow gap for traffic to pass through. The ground all around is churned up. Boy and Stroschn are lying in the grass close to the barrier with several Panzerfausts. A white poster with red lettering is fastened to the barrier: 'Panzerfausts and German soldiers are stronger than Red tanks!'

Bayer gives his submachine gun to the staff sergeant and I give one to Sergeant Weerts, our section leader. He gets up stiff-legged and struts around in his boots, looking very self-important.

I am allocated a place in the trench with Wegner on my left, and

Poziemba and Volke on my right. I take out my handkerchief and polish my gun, placing the cleaned components on a rag and then oiling them. Now I can see how it works. Then I place the ammunition and gun on the parapet and cover them with grass. Tired, I lie down on the floor of the trench, where the sand is white and warm.

Suddenly low-flying aircraft cross over the trenches, and again, before one can hear them bombs are falling on the road. We watch them fall, as if drawn to earth by magnets, and then bursting on the asphalt. The planes cross and approach from every angle. Boy and Stroschn streak round the barrier. Now the planes are attacking out of the sun with their tails up and fire ripping from their wings. Only later does one hear the sound of the discharge and the humming of the bullets. Everyone dives into the trenches and crouches in corners. I lie on my back and remain indifferent to it all. Eventually they fly off, the wind carrying the tacking of their weapons far across the land. Döbberin is burning in the background.

Whenever things start getting uncomfortable, Sergeant Weerts vanishes to the rear with his submachine gun slung, making for the command post. Klabunde is afraid. There is foam around his mouth and he wants to jump out of the trench. We have to knock him down and tie him up in the dugout.

Later, when things have quietened down, I go back into the village. A twin-barrelled, anti-aircraft gun stands beside the first house on the right, its crew smoking silently. I take a drink from the pump and help myself to two cases of pistol ammunition. As I am about to leave, aircraft dive out of the sun and I dash into the cellar. The bombs hit the village with a whistling sound. A dud lies in the street.

At noon I collect welfare stores for my section. The railway gun is silent. Bombs have destroyed the station, ripping up the tracks, and the command post has been badly knocked about. Doors have burst open, walls gape and windows have gone. Each man gets a hundred cigarettes, two packets of tobacco, two front line packets, buttons, razor blades and writing paper. There are even combs and pipes. I take a pipe and stick it in my pocket.

Volkssturm are lying in the trenches at the windmill and two farmers are already slaughtering a sheep, the blood flowing brightly from the cut.

As the sun begins to sink, I go to the rear again with Stroschn, Zander and Schomburg. We have taken the mess tins from our packs and are looking for something to eat. Aircraft are roaring over the front. American bombers? Their bomb bays open and silver objects plunge to earth. I lie in the trench as if it were a cradle rocking and want to die. The earth in the meadows has been ripped open, the craters filling with dirty water, and big openings and cracks have appeared in the roadway.

Darkness descends slowly. We eat a ladleful of pea soup, the grease running down our cheeks. A whole pig went into the cooking pot. Sand grates in our teeth, but now we are happy. Then I nibble some chocolate and biscuits taken from the front line packets and fill my pipe for the very first time. The smoke tickles my throat and brings tears to my eyes.

The staff sergeant arrives and the section gets together. The older men have suffered the first casualties with a direct hit on a foxhole. The three men were killed instantly and their remains have been taken to the cemetery. He reads out a Führer-Order: 'Berlin remains German. Vienna will be German again, and Europe never Russian. Form yourselves into brotherhoods. At this hour the whole German people are looking at you, my East Front warriors, and only hope that through your resolve, your fanaticism, your weapons and your leaders, the Bolshevik onslaught will drown in a sea of blood. The turning point of the war depends upon you!'[3]

We separate deeply thoughtful. We collect our packs from the windmill trenches and go into a dugout on our new position. The comrades lie down to sleep and I go outside with Boy to stand watch.

It is cool. We stand and stare into the dark night. I feel weak, tired and empty. It is difficult to maintain one's beliefs after what we have been through![4]

Tuesday 17 April 1945

We have hardly slept when we are woken up again. Freezing, we grab our weapons and slip out into the early dawn. We stamp about in the trench and look out at a new day.

The darkness slowly lifts, the sun comes up, unbelievably beautiful, to shine over us. Low-flying aircraft roar over the trenches, infantry fire flares up and occasional artillery barrages roll muffled and heavy. We lie in the trench and look longingly at the sun. I smoke my pipe again. The tobacco tickles my throat, but I want to get used to it, it looks so manly.

The sky gradually becomes busy. German aircraft dive out of the clouds, suddenly changing direction to dive like hawks on the windmill. There is a clattering and a roaring, and flames leap from the building, the windmill burning with a loud crackling sound, and the soldiers accommodated in the mill jump out of the flames. The singing propellers pull the aircraft back up into the sky, but they soon dive down again and start shooting up our trenches. We rush here and there to keep in the dead angles, depending on their line of approach. Are they crazy? They are *German* planes!

The staff sergeant sends a runner. Look out for aircraft captured by the Russians. We look up. Yes, these are German aircraft, Me 109s, but without either the Balkan Cross or the Swastika.

The aircraft cross over the trenches throwing out leaflets that flutter slowly down to earth. Then they fly off across the front and vanish into the hinterland. We breathe out again. We carefully climb out of the trench and run to collect the leaflets that lie quite distinctly on the dark fields. They are in large format with a black-white-red strip right across the heading. We pretend that we are collecting them up to hand them in later, but practically everyone of us keeps back a copy to read in secret. They are like a glimpse into an incomprehensible foreign world.

More wounded are coming back. At noon I go to the windmill with Stroschn. It is still burning and crackling, and the houses are now just ruins. The Volkssturm have vanished. We go down into the cellar and take some preservatives and enormous sides of bacon from the shelves. The cellar is soon empty and our knapsacks stuffed full. A few hens are running about the hilltop.

Later on I go into the village with Boy. There is plenty of food in the larders. We fill our stomachs and take away whatever we can. Cattle are lowing in their stalls, the milk burning in the udders of the poor suffering creatures. We hear them and yet we don't hear them. Have we become heartless? We take two rabbits from a house, and I break the neck of a startled goose. A little piglet is trotting along the street, and that too is taken. A soldier appears here and there among the farmyards carrying a sack. Geese gabble and are quickly silenced. Sometimes a door grates. Over all the burnt-out farms lies the smell of cooked meat.

We light a fire outside the dugout. Poziemba has brought back a whole hundredweight sack of semolina. Delighted, we make pudding out of it, taking water from the pond. Later we have a wash and in the evening we have semolina pudding with jam. Sergeant Weerts kills the piglet and two others pluck the goose. The aroma of fresh meat rises from all the fires. An ownerless dog slinks up to the fire. Weert aims and fires at it, but misses, sending a burst after it. The hound slinks away, but he kills it, carries it to the fields and throws it into a fresh crater.

We lie with full stomachs on our bunks this evening. Sleep will not come. The sentries come and go, and at last I fall asleep.[5]

Wednesday 18 April 1945

We are soon woken up again. 'Get up! Take post!' I turn over on to my other side and grumble that I have just come off guard duty. I am lucky, I am left alone. From outside come the tired voices of soldiers. They are collecting grass to camouflage the trenches. I slowly come back to the world. I can hear the voices of the sentries through my half slumber.

The comrades crash back in exhausted, having been digging all night. I get up feeling a little guilty, and together we finish off the remains of the goose.

Then we return to the trench. Low flying aircraft are roaring around as usual and wounded are coming back. The enemy has broken through on the right flank. Guben, Forst, Cottbus and Görlitz have been lost.[6] In the north he has pushed forward as far as Müncheberg, and Seelow has been lost. We are the last position left on the front between the Stettiner Haff and the Sudetenland.[7]

General Seydlitz is said to be in Seelow with tanks. A civilian apparently shot up his vehicle with a Panzerfaust. Is Seydlitz dead?

The front is quiet. We leave our trenches to fetch clumps of grass to camouflage our dugout and trench. I am carrying a tent-half with Boy to transport the turfs.[8] The howling of artillery fire can be heard in the distance.

Then suddenly all hell breaks loose. We find ourselves lying in an inferno of fire and horror. Fire strikes from the heavens and licks the earth, howling around us. I lie there half dead with fear, scratching the earth with my fingernails, ripping at the turf. If only one could sink into the bowels of the earth! All around us fire and dark smoke as the earth is ploughed up metre by metre. More keep coming – Stalin-organs[9] – God have mercy on us!

Have I been lying here for hours, days? The fire has lifted. I cannot believe it. I feel myself all over, nothing is missing. I am only covered in dirt and half shattered, but still alive.

A horrible silence now reigns. Here and there someone heaves themselves up. A human being? One of God's gifts? A ghost? We stand up, unable to believe that we are still alive. Perhaps death would have been more merciful.

We stagger back to the dugout. 'Water, water!' Soon life begins to course through our bodies again. The surrounding area now looks like a moonscape, bare and dug up.

The staff sergeant bursts in with an ashen face: 'All out! The Russians!' We grab our weapons, for there can be no holding back. Fleeing soldiers are coming from the front, most having thrown their weapons away. Among them are soldiers wearing black-white-red armbands, and Russians. The cry of 'Seydlitz-Troops!' goes up along the line. We aim and fire as we have been taught, always into the body. Tanks come up from the rear and reinforcements double forward. We advance, firing all the time. The Russians and Seydlitz-Troops fall back, slowly at first and then faster, finally fleeing. We are scarcely aiming any more. I empty magazine after magazine and the breach is soon red hot with firing.

A wounded man raises his hand: 'Help me, comrade!' He wears the black-white-red armband. We push on.

We reach the first row of trenches and stop, not wanting to go any farther. Reinforcements occupy the trenches. There is the occasional shot. The company commander appears and collects us together. We go back.

Dead lie between the craters, many of them in field grey uniform, nearly all German, some with swastikas on their chests, some with the black-white-red armband, their medals shining faintly. Now they lie close to each other, peaceful in death.

We are tired and despondent, burnt out. We have a big emptiness inside us. We have lost all hope.

Trench digging resumes at night and the fallen-in trenches are restored. I am in the older men's trench with Stroschn, the occupants having been attached to our section in an amalgamation. Yesterday still 140 strong, today we are only 110. Despite the hopelessness of the struggle, we remain in the centre of the battle.

We look out into the night over a machine gun, whose breech is as cold as ice. I have laid my submachine gun down in front of me. The night is cool and I move along the trench to keep warm, a cigarette glowing behind my cupped hand.

A flare goes up quite near. The field lies starkly in the falling light, the craters staring at the sky like big eyes. The light goes out and the darkness returns even blacker than before.

From across the way comes the sound of spades digging. A shot rings out somewhere and disappears singing. The front flashes to the north and south, and we are the last bulwark. Our flanks have been overrun and to the north and south the enemy is well behind our rear.

Time passes, the hours go by. It is midnight. Still another six hours of sentry duty to go. This time the whole night long. Boy comes over once from the section trench and we sit on ammunition boxes and chat, thinking about the hours just gone. There are new furrows, new lines etched on our faces. We have suddenly gone from being children to being adults, old people. We can kill, but we can't cry any more; we have learnt that.[10]

Thursday 19 April 1945

The night does not want to end. The staff sergeant comes along once through the trenches and looks us over. Just in time I am able to wake Stroschn, who had nodded off. Then we stand up again and move around, taking it in turns to walk along the trench to keep awake and not fall asleep. I go into the adjacent dugout to strike a match. We then take it in turns to lie down and sleep. The moon is like a ghost in the sky. The rattle of mess tins comes from somewhere, and I wake Stroschn up. We stand behind the machine gun again, our faces sunken and drawn. Boy brings our mess tins with hot food, which we gobble down greedily.

Our dead are buried in the cemetery. The cheerful Bittrich, only recently 17 and a blond East Prussian, whose father is a civil servant. The quiet, stiff Grigat with his broad Pomeranian skull. The well-loved Röder, who even in the worst circumstances could find a cheerful word, and always something to eat. Now they lie here as if they are sleeping, peaceful and still, united in death with children and fathers of families. They are lowered carefully into a mass grave. We throw a handful of sand on the sleepers as our last farewell, comrades. Soon a low mound covers the dead.

I go back again, leaving the twenty-three men – twenty-three comrades sleeping their last sleep. They are luckier than us who have to go on killing, waiting for death. Of the other seven comrades there is no trace. They were shredded to bits by the Stalin-organs, ripped to pieces.

We stand and stare into the night. The dawn comes up slowly.

Gunfire breaks out abruptly once more, right on our trenches. It explodes and whistles and the splinters strike all around us, humming like bees, deadly bees. The barrage moves on behind us. We lift our heads.

Figures are running across the field in front of us. Russians? We cram the belt into the feed and race it through. The salvoes bellow out. We remain calm, icy calm. Reinforcements enter our trench from the left. In front of us are fleeing soldiers, followed by Russians. We take our machine gun, I grab my submachine gun, and we move across to our old section trench, where everything is ready for battle, weapons grasped tight until it hurts.

Soldiers are running back along the road, coming from all over. Is everything lost? The Russians are coming up close behind. There is still heavy infantry fire up ahead. It is slowly becoming light and the sun climbs again as the troops flee back.

Tanks come racing up the road and SS jump off and spread out. The fleeing soldiers are stopped and rounded up. 'Forward march!' They are driven forward unarmed with a tank behind each group urging them on. Behind us on the right a tank stands in the fields and fires, sending its message of death to the other side.

Our sergeant stands on the road with his submachine gun and big steel helmet, his legs wide apart, and stops the fleeing soldiers who are still trickling back. Wounded are coming back, but even they are driven forward again. A young SS second lieutenant has driven his vehicle into the roadside ditch and is chasing around, herding the men together with his pistol.

We have to climb on a tank, which rushes forward, while another tank follows behind to prevent anyone jumping off.

Gradually things quieten down. The infantry fire indicates the fierceness of the fighting as it flares up and then dies down again. I go down to the pond and slake my thirst.

By eleven o'clock the situation has been secured and the attack beaten back. A sentry remains on the trench. I have the duty and lie down in the trench looking at the sky. A beetle flies by with a humming sound and a stalk of grass waves in the wind.

The Russians lay down a barrage and low-flying aircraft roar around dropping bombs on the roadway. Heavy artillery shells crash into the Komturei and flames rise above the trees.

As I am about to enter the dugout, shells strike and I quickly dive inside. There is a fresh crater smoking just outside the entrance.

The battalion commander comes forward and addresses us: 'Hold on another twenty-four hours, comrades,' he says in a moving voice. 'Hitler has issued an order: "Hold on another twenty-four hours and the great change in the war will come! Reinforcements are rolling forward. Wonder weapons are coming. Guns and tanks are being unloaded in their thousands. Hold on another twenty-four hours, comrades! Peace with the British. Peace with the Americans. The guns are silent on the West Front. The Western Army is marching to the support of you brave East Front warriors. Thousands of British and Americans are volunteering to join our ranks to drive out the Bolsheviks. Hundreds of British and American aircraft stand ready to take part in the battle for Europe. Hold on another twenty-four hours, my comrades. Churchill is in Berlin negotiating with me."'

We are going to win!

We listen to him breathlessly. Our troops need a break, for they have been burnt to cinders. We are boys scarcely able to carry our packs, but we know how to die in our hundreds, in our thousands at the front, from north to south. We can scarcely believe that this can possibly end sometime.

Infantry fire comes from all around us. The enemy is driving us back metre by metre from our ground, and the positions change hands several times. We advance with a 'Hurrah!' and we die with a 'Hurrah!', with hope in our eyes. After six years of war we are still attacking with 'Hurrah!' The big change is coming tomorrow.

But it isn't working any more. Little by little we are being forced out of our trench system, for the enemy is fighting like the very devil.

By evening the Russians are lying above on the road and the Seydlitz-Troops seem to have been fallen out. From the enemy trenches comes the sounds of bawling and shrieking, quite high-pitched, almost feminine.

A staff sergeant from some shattered regiment or other that had been in front of us stands beside me. He says that the Russians have their whores with them in the trenches. I look at him. He wears the Iron Cross First Class and the German Cross in Gold on his tunic, and next to them the small gold Hitler Youth badge. He has a coarse, barbaric, even brutal face, the barrack square bully personified. From his speech he could be an East Prussian. Perhaps in his early days he was a boy on a small farm tending cattle?

It has become quiet in the Russian trenches. We stare intensely into the night. I now realise that the staff sergeant has been drinking, for he reeks of rotgut.

There is a young major in the dugout, the commander of the regiment that was in front of us, now only seventy-eight men strong. His staff consists of the staff sergeant and three sergeants. He is making his plans as if we had not just gone through six years of war but were about to start a fresh campaign.

We listen in, unable to sleep. His words intoxicate us and revive our shreds of hope. The staff sergeant is drunk and bawling. The major says that the staff sergeant slips across into the Russian lines at night armed only with a knife and wooden truncheon and strangles them one by one. His hands are like sledgehammers. His best effort was five men in one night, which is why he wears the Iron Cross and the German Cross in Gold, and he would have got the Knights' Cross long ago if he was not always drunk. His awards are not for heroism, but for murder!

Before midnight the second lieutenant, the major and the staff sergeant leave on patrol, heading for the Komturei. Shortly afterwards we hear shouting, firing and hand grenades detonating, and they return triumphantly with a prisoner.

The intimidated prisoner stands outside the dugout entrance, while sounds of laughter and bawling come from within. The blanket screening the entrance flutters gently in the wind spilling light into the passage. I look at the prisoner. He is a human being like myself, with good-natured, warm eyes. I cannot hate him.

I go back along the trench. Solga has fallen asleep at the machine gun. I give him a jab and he wakes with a start. It is quiet, unnaturally quiet.

Later I return to the dugout and my relief goes to the machine gun post. Stroschn is standing at the entrance. He tells me that the Russian is being interrogated. Poziemba speaks Russian and is trying to question the prisoner, who is saying nothing. This makes Poziemba angry, and he strikes the prisoner. The major has to intervene. Shrugging, they give up the attempt. I slowly enter the dugout, where everything seems to turn in my direction: the dugout, the comrades and the men around the flickering candle.

Exhaustedly, I lie down on my bunk, but sleep will not come. The men's conversation buzzes gently in the room like bees, the flickering candle casting ghostly shadows against the walls.

The prisoner is taken outside by the staff sergeant. The sound of a pistol shot disturbs the silence of the night. I see his warm eyes before me, looking at me.

The candles have burned themselves out, the conversation dies.[11]

NOTES

1. Various times have been quoted for the opening of the attack. The Soviets used Moscow Time throughout and for them this was 0500 hours. The Germans were on Double Summer Time from 1 April to 6 October, and for them this was 0300 hours.

2. Some of the original trenches can still be found in the copse on the hilltop above the cemetery.

3. This Führer-Order had been written and despatched on the evening of 15 April, but did not reach the troops to whom it was addressed until the following day. Vienna had fallen to the Soviets on the 13th.

4. This first day of battle could not have gone worse for Marshal Zhukov and his 1st Byelorussian Front. Despite an opening barrage from over 40,000 guns of all calibres, Soviet casualties had been staggering and the day's objectives had not been reached. The German defence proved stronger than expected and the Seelow Heights positions had held, save for a minor breach due east of Friedersdorf.

5. By the end of the second day of battle, Seelow had been by-passed by Soviet armour on either side, heading for Diedersdorf at the northern end of the flooded valley on which Lietzen stood. The Seelow Heights front still held from west of Friedersdorf through Dolgelin to the south, masking the Lietzen position.

6. These had all fallen to Marshal Koniev's 1st Ukrainian Front farther south. Forst was Altner's birthplace.

7. In fact the Soviets did not reach and break through at Müncheberg until the following day, but Seelow did fall on the 18th. At this stage Lietzen formed part of the northern corner of a bastion of the defences still extending down to Frankfurt on the Oder.

8. German soldiers were issued with waterproof tent-halves that could be worn as capes or fastened together to make simple pup-tents.

9. The German name for the Katyusha (BM-21) multiple-rocket launcher.

10. On this third day of battle a German counter-attack against them by Soviet armour bunched at Diedersdorf exacted a heavy toll. Nevertheless, the Soviet armour thrust through toward Müncheberg and, concerned about the exposed southern flank of this thrust, reinforcements were brought in to exert pressure on the remaining German defence, including the Lietzen position.

11. The Soviet breakthrough was completed on this fourth day of battle near Müncheberg and the way to Berlin lay open, German resistance from then only being able to delay the advance, not stop it. Concern for the southern flank continued, hence the pressure on Lietzen.

CHAPTER VI

Retreat

Friday 20 April 1945

The breathing of the sleepers comes quietly across the room. A moonbeam streams through the blanket at the entrance on to the floor. Here and there a rifle shot whips through the night.

I had fallen asleep, but outside machine guns are bellowing, hand grenades exploding, shots whistling past and ricochets humming around. Somebody bursts into the dugout. 'Outside with your packs! The Russians!' He disappears into the night like a ghost, leaving his words hanging in the air.

A match flares. I quickly slip on my pack with unsteady hands, grabbing what I can in the dark, and stumble out. We stand in front of the dugout shocked and drunk with sleep. Figures are running across the hill, machine gun bursts are spewing over the roadway and grenades exploding with a flash in the darkness.

We move out. The anti-tank barrier stands threateningly on the road and the remains of the windmill glimmer red in the night. We only have one thought, and that is to get out of this bloody mess.

The village is under heavy shellfire with flames rising as high as the houses, the shells rushing over our heads to explode with a roar. We have no choice, we have to get through. We run along the street with the houses spurting fountains of sand and stone at us. Burning beams whirl up into the air. The howling and bursting of shells goes on all around us.

I am calm, unnaturally calm. I run through the hell, jump, fall and pick myself up again. There is no end to it. We race ahead as if pursued by demons in a race with death.

We have broken through the area of the barrage. Our tongues stick to our gums, our bodies are bathed in sweat, and our lungs suck in the fresh air in gulps. We have come through once more.

The dull thud of tank guns comes from the railway embankment.

The village lies behind us like a nightmare, with the fires rising into the night. We march off to the west. Wagons racing past in the dark into the unknown, sparks flying from the horses' hooves, forcing us aside into the ditches, and then we march on again. The horror slowly falls behind and our pace becomes easier. We can raise our heads again.

We stop at the battalion command post. The sergeants go into the farm while we lie in the ditches and wait. The night is cool and dark. It is two o'clock. We look around silently. A shower of sparks lies over the martyred earth. For us it is as if we have escaped from Hell. We have just been snatched from the jaws of death yet again.

The battalion staff have flown but Second Lieutenant Fricke is standing in the yard. We fall out and wait for further instructions. The sections split up inside the house. We go into the kitchen, where there is the smell of roast meat, and lie down on the floor to sleep. Occasionally the door bangs and a draught blows over our exhausted faces. The sound of the front comes through muffled to us. It suddenly occurs to me that this is the day of the big change. It has come, but not as we had expected. It is Hitler's birthday again and we are bringing him a fine present in the form of the enemy.

The door opens and the sergeant comes into the room. Köhler has been wounded and we have to help him. I get up with Stroschn and follow him into the barn, where the wounded man is whimpering in the straw. He has got a splinter in his leg. He only felt a slight blow, no pain, and hurried on. When we slowed down it caught up with him and he collapsed in the road. He is our youngest, only 16 years old. The pain shows in his eyes, but no tears. They have been burnt away and he would rather die than cry in front of us.

We pull the boots off his feet and carefully remove his trousers. His underpants are wet and red, blood pouring from the fresh wound. We cut the leg of his underpants off with scissors. He does not make a sound. What we human beings can take! I look for the splinter with the light of a candle. The skin has been cut just above the knee. We slowly pull the splinter out of the wound, then we put the leg in splints and bandage it up. We carefully pull his trousers on again. Blood is running wet and warm in his boots. Then we carry him outside. His features look as if they had been chiselled out, as if he were dead. He is our youngest and he has learnt not to cry.

The second lieutenant stops a passing tank and we lift him aboard. The engine roars and the tank thunders off into the night.

The artillery fire has died down, but the rifle fire continues. We are waiting for a runner from battalion. The second lieutenant walks about nervously. He has just come from there. The Russians are advancing along the railway embankment from the Komturei. A tank stands in front of the command post firing into the village. That should shake them up! They are coming through the gardens, fighting their way through. Only Köhler has been injured, and Alfons is missing.

The stars slowly fade and night gives way to a new day. Grey shadows lie over the fields and night still hangs in the trees.

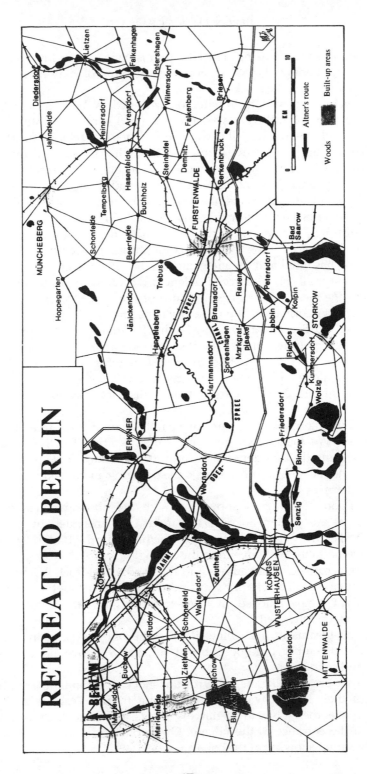

RETREAT TO BERLIN

We stand about freezing. The situation is confused and no one knows what is happening. Tanks, wagons and groups of marching men are fleeing back along the road.

Blaczeck comes back from battalion with orders. We are to go back to the collection point. We are all that remain of 150 men. We stumble over the field half asleep. The soil is wet and heavy going, clods of earth sticking to our boots, as we move through the mist like ghosts. The morning is cold, our packs heavy, and we have lost all feeling in our fingers.

We spread out. The trenches are before us and we go into the positions. Weerts goes to the right, Poziemba behind carrying a sack of hens and geese.

We sort ourselves out again. The dugouts are small and little light comes through the doors. I put my pack down on a bunk and go back outside. The voices of the comrades come through the gaps.

The fog has lifted and the view back to the village is clear. It is quiet in front, unnaturally so. The front is silent and soldiers are running over the fields to the west, ever more and more of them, without stopping. The front has been torn apart and the army is fleeing.

The second lieutenant comes. March off immediately! I run into the dugout and grab my things. The rest are assembling feverishly outside. Then we are off. We slip into the flood of refugees that is sweeping everything along with it, the second lieutenant going ahead of us, feather-light and supple. Our eyes are drawn to his back and our feet step out automatically.

Low-flying aircraft roar over our heads, skimming the treetops in the meadows. We look down and stay quiet, waiting for the tacking of machine guns, the thunder of their cannon, for death, silent and bitter, but nothing happens. The birds streak past singing in the skies. We are a defeated army.

The flood of refugees shows no signs of abating. Weapons and equipment are strewn all over the fields. All are ruled by the same thought: get away from the front into the haven of the hinterland. Let us have an end to the war, an end to the killing!

We go across fields, meadows and heath. Our feet hurt. A fence across the woodland path blocks our way and we clamber through the wire with difficulty. We have reached the V-Weapons factory, safe for the moment, and march on refreshed.

A pond gleams in the valley. Behind the hill lies Falkenhagen. Our stomachs are empty, our bodies burnt out, and we move like ghosts over heath and sand.

Now we are in Falkenhagen with the shocked inhabitants standing in front of their houses watching the fleeing troops. Wagons and tanks thunder over the asphalt in the narrow streets, and some dead civilians are lying at the entrance to the village. One woman is without a head, the bloody stump showing at the collar.

We pass by fields and meadows, and houses along the roadside. Villages appear out of the haze. Woods stand silent. The human column winds its way along the road to the west. The front has collapsed. The last bulwark has succumbed to the Red Army's blows. The road to Berlin is open.

We stop for a break in a wood, falling to the ground like sacks of corn. There is a monstrous emptiness and disillusionment in me, and also a great astonishment, for possessed and driven by the urge to survive, we have left the war and killing behind us. Weapons and bits of equipment lie in heaps on the road. Packs and steel helmets have been thrown aside, thrown away so that one can get on, but we still drag all our stuff with us, even though it seems to get heavier by the metre.

We emerge from the forest track and the main road[1] stretches ahead of us. The stream of refugees is converging from all directions and has become an unstoppable flood. There is a village on the left behind the hill, Arensdorf; shells are falling in the fields all around it. There is no respite, no rest for us. Heavily laden farmcarts sway and we cling to them like bees, letting ourselves be dragged along. The road forks in front of us. To Müncheberg 22 kilometres. On the left the road to Berlin.

The farmers stand at their garden fences at the side of the road and watch the flight with solemn faces, their wives tearfully dispense coffee, which we gulp down greedily, their eyes full of tears. We march and run, without rest or peace. With every kilometre we are distancing ourselves from horror and death. Our feet are like painful lumps of meat and the pack straps cut into our shoulders. We cannot go on like this much longer.

The sun climbs, driving the mist from the meadows. We stop outside the old church in Hasenfelde. It is noon and the bells ring as if this was just a normal day, but refugees are hastening past and vehicles race along the road. Boy still has some wine in his water bottle. The three of us pour it down our throats and it burns its way through. We move on slowly. A sign shows: 'Lietzen 16 kilometres'.

A tractor goes past with a steaming cauldron on its trailer. We are hungry. The stream of refugees on the road has thinned out into the side roads. We are to overnight and eat at a certain manor farm, but the road stretches ahead like an elastic band and the farm seems to get no closer. Stroschn, Boy and I take turns carrying our weapons. At last our goal glints in the sunlight. We stop among some dried-up trees and I sit down in the undergrowth and stretch out my legs, which seem to glow with heat. I would like to stay here and never have to get up again.

Sergeant Weerts drives us to our feet again. We have no idea what to expect. We walk up to the farm as if treading on eggs and stop at a barn. The vehicles of a delousing unit are parked at the edge of the wood. We sit on the ground and look up at the sky.

I pull the boots off my aching feet. The soles of my feet are white, as if dead, and covered in blisters. We are going to stay here for the night, but we have to find our own places to sleep, so we dig holes like graves in the ground and get straw from the barn to line them. One section is peeling potatoes, and half a pig is in the cooking pot.

The time goes past slowly. It is almost time to eat when the regimental commander's car draws up in the yard. The second lieutenant comes along. Get ready! I carefully pull my boots back over my aching feet. We fall in. Our holes and the pig cooking in its pot are left behind. Low-flying aircraft roar over the treetops firing their cannon into the village as we stand in the bracken and wait.

We follow the road keeping close to the trees. Coming towards us are some Volkssturm and firemen who have been hastily mustered and equipped, their solemn faces looking out from under their helmets. They are going into the fire, and we want to get out of it, but will we succeed?[2]

A race begins, a race against time over woodland tracks and open fields, through heath and sand, with fear at our backs. Somewhere or other soldiers are preparing a defensive position, flak moves forward, and tanks roll past, but we are going back.

Another village lies ahead of us, Demnitz. The inhabitants are unsettled and ask us whether they should flee. The SS are going from house to house rounding up the menfolk, who have to put on SS camouflage uniforms in the village square, then are quickly sworn in and sent forward.

It is Hitler's birthday...

We soon come to the main road to Berlin.[3] The feet hurt less on woodland paths than on the paved roads. Overnight we have become infantrymen from necessity and must keep going to get out of the trap. We advance in long files under the trees on either side of the road, our greatcoat pockets stuffed with ammunition banging against our knees with every step. I am carrying the submachine gun belonging to the sergeant, who is walking without a pack. Every half hour we change over carrying the Panzerfaust and the machine gun. I drop behind, unable to go any farther.

A bright inn stands at a bend in the road, where soldiers are busy packing files, and I ask for some water, which cools my throat. This gives me renewed strength, and I push on. The comrades of my company are taking a rest in the woods. Three men are missing.

Low-flying aircraft have set the woods alight. The undergrowth crackles and burns, bringing tears to our eyes. Big trucks rush past, their draught raising clouds of dust and causing the trees to flare up again. Our throats are burning, our tongues sticking to our gums. Will the pain never end? Machine guns tack in the woods quite close. The Russians. Was it all for nothing?

We run and march, our lungs gasping. We dare not discard our packs.

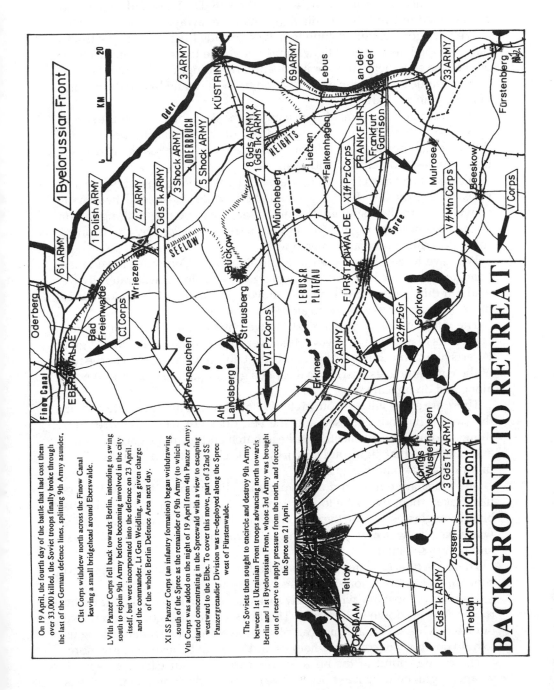

On 19 April, the fourth day of the battle that had cost them over 33,000 killed, the Soviet troops finally broke through the last of the German defence lines, splitting 9th Army asunder.

CIst Corps withdrew north across the Finow Canal leaving a small bridgehead around Eberswalde.

LVIth Panzer Corps fell back towards Berlin, intending to swing south to rejoin 9th Army before becoming involved in the city itself, but were incorporated into the defence on 23 April, and the commander, Lt Gen Weidling, was given charge of the whole Berlin Defence Area next day.

XI SS Panzer Corps (an infantry formation) began withdrawing south of the Spree as the remainder of 9th Army (to which VIth Corps was added on the night of 19 April from 4th Panzer Army) started concentrating in the Spreewald with a view to escaping westward to the Elbe. To cover this move, part of 32nd SS Panzergrenadier Division was re-deployed along the Spree west of Fürstenwalde.

The Soviets then sought to encircle and destroy 9th Army between 1st Ukrainian Front troops advancing north towards Berlin and 1st Byelorussian Front, whose 3rd Army was brought out of reserve to apply pressure from the north, and forced the Spree on 21 April.

BACKGROUND TO RETREAT

71

This is the last gap in the encirclement. We run. Darkness falls, the wood glows blood red and the machine guns hammer away.

We have got through. Behind us salvoes of rifle fire ring out. The trucks have stopped and a verey light hangs above the trees. The gap has been closed, the encirclement is complete and our strength is drained. We can only continue by creeping along. I go on tiptoe. I would like to drop dead. Has the pain no end?

We cross the railway line. A flare hangs in the sky behind us. We are saved.

We are in Berkenbrück. The sound of our footsteps echo hollow and dull from the houses, and a light blinks here and there as the disturbed inhabitants stand at their windows.

We take a rest at a crossroads, the moonlight playing on our exhausted faces, sitting on the steps of a small shop while the second lieutenant converses with the regimental commander. We have had nothing in our stomachs since last night. It is 48 kilometres to Lietzen by the country road. We really are infantrymen now.

We have to go on to Rauen to a supply depot. Comrades have taken handcarts from the houses and Boy has got a wheelbarrow. Gratefully we load our things into the barrow and move on. The disc of the moon hangs like a ghost in the sky as we go along the road half asleep.

The wheel of the barrow breaks, so we have to carry the stuff again. I have tears of anger in my eyes. Must everything turn out like this? I give Weerts his submachine gun back and stay behind with Stroschn as the rest of the company goes past, their weapons glinting in the distance. We are alone and do not care.

There are some villas on our right. We go through an open gate and up the steps. The door is closed and the bell does not work. We drop our things and pull our boots off. I strike a match and from the garden comes a shout: 'Put that light out!' Figures slink closer. Hitler Youths. They unlock the door and we go in.

The villas are empty and a company of Hitler Youth tank-destroyers have taken them over. We look around the kitchen as the boys bring us bread and glasses of malt, then go out again. We keep quiet and eat. Never was a meal so welcome. We eat and eat. Eventually the bread is all gone and we are satisfied.

There are tubs of water in the washhouse, so we sit down in them and cool our feet as the moon shines its silvery beams into the room.

Then we go upstairs, where straw sacks have been laid out in one of the rooms. We lie down and dream. The boys come and go, children like ourselves. One says that American planes have dropped leaflets asking us to hold on, they are coming to help us. But I cannot believe that any more.

The gentle sound of the boys' voices carries to our ears. I grasp my weapon tight, holding it as if it can save me, like a drowning man clutches a straw.

Saturday 21 April 1945

The house is shuddering and quaking, glass splintering, giving us a rough awakening. Bright morning sunlight shines through the windows and the boys are running all over the place. We grab our things and dive outside.

The wood, a pine plantation, begins at the road, which is blocked with wagons, automobiles and horses in an inextricable tangle, and we can only get through with difficulty. Flames are rising high in the village with clouds of smoke billowing over the rooftops. Everywhere there is frenzied activity.

In front of us extends the silver grey ribbon of the Frankfurt on the Oder/Berlin Autobahn. Military police are trying to bring some order into the columns of traffic, while defensive positions are being thrown up on either side of the Autobahn, with Volkssturm and Hitler Youth digging trenches. Troops are flooding back along the Autobahn verges, while fully filled automobiles race by. We try and stop one, but without any luck.

Uphill, downhill the ribbon of the Autobahn runs along exactly the same. The bridges have been destroyed and the underpasses camouflaged, but the road remains exactly the same every metre, making marching along it very tiring.

Another bridge appears with a staff sergeant standing on the road directing the traffic. The Autobahn has been blown up and vehicles have to make a detour. The staff sergeant is busy, his brand-new bicycle behind him on the bridge.

I swing on to the bicycle and pedal off with Stroschn running after me. I cycle to the next bridge, put my pack down and wait. A soldier is working on a commandiered motorcycle, while a civilian complains about the war. I cycle back cheerfully and Stroschn comes toward me smiling – he has found a big salami sausage. Empty cigarette and chocolate wrappings are scattered over the roadway. I recover my pack from the bridge and we cycle on with Stroschn sitting on the crossbar. With both of us and our packs, we make a heavy load and we are running on the wheel rims, but we are making far better progress than before. There is a little town on our right and a closed petrol station on the Autobahn.[4] A little farther on there is a demolished bridge, where the blast has torn off the roofs of the nearby houses. Stroschn gets off at the petrol station. I quickly stick a slice of sausage into my mouth and cycle into the village, Petersdorf, which has already been evacuated. The male inhabitants who are left stand in front of the school as Volkssturm and the Party District Leader in uniform goes through the ranks in uniform counting them. The men stand around sullenly as they are detailed off, and no one can tell us how to get to Rauen.

I cycle back. Occasionally a distorted face appears at a window and vanishes just as quickly. Soldiers are streaming back along the Autobahn towards Berlin. We pick up our things and cycle on, and have difficulty pushing the bicycle up the steep bank on the far side of the destroyed bridges. We then change our method of movement. One of us cycles two kilometres measured by the marker stones on either side of the Autobahn and taking the other's pack, then waits for the other to arrive. Then we change over. Thus we make good progress, leaving kilometre stone after kilometre stone behind us.

There are some houses down below to the right, and a young girl is tending cows. We call out to her. It is Rauen. We follow a woodland path until we come to the village, which the inhabitants are just leaving. We ask them about our company, but no one has seen it. We lean the bicycle against a fence at a crossroads and go into a farmyard to look for water, but there is no pump. Stroschn goes back to the street, and when I get to the gate, two second lieutenants are standing over him. Then they accost me. I have to go to Fürstenwalde straight away and report to the Hindenburg Barracks there. One of them takes the bicycle and I feel crushed. Stroschn is nowhere to be seen. The second lieutenant points to the submachine gun and says that it is urgently required. I must hurry. I set off angrily. I could cry with rage. We have been lucky until now, getting away from the Russians, but was it all for nothing? The two second lieutenants have gone ahead but keep turning round, and then come back.

Weapons are being handed out to the inhabitants on the village square and barricades erected. Both the second lieutenants have disappeared. A sign at the village entrance says: 'Fürstenwalde 12 kilometres'. I turn round and go back to try to find a transport column to take me on to Fürstenwalde. I go back into the farmyard and put my pack down in front of a shed. There is a supply column on the street with straw for the barracks in Fürstenwalde and a staff sergeant riding alongside it. I take my pack and climb aboard the last wagon. It does not matter any more, the main thing is that I do not have to walk. Randomly assembled companies are moving past, all having been stopped on the Autobahn and pressed into new units, soldiers and civilians together, boys and old men, most of them without weapons. This army of despair marches on in silence, a grey, tired mass, their footsteps sounding dully. The dying goes on.

The wagon is ready to move off, so I settle myself down, feeling alone and abandoned. I dare not think about it. Firstly the comrades with whom one has become a bonded part with all the emergencies we have been through together, and now I have just lost my best friend.

The wagon moves off and we are on our way. I look back. I must be dreaming. Stroschn is coming out of a side street without his pack. I call out, throw my pack off the wagon and jump down. We have found each other again.

He had quickly slipped away up a side street when the second lieutenants accosted me. Later on he had found the company and the supply NCO. The company is resting in a wood next to the Autobahn, and if we had gone a bit farther we would have found it.

We go back to the entrance to the village. The emergency companies are coming along the road towards us with blanched staring faces and go past. It has started to rain. We go along the road, the Autobahn appears and then the wood with our comrades. I put down my pack and report back to the second lieutenant, who shakes my hand. I am back where I belong, with my comrades.

The rain increases. We are lying on moss and get very wet. Sergeant Weerts runs around collecting wood for a fire. Heavy wagons are thundering past on the Autobahn and from one of them the face of Klabunde appears for a second, and then they are gone.

The regimental commander's car draws up and stops. The second lieutenant goes up to it. Then it drives off, only to return again after a short time. We fall in, except for the sergeants and the radio section of older men who had joined us. We have to give up the Panzerfausts and machine guns. I put mine down on the wet ground and hand over my submachine gun and the ammunition from my pack and greatcoat pockets to Staff Sergeant Köster. Only the second lieutenant and the staff sergeant remain with us. The regimental commander drives away, and we march off.

There is food for us in the village, so we go back in the pouring rain and eat the thin soup hungrily. Then we set off again, but the road is closed to us for the Russians are in Fürstenwalde and in Erkner, a suburb of Berlin. We are numbed. How are we going to get through?

We will try to go via Storkow. That route is supposed to be still clear. We march south along woodland tracks and it gradually becomes brighter as the rain eases off. We take a rest, sitting shivering on the wet ground, the rain numbing our faces. A Wehrmacht camp lies empty and dead, the doors flapping in the wind, and there are weapons and bits of equipment scattered all round the huts.

Occasionally we come across someone, someone as harassed as ourselves, slinking cautiously through the woods. A man shows us a short cut. We do not need to go through Storkow, we can pass it to our left. We go through woods and across fields. At the track junctions the second lieutenant goes ahead to reconnoitre, while we lie in the grass and wait. Then we go on, marching along inconspicuous tracks through woods, across fields and along byways, navigating by map and compass. There are said to be Russian tanks in Storkow.

A lonely farmstead appears. The owners have seen us long before we reach it and we are met with hot milk and coffee as we cross a bridge over a stream. These people are still untouched by the war here, being out of sight of the rest of the world. The farmers invite us to stay and the second lieutenant has a conversation with them. We are staying. We go into the barn and I climb the ladder to the loft, followed by Boy and Stroschn, and we lie down in the straw, pulling our wet and heavy greatcoats over us. There are big holes in the floor through which we can look down on the threshing floor. I go down to the yard and wash my feet. Some comrades are peeling potatoes, and the smell of warm blood comes from the washhouse, where a sheep is being slaughtered. The farm girls go clacking across the yard in their wooden pattens carrying buckets of fresh warm milk, which we drink gratefully.

Blaczeck has been into Kummersdorf, from where a train is leaving for Berlin tonight.

There is much activity in the yard. Soup is being dished out. It slowly gets dark. Laughter comes from the stalls, where fat Reinicke has fallen through to the threshing floor from the loft. He looks around in astonishment. His bottom is a little bruised, but no bones have been broken.

We talk to the farm folk in the yards. They get no news here in this hidden corner and have been spared the war; they hope that they will continue to be so. The farmer is smoking, puffing a long porcelain pipe with foul-smelling smoke swirling round his head. He smokes his own tobacco and swears by it.

The blanket of night sinks slowly. We go into the barn and climb the ladder carefully not to waken the sleepers, then I roll in the straw. Boy is thrashing around in his sleep. The starry heavens shine through the gaps in the roof. A shaft of moonlight plays over Günther's face and the hearty snoring of a sleeper comes from below. I recall the horrors and death, and want to despair.

God, what is the meaning of our lives?

Sunday 22 April 1945

We are woken up before midnight. I have been unable to sleep properly for my uniform is cold and wet. Shivering, I put on my damp and heavy greatcoat and go down the fragile ladder step by step. The comrades are moving around in the barn. A faint light blinks here and there.

We stand in the yard half drunk with sleep and then pass quietly through the village. Somewhere a dog is barking loudly and complainingly. We march along a narrow woodland path with the wet branches brushing against our faces, moving along in the shadow of the trees. The grass shines with the night dew. We have to be careful. The Russians could have already broken through and be forming a new encirclement, or have even already closed it. I chew a piece of bread and sausage as I walk, the pack of the comrade in front of me swaying before my face. We move along silently into infinity.

A narrow gauge railway runs through the wood and in the distance a locomotive's whistle cuts through the night. Our heads lift up and our breathing quickens. That is our train, our train!

The wood is behind us. The wind sighs across the fields. The red of a railway signal glows in the distance and a station lies sparsely lit in the night. An engine releases hissing steam into the air and stamps impatiently.

The second lieutenant talks to the station master. The goods train is bound for Berlin and has to leave straight away. We climb into the cold wagons and wait, lying tightly packed together. The floor is wet and cold. A match flares and shows up our tired faces in the darkness for a second. A word is dropped here and there. The engine stamps. The voices of the railwaymen come from outside the wagon. I fall asleep.

The door of the wagon squeaks open and the wind sighs. Light rain is driving across the sky. 'Everybody off!' The Russians have blocked the line.

I could cry with disappointment. Another hope has gone with the wind. Behind us the engine stamps, sending steam whistling into the night. We march on, having lost a valuable hour. We cross the fields in a long, silent column, half asleep from exhaustion as we stumble along, automatically following one after the other, without hope and without a sure objective.

We soon come to the main road. Occasionally a vehicle passes, briefly lighting up the night. There is an airfield on our right[5] and a dense wood on our left. We sit down on the wet ground and sleep. Cyclists come past, girls' voices hanging in the air. Then we go on again, each in his own way.

There is a village up ahead. The road forks. A river[6] shimmers under a bridge. We traverse the sleeping village, no sound disturbing the silence of the night. A sign gives the name: 'Bindow'.

The night is becoming lighter as dawn approaches. The sun comes up early and shines on empty streets. Another village. I go into a farmyard with Boy to fill our water bottles. The company goes on ahead and it is difficult to catch up those few metres.

Packs, clothing and weapons are lying scattered in the roadside ditches. Little summerhouses glimmer in the gardens. We take a rest and march on again. There is a wood with dense undergrowth on the left, in which the bright sand from the trenches that have been dug there makes a strong contrast. Another five kilometres to Königs Wusterhausen, from where the suburban railway should be able to take us on.

Sunday, another Sunday. Women are walking along the street with their milk cans and standing in queues in front of shops, and children are going to church. Swastika flags hang from some houses and Volkssturm are building barricades and firemen are practising cleaning weapons on a square. Some of the women bring us hot coffee. There are some fenced in barrack huts on either side of the railway station with French prisoners of war standing looking at the street through the barbed wire.

The station looks dead. The trains are no longer running to Berlin for the Russians have blocked the line. We feel ready to collapse. This was our last hope. We are on the brink of despair.

Many stay behind, their strength gone. With every step we take, our packs seem to grow heavier. Helios has tears running down his cheeks and keep on murmuring: 'What have we done to deserve this?' Blaczeck collapses in the roadway. Two others are lying groaning against the fence.

We stop on the roadside. There is a crossroads in front of us. 'City Centre 44 kilometres'. We must make another attempt. The road turns off on the left to Dahlwitz, 12 kilometres. In just two hours Stroschn and myself could be home. But he does not even look at the sign, instead he just marches on.

Women bring us bread and things to eat. We thank them as we march along, biting hungrily into the food. Our column is long and well spread out and the staff sergeant goes along the column urging us on. Women stand in the roadway and hand out cigarettes, many of them crying. I take a Juno that is a little damp and a green, and greedily suck the smoke into my lungs. The staff sergeant warns us that smoking will make us even more tired, but it gives us a little pleasure.

Local people – men, women and children – come up to their garden gates bringing us bread. We can only thank them and stuff it down as we march on.

We stop while the second lieutenant and the staff sergeant check the company. The Russians are already in Berlin. The S-Bahn station at Köpenick has been taken and part of Prenzlauer Allee cut off. Their artillery is firing on the city centre from the east, and their aircraft dropping bombs. Berlin has become part of the front line.

We have to hurry. The Russians are trying to seal off an encirclement between Zeuthen and Glasow, and are said to be already close to the road.

A truck stops beside the second lieutenant. 'Climb aboard!' We throw our packs on to the truck and jump in after them. We race along the road, rushing through villages with shells bursting in the fields on our left and machine gun fire coming from the woods on our right. We were only just in time. We have escaped from the third encirclement.

We go on at full speed and a wire hanging over the road snatches the cap from my head. At last we stop, climb down and unload milk churns on the village street. The truck turns round and drives back to collect the rest of us. Will it make it?

We sit around on the churns and our packs. On the other side of the road are the vehicles of a field bakery, and the smell of freshly baked bread wafts towards us. Boy and myself go over and come back heavily laden with bread that is still warm and soft. We plunge our teeth into it and swallow it down.

At last the truck returns. It only just got through and there are machine gun bullet holes in the cab. We have been lucky.

We march on. Military police are directing traffic at the village entrance, their silver gorgets flashing.[7] There is a stream of people on the road to Berlin, both civilian and military. The road to Brandenburg turns off to the left, to the west. Long rows of heavily laden vehicles carrying generals, people wearing Nazi Party insignia and Party officials, as well as high ranking civil servants, are making for the last remaining exit from Berlin. Civilians with handcarts and cyclists are also going that way. The rats are deserting the sinking ship.[8]

The grey ribbon of the roadway stretches to the left and the lines of an industrial railway shine in the sun. On the left is an airfield[9] with its hangar doors open. A Fieseler Storch[10] flies over the road, its surfaces flashing brightly as it lands. From the right comes the sound of aircraft engines and tacking machine guns. Low-flying aircraft cross over the village and dive down, one after the other, like deadly black birds.

Occasionally enemy aircraft fly frighteningly close and the road then looks as if it has been swept clean in the sunshine, as we lie in the ditches pressing our faces into the grass. Erkner has been lost, Nauen occupied and there is heavy fighting in Oranienburg. The Russians are almost in the city centre and we have not even reached the city boundary yet. They have beaten us to it.

There are some friendly looking little summerhouses alongside the road, set well back behind flowers. The sun shines Sunday-like on this peaceful scene. It is spring, but nobody seems to notice. The houses are empty, their owners fled, although occasionally one sees them sitting on the hump of a dugout that they have dug in their garden.

We stop in Waltersdorf. We have to change direction. The Russians are already in Köpenick, so we will now have to try and get into the city via Tempelhof. Just to be wiped out?

The anti-tank barriers have been closed at the crossroads. The situation is completely confused and bewildering. The enemy seems to be everywhere and can appear suddenly at any moment from any direction. No one knows, and wild rumours about tanks circulate from mouth to mouth. They are supposed to be everywhere, appearing and disappearing like ghosts.

Across the street in a garden some Volkssturm are washing their eating utensils. We sit on a doorstep and wait, and a woman brings us some hot coffee. The Volkssturm are using an inn for their catering. Boy and myself take our mess tins from our packs and walk across. Some women take our mess tins and fill them for us, then we sit down on the doorstep and happily spoon the soup down. Children are playing in the yellow sand by the anti-tank barrier, and men wearing armbands are walking busily along the street. A bird sings somewhere, and a dog barks. From the distance comes the dull thump of artillery, but this is an oasis of peace.

The second lieutenant returns. He has been to the village commandant of Waltersdorf to seek information. We have no alternative, we will have to try to get into the city from the south by means of a big detour to the west.

We get ourselves ready once more and march off. Poziemba would like to requisition an abandoned truck, but it is unfortunately no use to us, as all the anti-tank barriers have already been closed. We march through several villages where the inhabitants are feverishly ripping up the streets, reinforcing barricades and laying mines under Party supervision. Children and youths, women and even old men, everyone has to join in.

Later we cross the Mittenwalde/Britz railway line: both termini are in Russian hands. Two women passing with handcarts take our packs for us. We then march through Klein-Ziethen and have reached our goal for the day. We turn right into a big farmyard, but the farmer does not want to take us. He is scared that the Russians will be here quicker than we can leave. Blaczeck has caught up with us again. The staff sergeant asks him about his Panzerfaust. He left it behind in Königs Wusterhausen, and the second lieutenant threatens him with court martial. Blaczeck has to carry another Panzerfaust all the way back to Berlin as a punishment.

We go across to the manor farm, where the tenant directs us to a room over the stalls. We can hardly climb up the steep stairs – the floor is rotten with big holes in it. There is enough room for twice our number, but the windows are broken and the wind whistles through the room.

I unbuckle my equipment. There is no straw available, so I lie down on the bare floor. Boy, Stroschn and myself tuck our greatcoats around us and snuggle up together. I pull off my boots and go barefoot down to the yard. I work the pump like an invalid, keeping my feet under the cold water. The soles of my feet look dead, sweat has made big holes in the calluses, and there are big blisters on my heels and between my toes.

I look around the yard as I cool my feet. Wagons are hurriedly pulling up in front of the manorhouse and are being loaded with clothing and furniture. Parked in one corner are the carts and wagons of some refugees, whose children are playing in the barn.

Upstairs Günther and Heinz are studying a map, working out the route that we have taken. The last three days we have been making an enormous detour, marching 160 kilometres. In two nights we have had a total of seven hours' sleep, marching the rest of the time. For three days we have had nothing decent to eat, only a bite here and there and some soup. We have another twenty-five kilometres to go before we can continue by rail.

I pour powder over my aching feet and pull my socks back on again. Then we roll up tight together and fall asleep. The wind sighs over the roof and the cattle paw the ground below in the stalls. We fall asleep from exhaustion.

It is eleven o'clock. We have to parade outside in the dark. We go carefully down the narrow stairs and assemble in the yard. The Russians are close behind us and Waltersdorf has been taken. The yard dog barks as we march off through the sleeping village. The hour of midnight strikes in the distance.

Monday 23 April 1945

We march silently in the night through the sleeping villages. Most of the anti-tank barriers on the road have already been closed, the pavement stones ripped up and mines laid in the gutters, waiting for their victims. No sound disturbs the silence, only that of our footsteps reflected by the buildings as we pass. Occasionally a civilian emerges from the gloom from behind a barrier and speaks to us. Our weapons shine dully in the moonlight. We are now on the main road to Berlin.[11] Lichtenrade goes by, then Mariendorf. We have reached the city boundary and apartment blocks rise high in the sky. Occasionally a faint light flickers. Some inhabitants standing in the doorways recoil in alarm as the sound of our marching feet resounds from the walls, and then breathe out again when they realise we are German.

Scraps of cloud race across the sky. Tempelhof airport is on our right. We carry on tiredly. The road seems endless. Then some BVG[12] trams loom out of the darkness. We stop and slowly climb aboard. The moon shines through the windows. A poster summons people to die for the defence of Berlin, even women, children and old men. I fumble in my pocket for bread and hungrily eat some crumbs. Boy sits next to me looking out into the night. The moonlight reveals our exhausted faces. My head slumps, but we are too tired to sleep, overcome with exhaustion.

The second lieutenant goes by rapping the windows. 'March on!' The night swallows us up step by step. We keep close to the buildings. The trams loom behind us. A door scrapes somewhere and a child starts to cry. The beam of a torch cuts the darkness for a second. Two candles are blinking faintly in the night ahead of us. The wind is rustling in the dry branches. We stop and wait, then go down the steps of an air raid shelter. A pleasant warmth meets us and two lamps give out meagre illumination. The shelter is packed full of men and women sitting on their belongings. Nevertheless, they seem to be comfortable here while overhead the distress of this dark April night with its threat and uncertainty hangs over the street.

Astonishment shows in their eyes. They look at us as if we were ghosts. Did they think that the Russians are so far off that the fear will be behind them by the morning? The eyes of several of them show anger, even hatred. Hatred of us because we are continuing the fight. Hatred of us for having not yet cast aside the fetters of duty. They shyly draw aside to make room for us and the comrades collapse on the benches or roll on the stone floor. I lie on a bench with my pack under my head. My legs are stiff and my skull aches as if to burst. We soon go out again, leaving the people behind sleeping, waiting and hoping.

We stand shivering in the morning fresh street. The dawn is just breaking and the street is still in semi-darkness. We are in Berlin among the ruins of the night bombings, the facades looming high into the sky. Occasionally someone scurries across the street and quickly disappears again.

I march along next to Boy and Stroschn with the second lieutenant well ahead in front of us. Uncertain footsteps sound behind us. The staff sergeant goes past, urging us on. We are still carrying our full equipment, from the second issue of underwear to the last pocket handkerchief. The world is collapsing around us and the war is lost, but we are still carrying our full equipment.

We stop again. We have become fewer in number and need the last of our strength to drive our bodies forward. While we are stopped, Boy looks around for a cart to carry our packs. There is a wheelbarrow in the debris behind the facade of a burnt-out building. We push it into the street and put our packs in it, and it runs forward as we are still trying to get the hang of it.

Time passes relentlessly as it comes to the final hours. A group of women appear from the south. Men rush along the street looking furtively around them. SS patrols in cars are driving along the streets, stopping a man here and picking one up there, their engines humming. Volkssturm, here mainly in SS uniform, close the anti-tank barriers behind them, while Hitler Youths go about proudly carrying Panzerfausts.

There is a big square to our right lined with the facades of burnt-out buildings. Two SA[13] men are standing beneath a lamp post, from which a handcuffed civilian is hanging with a red electricity cable around his neck that has cut deep into his flesh. His face is blue and his eyes hang deep in their sockets. Around his neck is hung a white cardboard placard, on which is written in red in shaky writing; 'I, Otto Meyer, was too cowardly to fight for my wife and child. That is why I am hanging here. I am a swine.' I feel I am going to be sick. I want to look away but cannot take my eyes off this gruesome sight. The SA men are laughing and smiling as the dead man swings slowly in the wind. A passing civilian tells us in a low voice why the soldier has been hanged. Like us he had come back tired and burnt out from the fighting and encirclement before Berlin. He was young. His wife begged him to stay. He gave in and was then betrayed by a neighbour. The SS came and murdered him in front of his wife and child. The SS smirkingly dictated the text, made him write it out and then hung him. The cable cutting into his neck soon killed him while his wife lay unconscious on the ground. The SS drove away and the SA took over. A man was condemned. Condemned? Murdered!

And life flows on past the dead man. The expressions on the faces of the passers-by, show that their despondency over the senselessness of the fighting and their fear of the collapsing regime's thugs is deeply etched. We march on shocked to the core.

There is a road junction ahead of us and on the left the entrance to the

Belle-Allianz-Platz U-Bahn station with its familiar blue signs. We leave the wheelbarrow outside the entrance and wait for the stragglers. Then we go down the steps quite slowly, almost solemnly, wanting to relish the sensation of being back in Berlin.

People are standing like walls on the platforms. The train pulls in and a gap opens up. We enter the carriages and sit on our packs. The doors roll shut and the journey begins, a familiar rhythm. The tunnel lights flash by and the stations go past. People come and go. We get off and go through a long tunnel. We are right under the centre point of the city at the junction of Leipziger Strasse and Friedrichstrasse, without seeing anything. We board another train that takes us underground through Potsdamer Platz, then daylight comes through the windows and the train passes high above the buildings. Ruins show up clearly and low-flying aircraft are criss-crossing and diving in the distance. Somewhere or other columns of smoke and flames rise into the sky. Soon we are back underground again, as one station after another flashes past.

Daylight breaks through again and the train stops at Ruhleben. We go down the steps like old men. We fall in in front of the station and march slowly back along the street. The railway embankment is on our right and the barracks loom up on our left. The trees are green and heavy with buds. There is the sentry and the barrack gates. We wheel left and pass over the threshold one by one, the gates rolling shut behind us, clanging heavily on their hinges. We are back. Our race with death has been won this time.

When we passed through the gates two weeks ago – it seems an eternity, a whole lifetime ago – we were 150 men, children looking into the future. Only fifty-eight of us have returned today.[14]

NOTES

1. The Frankfurt on the Oder/Müncheberg road, today the B-5.
2. Some of the reinforcements dispatched by Goebbels to the 9th Army, but far too late.
3. The pre-Autobahn main road from Frankfurt on the Oder to Berlin via Fürstenwalde.
4. The Fürstenwalde Autobahn turn-off.
5. Friedersdorf airfield.
6. The Dahme.
7. German military police wore a large silver metal gorget hung by a chain on their chest bearing the word 'Feldgendarmerie'.
8. Hitler had given permission for such an evacuation on the night of 20 April.
9. Schönefeld airport.
10. The high winged, short landing and take-off Fieseler Fi-156 three-seater mainly used for reconnaissance and liaison purposes.
11. Today's B-96.
12. The municipal transport company.
13. *Sturmabteilung*.
14. That day the advance elements of Marshal Koniev's 1st Ukrainian Front

reached the southern outskirts of Berlin, spreading out thinly from Potsdam to Schönefeld, but it would take another day for their supporting elements to catch up. Meanwhile Marshal Zhukov's troops had taken Köpenick and were well into the city from the east and north-east, and the 47th Army crossed the Havel river north of Spandau that night.

CHAPTER VII
Defending Northern Spandau

We are passing through the gates into the barracks for the second time. Four weeks ago we were not so happy to go in, but today? Today it seems like an oasis of peace, if perhaps only for a few hours.

We go past the buildings to the barrack square. Civilians who have fled from those parts of the city where fighting is taking place are standing in front of the barrack blocks, and children are playing between the buildings, while troops are marching off to fight in the city. We are just tired, absolutely exhausted.

We form up in front of battalion headquarters. Our ranks are thin, only fifty-eight young faces under grey helmets, pale and drawn, one just like the other, the face of our generation. The second lieutenant comes back. We can fall out. We go past the quartermaster's stores in the East Block. Every building is packed with troops and refugees from the city, so we will have to sleep in the stables.[1]

We stand around in front of the stables. It has started raining and a cold wind is sweeping over the buildings. Eventually we can go in. The attic is to be our temporary accommodation. We put down our things at random, glad to be shed of them at last. Some slates are missing from the roof and the rain drips through. We roll up tight together, pull the boots off our aching feet and try to sleep.

The cold drives us up again. We go round the room trembling, only daring to tread very carefully, as our abused feet are covered in blisters and only poorly protected by our tattered socks. Later a couple of medical orderlies come over from the sick bay and treat us one by one. They try to restore our feet with the aid of scissors, needles, iodine and ointment. The blisters are cut off and quickly dabbed with iodine, but we all very much doubt that this will help.

We then wander off individually through the barracks. We have not eaten all day and are looking for something to eat, but without success. Children and refugee women are going through those barrack rooms still occupied by soldiers begging for food. Their menfolk were thrust into uniform as soon as they entered the barracks and have been thrown into the fighting for the city. The anti-aircraft guns that stood on the barrack training area have been sent with their crews into action. A few Hungarians, the remains of regiments that have been completely destroyed, as one woman informs us, slink past keeping close to the walls. I am looking for Windhorst to see if I can perhaps get something to eat from him.

Windhorst is in his old barrack room and looks up at me in astonishment. That we should have just come through the encirclement to the south of Berlin he takes to be extremely fortunate. He thinks that we have done enough already, and that we should not now have to take part in the battle for Berlin. I ask him what the situation really looks like, and he paints a picture that is so terrible that I can hardly grasp it. It is for this that we have marched day and night, and undergone the suffering and horrors of the retreat, just to get involved in more chaos! And we do not know whether we will escape this time.

I go back down to the barrack square. Grey bands of cloud are scudding across the sky and dull discharges and cracking explosions can be heard in the distance. Satan's legions seem to be roaring over the unfortunate city, bringing death, horror and destruction to this last bastion of defence.

I go along to the sick bay and stand in the doorway. A woman who has fled from the inner city is talking about the fighting in Berlin, saying that children and old men have taken up arms and have been thrown into the fighting in the ranks of the Volkssturm units. Those parts of the city in which the fighting is raging, drawing ever closer to the city centre, are sinking in dust and ashes under the Russian attacks and despite the futile efforts of the soldiers and civilians. The women and children who so far have been lucky enough not to be drawn into the 'defence' of the city, are sitting in their cellars being buried alive by the collapsing buildings. There has been no electric light for days and the mains have been destroyed and provide no water. She says that it is a wonder that she was able to escape from the witches' cauldron. Many of those who tried to get away have been killed, and now it is too late, the ring has been closed. And then she says that the men of the Waffen-SS have formed a horrible regiment with which to drive the Volkssturm units mercilessly into battle. No corner or apartment, no cellar or shed is safe from the patrols that drive anyone capable of bearing arms out into the streets.

There are more civilians than soldiers fighting in the city, the woman says. She fled from Weissensee and makes the serious allegation that the district was given up without a fight. She says that reinforcements are on their way, but they seem to be the same reinforcements that we were expected to believe in to keep us fighting. The rumours that the Western Powers want to make peace with us, and that the Russians will then be our only enemies, keep appearing in all shapes and forms.

A soldier says that the towns and places around the city are being rapidly occupied by the enemy. Oranienburg, Velten, Nauen, Erkner,

Rummelsburg, Frohnau and Köpenick have been lost. Fighting is supposed to be taking place in Potsdam, and Bernau and Reinickendorf have been occupied. Berlin is a defensive position from which ever larger pieces are being broken off and vanishing. It has become a slaughterhouse. The last act is being played out. The world is being ripped apart in an abyss of blood and horror, and our whole nation, staggering blindly to its ruin, is falling into this abyss.

I go back to our accommodation and wearily climb the steps. The second lieutenant has arranged something for us to eat – a thin, hot, watery soup with a few cabbage leaves that hardly satisfies, but does put some new strength into our bodies. Then I go to the quartermaster's stores to exchange my boots and get some new trousers. The quartermaster issues them reluctantly. In his eyes we are still recruits, for whom the old stuff should be good enough. Then he calms down and makes the issues. It is quite laughable even for him. We are recruits, but recruits who were considered good enough to die, even when we hadn't had any training.

In the canteen Volkssturm are being fitted out with uniforms, old peacetime uniforms with shiny accessories. Some young girls are walking about the barracks in SS uniforms with their caps pulled down over their curls. They are wearing pistol holsters (they want to look warlike, even if the holsters are empty) and walking proudly. They are members of an SS 'Death Battalion' and have sworn not to fall alive into the hands of the enemy, but rather to die in the ruins of the city. These are the fruits of their weapon training. A few days ago they came in with their shopping bags and pinafores to try out the new 'sport', and now they are already in uniform. Whether the 'sport' will prove so appealing to them when things begin to get serious, we all very much doubt. Their tight trousers incite the troops to thoughts other than viewing these 'ladies' as fellow combatants, and they themselves appear not unamenable to a less warlike role. The troops see them merely as a convenient means of sampling the pleasures of this earthly existence, and so the girls go proudly by with their heads held high and 'fight' on.

A large yellow omnibus has drawn up outside the quartermaster's stores and is being unloaded. A clerk stands by checking every single item. Wagons carrying arms and ammunition, old booty weapons from all over the world, including machine guns, are driving into the barracks. They are considered good enough for the troops whether they can fire or not. I pick out a passable cap from a cartload and throw my old recruit's cap into the bushes. Shortly afterwards the comrades come by one by one and help themselves to headgear until the quartermaster emerges from his stores and explodes with anger. But it is already too late, everyone has a new cap and no one is prepared to give it up. We have already been through what his lordship fears most, and we have other things to make us tremble than this braided flowerpot, but he gives us no peace.

We stroll on through the barracks. Staff Sergeant Becker, the former commander of the Recruit Company (how long ago that seems!) has gone to the front. 'The Scarecrow' has been killed, and only Sergeant Rytn has held on to his 'position'.

There are some large propaganda posters on the walls of the Convalescent Company building, according to which the Russians will maltreat and kill us if they take us prisoner. One does not know what to believe any more. A poster, on which the ink has hardly dried, and signed by Goebbels, proclaims: 'The darkest hour is before the dawn.'

A map of the Berlin area covering as far as the Oder (the Oder positions are still shown) clearly indicates the hopelessness of our situation. Today, as we once said jokingly, the front line is denoted by the S-Bahn termini. Erkner, the eastern front. Oranienburg and Frohnau, the northern front. Potsdam and Werder, the southern front. Only Spandau-West is still in German hands, but for how much longer?

I go back to the attic. Lieutenant Stichler sits down with us and talks to us as if we were invalids. We will have to go back into action again this evening. We were hoping for a least one day's rest, but there is no rest in this life so overshadowed by death.

It gradually gets dark. The rain has stopped. The barrack blocks have no electric light. Even the water supply has failed and water has to be hauled from the pumps in the yard. Someone brings us an allocation of welfare items. We get half a litre of schnapps each. They must have realised that we need to be kept quiet. Then there are cigarettes galore and chocolate. We share out these items by the light of several candle stumps, and lively haggling begins. I exchange my cigarettes for chocolate, and am soon the possessor of a considerable quantity. Then I go with Boy and Stroschn to the canteen kitchen, where the schnapps is being issued. We come back with a big container of it to share out jubilantly.

Later on we are divided up into new sections and have a section sergeant allocated to us. We do not say anything more but go straight to our new sections as it suits us. I am in in the same section as Boy and Stroschn. Then we go across to the armoury by sections and draw some rifles that have been overhauled with some ammunition.

It is ten o'clock when we eventually parade in front of the dark stable block. We have our full packs on, including our dirty washing. It is Wehrmacht property and must be properly looked after, even if it is useless. As we pass along the silent barrack streets, I take a quick slug of schnapps, which warms my throat. The moon shines occasionally through the racing scraps of cloud to illuminate the doomed city in its peaceful glow. We pass battalion headquarters in long rows, our footsteps pounding hard on the roadway, then we pass through the gates and leave the sentry behind. The long barrack wall begins. We have emerged into the world once more.

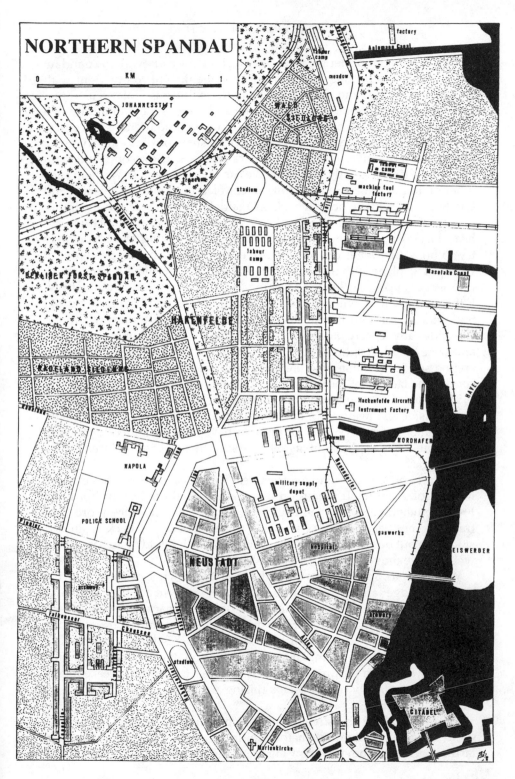

NORTHERN SPANDAU

0 KM 1

JOHANNESSTIFT

WALD SIEDLUNG

factory

Aslemann Canal

labour camp

meadow

labour camp

machine tool factory

stadium

labour camp

Maselake Canal

GEVIEDER FORST SPANDAU

HAKENFELDE

Hackenfelde Aircraft Instrument Factory

KAGELAND SIEDLUNG

HAVEL

NAPOLA

sawmill

NORDHAFEN

POLICE SCHOOL

military supply depot

gasworks

EISWERDER

hospital

NEUSTADT

brewery

brewery

stadium

CITADEL

Marienkirche

89

Well spread out under the trees, we go along the causeway to Spandau. An oil wagon is burning on the railway embankment to our right with yellow-red flames, and the sky over Charlottenburg is violet-red from a fire. A shell bursts somewhere in the city and there is the dull thump of a gun firing. The sound of an engine comes from behind us along the street, then it reaches us. Second Lieutenant Fricke steps out into the roadway and waves it down. A tractor towing a trailer stops. The second lieutenant talks to the driver and then calls us. We can take a ride on it. We help each other on to the trailer. Someone has uncoupled the trailer by mistake and the driver is trying to hook it back on again. I jump down from the trailer to help. The burning oil wagon sheds a bright light. In the distance one can hear the tacking of an aircraft engine slowly approaching. We desperately try to hook the trailer on, but the driver is nervous and keeps getting it wrong. The plane with the tacking engine flies over us like a gigantic bird. It must be one of the 'Sewing Machines' that the enemy used at the front. I throw myself down behind the tractor wheel as the bombs drop. Splinters fly through the air and cries come from the trailer, where the comrades are densely packed. I feel something wet running over my eyes and taste blood. A splinter has torn a tiny cut above my eyes. The tractor engine suddenly bursts into life and it vanishes into the darkness at top speed. The tacking of the aircraft engine continues in the distance.

The comrades have meanwhile jumped off the trailer and are lying on the roadsides. However, we have been extremely lucky, sustaining only some minor injuries. Wegner and Bräuer have been wounded in the arm, and another has a splinter in his leg. The six who have been injured return to barracks.

We carry on spread out under the trees. The battle for Berlin has exacted its first toll from us. If it goes on like this we shall not last out for long. From somewhere comes the sound of a motor engine once more. The tractor comes back, drives past us and turns, then comes back again and stops. We put our stuff aboard and climb in after it. I hold on to something wet, and we move off.

We come to Spandau, passing through the town's ruins, and drive across a bridge[2] and turn towards Spandau-West. We are both tired and shattered. We have left the trailer sides open, so that every time we go round a bend we sway to and fro, in danger of falling off. The tractor stops almost without our noticing it. Everyone grabs his things and we are standing on the street again. The tractor drives off, the sound of its engine gradually fading in the distance until it vanishes completely. Peace reigns over the streets, only our footsteps raising a loud echo from the walls of the passing buildings.

We march along the streets half asleep. Then we stop at an air raid shelter and rest for a minute before going on again. The buildings are set farther back from the street now and gardens begin to appear. The second lieutenant says that we are approaching Hakenfelde. Slit trenches have been dug into the verges and the foundations of an anti-tank barrier await completion. On our left the wood piles and sheds of a large sawmill are burning fiercely, throwing a bright light across the street.[3] Another aircraft clatters over and we throw ourselves down and wait for the howling of the bombs, which hit the the burning sheds and scatter sparks, sending burning planks whirling into the air. And again one hears the tacking of the engine as the plane flies at its target, the whistling and the exploding bombs. The street is lit up as light as day. We press ourselves tight against the wire mesh fence, as if it could give us cover, clutching at the earth with our fingers. Across the street the bombs continue to strike into the flames, whipping them up even higher. Our hearts beat wildly, praying for it all to end.

Then it quietens down as the humming of the aircraft engine dwindles in the distance. We brush the sand off our uniforms and march on. An apartment block looms out of the night on the left, and on the right a vast building with hundreds of windows reflects the flames. A long, high brick wall separates the Hakenfelde Aircraft Instrument Factory[4] from the street. Suddenly the hum of aircraft engines returns and they are overhead again. The roaring resumes and we throw ourselves down, pressing tight against the brick wall and wait, wait as we have already done so often. Then come the bangs and splintering as the bombs strike the stone colossus next to us. Splinters and masonry shower down around us, falling on our steel helmets and our bodies. The explosions in the street go on and on. The lights in the stairwell of the building across the street suddenly come on. We shout, and it goes dark again, except for the fires burning everywhere, lighting up the street.

At last it is quiet. We run across the street and dive into the building, then go down the steps into the cellar, where a burning candle spreads a little light. The second lieutenant is sitting in a corner asleep, having fled into the cellar as soon as the bombing started. I sit down in a corner and try to sleep. Outside the bombing has started again. A bright light comes from the entrance an air raid shelter and a man comes out. A radio is quietly playing marches. Suddenly a voice comes from the set: 'The fighting for the capital has intensified...Köpenick railway station, which had been lost, has been retaken by counter-attack and an enemy attack on it driven back. A breach by Soviet troops on Prenzlauer Allee has been contained. The enemy is pressing through the northern suburbs of Berlin.' Then come marches again and 'Deutschland, Deutschland über alles!' As Goebbels says: 'The darkest hour comes before the dawn.'

The candle has gone out. The air raid shelter door is shut tight. Hearty snoring comes from a dark corner and someone is talking in his sleep. I curl up and try to sleep, but sleep will not come. My thoughts allow no rest, going on and on, swirling around. I look at the time. It is late. The old day has ended unnoticed and a new one has started while we have been lying here waiting. Why, I do not know.[5]

Tuesday 24 April 1945

It is about three o'clock when a runner comes hurtling down the steps. We are supposed to be in the Police School near the Johannesstift,[6] where the staff sergeant and a few of our comrades are already sleeping peacefully. We pick up our things and trudge up the steps to emerge into the clear, cool night. The great bulk of the administrative building looms threateningly across the way. The remains of the sawmill sheds glow red in the night. A mist lying over the ground makes us to shiver.

We hurry along the streets almost asleep on our feet, paying no attention to our surroundings, which are all the same to us. We only want to rest, a place to stretch out and be able to sleep. Then we pass through a gateway and a torch flashes for a second, revealing a sentry box. We pass it and cross a square, passing over soft sand. Some light-coloured barrack huts appear and we go through a glass door that swings to behind us. The runner opens the door of a barrack room, from which shines a bright light. We throw our things down and roll on to the beds, wanting only to sleep.

A voice says that we can get some soup. We get up again and grab our mess tins. Two men collect them up and go out, returning with full containers. We eat the thick porridge that the police company must have left behind when it was sent into action. Then we lie down again to sleep, full and content.

Bright daylight is streaming through the windows as the staff sergeant races along the corridor blowing his whistle to haul us out of bed. As soon as there is a quiet moment, their lordships have to revert to their old barrack habits. We stand around grumbling, tired and sleepy. In the kitchen Erich the cook has prepared coffee that is ready for collection, but first a few slugs of schnapps to wake us up. Then we have to move to another hut. We are divided up into new sections again as a result of losing the wounded comrades last night, and also another sergeant has turned up from somewhere. Then we have to unpack our stuff into the lockers for there is to be a rollcall at noon with bed and locker inspections.

The rooms are in terrible state with dirt and dust all over the beds and lockers. The kitchen is a pigsty with trampled bits of food and items of uniform thrown on the floor; a truly marvellous example that the guardians of law and order have shown us. The staff sergeant wants to take over the police company commander's room, so Boy, Stroschn and myself are detailed to clean it out. We discover a litre bottle of good schnapps behind the desk and take turns in taking swigs from it until it is empty. Then we fill it with water and vanish quickly into another barrack room that we proceed to 'clean'. Boy finds another bottle of schnapps,

'*Kosakenkaffee*'. The gentlemen of the police do not appear to have lived badly. Now they have had to leave all this behind and do what they never expected they would have to; go into action. But we are not angry with them; we can enjoy their 'provisions'.

We feel tired suddenly. We have been drinking too much and sampling too much of the good things. I take some books I have found in a locker and we return to our barrack room and lie down on our beds. Boy is lying next to me, and Stroschn on the other side of him. Fortunately they are not double-deckers or I would never have managed it.

My skull is throbbing when I wake up. Boy says that we have to go outside, there is an alarm. We are only taking fighting order, as we will be back by evening. My limbs are limp when I get up, and my head is churning like a carousel. I quickly stuff a can of meat I have found into my pocket and put my cigarettes into my haversack. I grab my weapon, and am about to go outside where my comrades are already standing in front of the entrance to the hut, when I turn back once more and stuff some socks and my photo album into my pockets. They are calling for me outside. The second lieutenant appears and we march off.

Now in daylight we can see where we are. We go back across the asphalt, which has tall buildings and stables on either side, the Napola and Police School, says the second lieutenant. Then we halt in front of a building where Waffen-SS and Hitler Youths from the Napola are standing around.[7] We are handed out weapons and ammunition. Each section gets a machine gun and two Panzerfausts. The others have to carry the ammunition. The second lieutenant is anxious to get on. We are loaded down like donkeys, and still the Hitler Youths keep bringing out more weapons and ammunition. One section has been give a First World War machine gun that nobody knows how to use, but they still have to take it. And then we are off.

We pass through the gateway we came through last night. I have several belts of ammunition around my neck like chains and two linen bags in my hands that look almost like shopping bags, but are filled with machine gun ammunition. Policemen armed with rifles and Panzerfausts are standing in the street, and there are some Waffen-SS flame-thrower tanks parked under the trees ready for action. Now we can hear the sounds of battle coming from the streets up ahead. There is a wood on our right and some private houses on our left. Hitler Youths are coming back along the chaussee. The odd rifle shot hits the trees and the din of combat gets closer with every step we take.

The second lieutenant talks to a Waffen-SS officer, then we turn off to the right and go through a wood alongside a railway line. The staff sergeant says that the line goes to Bötzow. There is a large building in a garden on the left that looks almost like a hospital or a convent. The second lieutenant says that it is the Johannesstift and that the Russians are on the road behind. A Red Cross flag flutters over the trees. Then we turn right again and go deeper into the wood. Some houses appear in front[8], little family houses with a few women standing on their doorsteps, wondering whether to be more afraid of the sound of fighting coming from the Johannesstift on the left or the noise from the tramline behind the wood on the right.

We go along the tram tracks, but Boy, Stroschn and myself hold back for the enemy seems to be at the crossroads ahead, and there are thick hedges either side of the street. A Volkssturm detachment comes out of a sidestreet and tags on to us. Suddenly low-flying aircraft roar over the treetops and shoot up the roadway. I slip through the hedge and throw myself down on the ground as I do not want to go back on the street, which would only mean getting caught up in the fighting again. One is slowly losing one's nerve, although one has to get used to the killing in the long-term. The comrades who had been in front come back and the second lieutenant comes past. We creep out of the hedges and tag along. A German tank is standing at the crossroads firing along the street and some soldiers dash across the way, but we are going back. They can do what they like, but the main thing is for us to be left in peace for the moment.

We stop by the Bötzow railway line in front of the Johannesstift, where the Volkssturm have prepared some trenches. Their four-pip commander[9] (he thinks a lot of himself) does not want to let us occupy them. In fact, because they are laid out facing the woods, they are not all that much use to us for the moment, as we have to aim towards the Johannesstift fence, which has a thick hedge behind it. When the Russians come they will be able to shoot us like rabbits if we do not see them first.

Behind us the Volkssturm have made themselves comfortable in their trenches. Our own do not seem to be all that bad, as they are not too far forward. The noise from the Johannesstift swells up again. The second lieutenant comes along the trench and tells us that there are some 500 severely wounded in the buildings in front of us and that the doctor in charge has been discussing with the Waffen-SS commander handing over them to the enemy without bloodshed, but the commander will not agree to it.

I have put my ammunition down. Brushwood and fir branches have been laid over the trenches as camouflage, so that one has to virtually crawl along the bottom of the trench to get from one firing position to another. Boy happens to be next to me, so we are able to talk. We are both hungry. The pain in my head from the sleepless night and overindulgence in alcohol has eased, but the hunger will not go away, for we have not yet eaten today. Later on the Volkssturm get enough hot food that we also get a ladleful. Unfortunately I do not have the essential mess tins and spoon with me, but a Volkssturm man helps me out. Later Blaczek brings along a large container of hot tea to warm us up.

Time goes by slowly, and it has become almost quiet. I open my can of meat and we eat it together, then we do some digging in our firing position. We are going to have to spend the night here after all. The Volkssturm have decided to disband themselves, the complaining men wanting to get back to their wives before the Russians arrive. Ignoring the pleas and threats of their battalion commander, they disappear between the trees and, realising that he has no one left to command, he too disappears.

It has got dark and cold. The night is quiet. The staff sergeant comes along the trench parapet from time to time warning us to stay awake. The trench runs under the fence at one point, and I go along the trench with Boy and climb up into the garden on the far side, where we find some straw in a shed and put it in the trench, then find a stack of planks and throw them over the fence. We lay the planks on the bottom of the trench and spread the straw on top of them. We put some brushwood over the firing position like a blanket, but it is no use against the cold rising from the ground. We lie down close together, side by side, and curl up, then get up again shivering. The night is endless. Mist creeps over the ground, shimmering like silver. A voice comes from somewhere and a shot rings out in the far distance. We take an occasional drink of schnapps which is like ice. Our feet and bodies ache from the cold. Then we sit down again, drooping with fatigue. What is the point of the order to stay awake when our bodies simply cannot take any more?

The cold drives us to our feet again and again, so we climb out of the trench and walk about in the Johannesstift garden, where we collect some more straw to snuggle down deeper in, but there is no proper protection from the cold in our thin jackets and with nothing in our stomachs. These April nights are cold.

The new moon climbs slowly. Occasional scraps of cloud race across the sky and obscure its light. The canopy of stars hangs peacefully over the world. There is a slight rustling of branches from the wood. The time moves slowly, seemingly bit by bit, as we count the minutes of this endless night. Then we take another drink of schnapps like old sweats, but what can possibly help us when the cold is so deep in our limbs and stiffening our bodies? It is not long before we are shivering again. We walk around in the garden dead tired and just longing to sleep, but unable to. We lie down in the straw at the bottom of the trench and rest for a few minutes until we are forced up again by the bitter cold. The time goes so slowly, and then suddenly a clock strikes one o'clock through the silent night, the sound ringing on. A new day has begun. I lie down again and try to sleep, rolling myself into a ball, and sink into an exhausted sleep.[10]

Wednesday 25 April 1945

I wake up. My whole body is numb from the terrible cold of the night. I climb out of the trench and walk along the edge of the wood to try and warm myself up a little. The stars are beginning to dim and a thin mist lies over the ground. I look at the time. It is almost four o'clock. Boy comes from the trench and joins me, and together we go along to the second lieutenant's command post. Hardly any of us have been able to sleep. We are all standing trembling in the trenches or walking about to warm ourselves up as much as is possible, for our thin jackets are unable to keep out the night's cold. Had we realised yesterday what being 'back by evening' entailed, we would have dressed more warmly.

It is gradually becoming light, the night receding as the new day dawns. A few Volkssturm men have reappeared, having been hauled from their beds, and stand around complaining. Explosions resume on the road on the far side of the Johannesstift, the din of battle swelling. We climb into the trenches and watch the hedge in front of us, although we would be unable to see the enemy if he suddenly came up behind it.

Then Erich arrives with a horse and little cart that he has acquired from somewhere, bringing us some hot tea. With it comes half a litre of schnapps each and some soup. At last we warm up again. Blaczeck, the second lieutenant's runner, says that the Johannesstift will be handed over at noon, so we should not have to stay here much longer.

We leave most of the ammunition behind in the trenches when the second lieutenant has us fall in. The Waffen-SS company that was covering our rear yesterday from its position at the crossroads behind the wood withdrew early this morning. Consequently, our group has been left out on a limb again. We withdraw quickly along the railway line. The odd shot whips through the trees and vanishes. The noise of battle on the road behind is steadily increasing and now one can also hear the sound of tank guns. Then we pass by the new positions manned by Waffen-SS and Hitler Youths.

The second lieutenant talks to the Waffen-SS officer, who wants to stick us in his trenches, but we go on. We have to report to the aircraft instrument factory in Hakenfelde for further orders. The occupants of the houses along the road are standing on their doorsteps listening anxiously to the approaching sounds of battle. Some Volkssturm groups have been dressed by the Waffen-SS and look a strange mixture. Young faces from the Hitler Youth to old men of up to 70, all having to wear Waffen-SS camouflage uniforms, then given weapons and sent forward by sections. Some of the barriers have been closed and have Hitler Youths armed with Panzerfausts lying behind them.

The sun has broken through to shine over this scene of destruction and the preparations for it. The odd armoured personnel carriers of a Waffen-

SS unit are standing around and an occasional flame-throwing tank. But this is all we seem to have as heavy weapons. Only manpower is not lacking, and there is plenty of that, even if consists only of children and old men shedding their blood. Once they have been used up, the women will be taken. The SS officers have found the ways and means of filling the defence's ranks.

We march along the streets. The sawmill that was on fire the night before last is a charcoaled shell. Even the apartment block where we took shelter that night has been partially damaged. Only the instrument factory appears to be immune, standing like an indestructible block in the middle of hopeless destruction, but its windows are empty, the shards of its broken window panes lying in a thick carpet on the pavement.

We stop at the factory gate, where the guards are digging slit trenches. The second lieutenant goes in to report to the regimental commander for new orders, while we sit against a hut and sun ourselves. A Volkssturm unit is already getting its food, so we take our mess tins and line up too. We all get a ladleful of milk pudding with baked plums. Actually we should not be eating, for we do not know what the next few hours might bring, and a stomach wound is better on an empty stomach. However, what concerns us most is that we are hungry and what we are probably eating is the condemned man's breakfast. We do not know whether we will be getting our last meal today or tomorrow.

There is frantic activity going on in the yard, with runners and liaison officers running about and driving off on motorcycles to the various units. Some Volkssturm officers, most of them wearing Nazi Party uniforms, leave the building and set off down the street with their men. Even the factory guards in their blue uniforms have been paraded.

A tank swings into the yard with squealing tracks and a general climbs down from the turret with lots of gold and decoration on his collar, his chest covered in medals. He strides theatrically between the men preparing for action and snarls at a soldier who fails to salute him properly. He then disappears into the building that houses his command post.[11]

The second lieutenant returns. We are now a special task force under the direct command of the regimental commander and will be going back into action straight away. The machine guns and nearly all the Panzer-fausts are to be left behind at the command post. The sergeants get their instructions about drawing rations and later we each receive five front line packets. That clearly means that it is going to be hot for us again, because they never dish them out otherwise. Then we fall in. Blaczeck comes along and informs us that the huts in which we left all our kit have been burned down by the police troops to clear a field of fire, and all our things have been burnt. So it was for this that we struggled back to Berlin with full packs, including the Wehrmacht second issue of underwear as per instructions, just so that they could be burnt here! But it cannot hurt us any more, even if the last of our personal belongings have gone up in flames, for we are now truly 'soldiers' in the fullest sense of the word. The battalion commander back in barracks has got his way at last. 'Personal memories are not worthy of a young soldier...'

We pass the factory guards as we go through the gate. A few women and young girls are standing in front of the apartment blocks handing out bread and hot coffee as troops move forward on both sides of the road and disperse up the sidestreets. Going along the street opposite us are some Volkssturm, and one sees in their despairing and tormented faces the compulsion that they must be under. Up ahead goes a Waffen-SS second lieutenant with a drawn pistol turning round all those coming back whether wounded or not, it makes no difference. Even two soldiers carrying a container to collect food for their unit are driven back.

The staff sergeant passes along warning us to look out for that second lieutenant. He is shooting anyone who does not instantly obey his order to turn back, wounded or not. He holds the Knights' Cross and previously commanded a punishment battalion renowned for its enormous losses. The men were driven unarmed against the enemy positions, and as soon as the battalion had run out of men, he was sent political detainees and criminals who had been reprieved 'for front line action'. Once that battalion too was wiped out, he was given the Knights' Cross and now it seems that he is out to get the Oak Leaves to it before the fighting in Berlin comes to an end.

The apartment blocks are now behind us and the street widens out. On the right is the fence of the aircraft instrument factory, and on the left some small family houses set in their green gardens.[12] Slit trenches have been dug under the trees in which Hitler Youths with Panzerfausts and steel helmets far too big for their heads are watching the street. Distant sounds of battle come from the right, where things appear to be hot towards the Nordhafen. Shots are coming from up front and smashing into the trees. The houses fall behind us and the chaussee runs into a wood, where a sign stands on the roadside with 'Gross Berlin' on one side and 'To Velten 17 km' on the other. We are at the north-west edge of the city, the part that the enemy have not yet succeeded in penetrating. There is a field in front of us that runs up as far as the wood, and on the right the chaussee runs under the first trees of the wood.[13] Waffen-SS and Volkssturm are moving forward along the roadsides. We have to run across the field and occupy some trenches on the edge of the wood. On the left is a foreign workers' camp belonging to the instrument factory, from behind which the enemy is showering us with machine gun bursts and single shots.

We race across the field with bullets striking the ground and whistling through the air. The field is as flat as a pancake and offers no cover, so we have to hurry. The trenches are empty, but if we do not get to them fast enough, the enemy could occupy them before us and then we would be running straight into their open arms.

At last we reach the wood, which offers us some protection from the infantry fire, and there are the trenches into which we are already jumping. The second lieutenant and the staff sergeant come forward safely from the road along a communications trench. The foreign workers' camp is only a few metres from us. A factory chimney rises behind the trees beyond the chaussee on the right, where the factory appears to be occupied by the enemy.

The trenches barely come up to our chests. We kneel down and fire into the thick plantation in front of us, even though we cannot see the enemy, but shooting steadies our nerves. The second lieutenant allocates our sections to different parts of the trench. No.1 Section is to go to past the foreign workers' camp and occupy the trench beyond it that leads to the plantation via a clearing. I follow them as the link man from No.2 Section.

We crouch down along the trench with the section leader carrying a Panzerfaust leading. When we reach the foreign workers' camp we have to leave the trench and run across a pathway into the other trench. The plantation is now on our right. The enemy does not appear to have spotted us, as his fire continues to be directed at the trench in front of the plantation as before. A tank is standing at the edge of the woods and, as far as one can tell, appears to be burnt out.

It is uncomfortable advancing along this trench, as we do not know what is lurking behind the plantation. Not to draw enemy attention to ourselves, we move in a crouched position without firing at the plantation. Once the section has advanced far enough, I turn round and race back to my section. We dare not lift our heads above the trench, as machine gun bursts and rifle fire are whipping into the trees.

Suddenly there is the sound of a tank gun firing and cries can be heard. Two figures race across the pathway at full speed and dive into our trench. Their faces are in a state of shock and they have lost their weapons. They are shaking like leaves and can only give the staff sergeant a garbled report on what has happened.

They had advanced farther along the trench and had almost reached the edge of the wood, and with it the end of the clearing where the tank was standing, when suddenly its turret turned and aimed at the trench. The sergeant was aiming his Panzerfaust when it fired and hit him in the body, and the Panzerfaust exploded. The sergeant's head was blown off, although he still went on a few steps. A few others were killed immediately. Helios and Reinicke got away because they were behind a bend in the trench. Their faces and uniforms are splattered with blood. It is only then that Helios notices that he has a gaping wound in his shoulder from which the blood is pouring. He begins to whimper and tries to jump out of the trench and run back. We only stop him by force.

The firing from the plantation has increased. Two comrades bandage Helios, who then lies listlessly at the bottom of the trench, letting things happen. He lies there with bloodless lips and only moans a little when the pain gets too much. Reinicke suddenly begins to shriek and tries to get out of the trench. Reinicke, who has always taken things with composure and humour, who lifted our spirits with his jokes in the bad times and made us forget our circumstances. We have to hold him down on the ground, not to be carried along with him. The horror of his last experience, which is only now getting through to him, has given him extraordinary strength.

As soon as things quieten down a little, both of them jump out of the trench and run back crouching down to vanish between the bushes chased by enemy fire. Another section less. Our little group is collapsing around us. Will this be our last action? Are we all going to bleed to death in this trench?

We lie in the trench and shoot, reload and shoot again. The enemy must not know how weak we really are, for an attack would completely knock us out. The trench walls are dry and sand falls in with every impact. Our weapons are completely covered in sand, and one jammed round follows another. It takes a considerable effort to extract a round from the chamber, only to have the next round do the same thing. Then suddenly one round refuses to budge. My ramrod is bent and cannot force it out. I give up; the weapon is useless.[14]

A figure can be seen climbing the chimney of the factory on our right. All who can still shoot try to hit him, but there are not many left still able to use their weapons. Nearly all have stoppages from the sand getting in. But he is hit and falls from halfway up. After him falls a small box, presumably the telephone. We only hope that night will come soon and that we will be able to withdraw.

Suddenly there comes the rattle of tanks tracks and the roar of a tank engine. We raise our heads and look out towards the road. A vast tank is emerging from behind the plantation. It stops and slowly turns its turret. The staff sergeant calls for a Panzerfaust, but there are no more available. The gun barrel drops a little and suddenly there is a flash of flame. There is a splintering among the trees and branches fall. Our ears are deafened by the gunfire as we lie cowering against the earth. The trench runs straight up to the road without scarcely a bend or zigzag. It only has a bend close to the foreign worker camp that protects me, as the last man in the section, from the firing.

The roaring of the gunfire and the cracking of the explosions come faster. The tank is firing straight into the trench. Screams can be heard above the sound of the gunfire and exploding shells. Someone suddenly runs along the trench, jumps out and dashes to the rear. A brief streak of fire comes from the tank's machine gun and he collapses. The tank is firing into the trench with frightening precision, digging it up metre by metre, and the trench walls are falling in on the living and the dead. I crawl into the earth waiting to be hit, thinking that I will not be able to take the roaring of the gunfire and the screams of those hit any longer. I have only one sensation in my head, a single mighty hammering, which makes it impossible to think clearly. Is anyone else alive near me? It is possible that some men are still breathing in this mass grave the trench has become for us. Have I been wounded and not noticed? My rifle is buried and I myself am half covered in sand. The thundering of the tank gun goes on. There does not seem to be anything but the roaring of the gunfire, everything else is pure fantasy.

The barrack huts are burning behind us accompanied by the screams of the wounded. From the air raid shelters, dug in the sand for the foreign workers, come the death cries of the dying as wounded German soldiers are burnt alive in the dugouts there, and nobody can help them. Even some trees next to the huts have caught alight, the flames leaping up with the blast of every exploding shell. Then it is suddenly silent. The ears hear it but the mind does not believe it, not believing that one is still alive. Even louder in the silence come the cries of those who have been hit, and the whimpering of the wounded. Then the roaring resumes, the tank tracks screech and the messenger of death slowly withdraws step by step to disappear between the trees. Only the gun barrel remains threateningly visible between the bushes by the roadside, but now I can dare breathe out again. Perhaps it is only giving us a short break. Is there anyone else alive apart from myself in this mass grave? Has anyone else survived that Hell, or am I alone?

But yes, a face appears around the corner and a voice calls out: 'We are going back!' Here and there a figure digs itself out of the sand, stands up and stumbles away. I get up and look around me. I am the last. I quickly crawl forward, frightened of losing contact and being left behind. The trench walls have fallen in nearly everywhere, burying the dead and wounded. The trench is narrow, so one cannot avoid the dead. Shots are coming from the plantation again. It is time to go. I climb over the gently yielding bodies with my teeth tightly clenched. I could scream with horror when one of the wounded with shattered limbs – there are only the dying left – begins to whimper when I climb over him. And then I come to one with a shattered face and empty eye sockets. His face is half destroyed, his nose torn off and his jaw smashed. Blood is dripping slowly from his mouth and he is still groaning. There is still the spark of life in his shattered body, and I have to climb over him. But I can't.

Shots are coming from the wood and the enemy seems to be getting closer. The man ahead of me has vanished. I am alone among the dead in the middle of all this horror. I shut my eyes, get up and crawl slowly over the wounded man. My hands grasp blood and sand, sticky bits of brain dripping from my fingers, and I can barely go on, can hardly keep calm. A red veil dances in front of my eyes, and my heart is beating as if to burst. Then I am over. I let myself slip to the ground and lie still, breathing out and trying to regain my senses. Then I force myself on again. The whimpering and groaning comes from all around. I plunge out of this horrible graveyard, forgetting all caution just to get away and not to have to see those shattered bodies with their spark of life. I suddenly feel guilty about still being alive and start running along the trench. I stumble over a Panzerfaust lying half-covered in the sand, then turn into the communication trench leading to the rear. Right up ahead of me I see the back of a soldier, and breathe out again. Away from death. I don't want to die! I want to live!

I slow down when I see the Waffen-SS officer with the Knights' Cross who is standing in a slit trench and shooting. Then I look back for the first time. Figures are running across the road and through the wood to vanish into the trees. Swarms and swarms of them appear. The SS officer is calmly aiming and pressing the trigger, handing the weapon to his orderly when it is empty for him to reload. An enemy falls with every shot fired and lies still, and the second lieutenant goes on firing as if he were on a rabbit shoot, but these are human beings.

My section sergeant is standing at the junction of the slit trench with Paulat. The officer has summoned them and told them to wait until he has finished. I too have to stay behind. I still have my rifle, but it is useless and will not fire any more. I can still see my dying comrades with their torn faces. I have a lump in my throat and could spit on everything going on around me.

As the officer goes on shooting for a long time, we slowly inch back. Dusk falls suddenly. The light finally defeats the officer and he goes forward with his orderly. He orders us to stay where we are, but as soon as he is out of sight we turn round and hurry back along the trench to the rear. On our right is the bushy field, with a few dead lying around, and on the edge of the trench on the left is a bulging officer's rucksack that I carry back with Paulat. The trench bends to the left and then ends at an anti-tank barrier, where some Volkssturm are standing around looking ill at ease into the gloom. They help us out of the trench, and we take a deep breath.

The troops have withdrawn and the Volkssturm are just waiting for their orders to withdraw as well. A steaming food container stands by the side of the road. The Waffen-SS officer comes back with his orderly and disappears to the rear. A dead civilian is lying on the ground in a pool of blood, and weapons and ammunition are lying about under the trees. Paulat and myself dig into the officer's knapsack we recovered and come up with schnapps, cigarettes and cans of sausages and meat. We stuff our pockets full and throw the rest into the ditch.

It is now completely dark. A staff sergeant comes up from the rear and gives the order to abandon the position. We tag on to the Volkssturm and go back with them. Dead men are lying on the road in puddles of blood, mainly Volkssturm in civilian clothes. The darkness closes behind us as we step out. Tomorrow, or perhaps even today, the enemy will penetrate as far as this.

The instrument factory fence runs along our left and the tall apartment blocks begin on our right. An anti-tank barrier has been built across the road in front of us. As we slip through it, we see the Waffen-SS officer stopping the returning men with his drawn pistol and placing them under the command of Waffen-SS soldiers. Suddenly shells start exploding on the street and everyone scatters. I dash across to the other side of the street and run past the barrier into a hallway, where the shocked occupants are hurrying down the steps to the cellar. Then suddenly I hear the voice of our second lieutenant, and I force my way to the door. The shelling has stopped. I go out into the street again, where the second lieutenant and the staff sergeant are standing together. Then Paulat emerges from the door of the next building. Soldiers and Volkssturm are streaming back in no mood to be stopped any more. Someone says that the Waffen-SS officer has been hit.

We make our way back to the factory. Soldiers are lying in the entrances and cellars of the apartment blocks, and occasionally a woman scurries across the street. Then we come to the gate of the instrument factory with the administrative building towering dark in the night. We go past the factory guards and through the big shattered glass doors of the entrance of the building, then down the steps to the cellar. The staff sergeant is sitting at a table in the passageway. He only asks if we are the last. We look for a place and lie down exhausted on the floor. Then the second lieutenant calls us back to the table. Faces appears here and there out of the darkness and come into the light shed by a small lamp. We stand around waiting for more to arrive, but there are no more. The second lieutenant counts us and gets to a total of twenty-eight. All the rest are dead, wounded or missing. The staff sergeant writes down our names, the names of the last of our company. Then the sections are checked. Only one sergeant has survived; all the rest are dead. No.1 Section is missing completely, all dead or missing, and I am the sole survivor of No.2 Section. Even my best friends I could always depend on, Boy and Stroschn, are missing. No.3 Section has survived, including the sergeant. Only one or two are left from each of the other sections. Then the staff sergeant reads out the names of the missing and our weary responses ring out: Dead – dead – missing, dead – missing, dead. A long list. Of those of us who have survived, some are wounded. We are all tired enough to collapse, our faces are bloodless, and hunger has made us ill-tempered.

Then we go back down the passageway and lie down along the sides.

Occasionally soldiers come down the steps and tramp past, feeling their way in the dark, and sometimes a door opens spilling a bright light across the passage and falling on the exhausted figures, lying there as if dead. Then two of our men go off to collect food. There are not so many of us to cater for now.

The food carriers return and the sergeant shares out the food. We all get bread and butter, for there is plenty of that. What was once intended for fifty-eight makes double rations for twenty-eight. There are also ten front line packets per head. Apparently they are being generous as all the cellar rooms are full of them.

I nibble exhaustedly at some biscuits, have a smoke and lie down on the cement floor. More and more soldiers arrive to fill the passageway. We take some planks that had been lying in a corner and put them down on the floor to lie on, then roll over and try to sleep.

Later a sergeant comes along and says that there is some soup going, but we will have to hurry. We go along the passage, where candles are flickering here and there, and soldiers have settled down to sleep. Paulat steps over the sleeping figures beside me, and Solga follows behind. We go up the steps through a broken glass door, where the moon is brightly illuminating the stairwell, and look for the canteen building. There are some thick green bushes alongside the path. Then the flat roof of the canteen building comes up on the right and we turn into it. Part of the wing from the eagle and swastika over the door has been broken off, and the doors have been ripped off their hinges. The moon shines into the room through a hole in the roof ripped open by the bombing. Our boots stumble over glass splinters and shards.

Food is being given out in a corner. A woman hands out plates and spoons, and a cook gives out big helpings of soup. We eat quickly and go back for a second helping. Then we hand back our plates and spoons and make our way back over the rubble to the cellar. A door is standing open and we can see boxes of supplies stacked up to the ceiling. A couple of civilians begging for bread are chased out again.

We enter the passage and shut the door, causing the candles to flicker wildly, then clamber over the feet of the sleepers. Some soldiers are playing cards in a corner. The remains of our company are all pressed close together. The second lieutenant and staff sergeant are sitting at the table trying to sleep. Here and there the tiny red points of cigarettes glow. Soldiers stumble by looking for space, and sergeants clamber over the sleepers lighting up their faces in the search for their men.

Some soldiers bring in a whimpering bundle of humanity. Later we hear that it is a 10-year-old who was sent by his mother to get food from some soldiers and stepped on a mine. His younger brother was killed instantly and both his legs have been smashed to above the knee.

I talk quietly with Paulat, who is lying next to me. Another day has gone by that has ripped so many from our ranks, and it is as if we can see the faces of our comrades who are now lying in their own blood somewhere with only the night to cover them.

The normally cheerful Reinicke, who suffered so much and then ran off to the rear. I think of his mother, a small, generous woman, who visited him in the barracks at Easter and asked us to look after him, as he was the last one she had. Now he is gone and she will be waiting for him to return. He could talk crudely about women and girls, although he certainly had never had one. With his large head that he always seemed ready to bang against a wall, and flax-golden hair, he was the liveliest among us, always thinking up and playing out new tricks. He liked to tease and tell tall stories, so that at times we could become quite annoyed with him and gave him a thumping, but one could never be really angry with him. Despite his age, he had hands like coal shovels and, while still a schoolboy, had worked for his father in his workshop. Whenever he spoke of this, an eager look would appear in his eyes and he would become quiet, which was not what one would have expected from such a scamp. When he was called up, he had to give up the troop of Deutsche Jungvolk[15] that he had been leading, which he was very reluctant to do, or so he told us. He fervently believed that German arms would be victorious and he absolutely adored Hitler. He even took the fairy stories about wonder weapons that we no longer believed in to be true. When something failed to appear that we had been promised, he would just say that Hitler could not be expected to see to everything himself, but then when we went to the front and went through Hell, he became quieter and quieter, and as we stumbled from encirclement to encirclement by night and forced marches, his cheerfulness faded with his beliefs, and he carried on quietly with us, bitter and without hope. Now he is lying somewhere, perhaps in the wood, perhaps in the field, perhaps on the road.

And Harry Tischwitz, what happened to him? He came from a small village near Berlin. He was an incurable bookworm and carried all sorts of books he liked to read with him, and would leave them lying around once he had read them. All his money went on theatre performances, and he was looking forward to going to good theatre after the war with no fear of air raid warnings and bombs driving the audience into the cellar during the middle of a performance. He lived with his mother and sister, and went to school in Berlin. Whenever his mother, who came to see him nearly every day with his sister and two large dogs and would not let the NCOs stop her, brought in a large packet of food, he would openhandedly share it out, silently pressing on everyone pieces of cake or ham or sausage, waving away all thanks, and then bury himself back in his books. Even when he went off to the front, he had a couple of books in his pack that he did not want to leave behind, as was always the case. Among us 17-year-olds he stood out. When the wounded and frightened cried for help, they only had to see him to calm down. He often armed himself with his own particular mixture of tactlessness and sensitive understanding. Now he is dead and will be attending no more theatrical performances, reading no more books.

And what about Czech, Stangenberg, Kranz, Mattern, Osterberg? Where are they now? Lying shattered in a trench? Who was the one with the smashed face? It is terrible to think that he was once a human being, a child like us and many others.

It is our own death knell we can hear, not a victorious fanfare any more, for we have lost faith. The list of these children is not complete, for it only has the names of those I knew personally. Who knows the nameless ones lying scattered on the streets? Those who have been thrown about as shattered bundles of bones? Where are the twins, where are Hüsing, Gerke, Wiethoff, Weissgerber, Lange and Schmitt? In which hole does Zander lie, the big East Prussian who loved his mother so much and wrote her long affectionate letters, who looked for the best in his instructors and drove away despair with his calm attitude, who never lost his sense of humour and lust for life, even when things were at their worst?

Sleep will not come to me. Their faces pass by like ghosts. I put another biscuit in my mouth and light a cigarette, the umpteenth today. The candles have gone out, snores come out of the darkness, and a wounded man groans somewhere. A faint light shines at the table on which the staff sergeant and second lieutenant are lying asleep. Occasionally a soldier stumbles past and goes outside.

It is quiet in the passageway, with only a cigarette glowing here and there in the darkness. I suddenly feel tired, the cigarette falls from my fingers, and I curl up, pressed to the floor. It is warm down here with the central heating giving out dry air. I hear nothing more, I only see the faces of my dead comrades as I fall asleep[16]

NOTES

1. The rule had been that refugees from outside the city were only allowed to pass through and not stop except for medical reasons.
2. The Charlotten Bridge between Stresow and the Alt-Stadt.
3. Francke Furnier und Sperrholz Werke, Streitstrasse 12–18.
4. The administrative buildings of the former Luftfahrtgerätewerk Hakenfelde GmbH still stand at 5–17 Streitstrasse, but are now used for other purposes.
5. The 125th Corps of the Soviet 47th Army, supported by the 50th Guards Tank Brigade, had closed in on the German defences around Spandau and Gatow airfield that day, but made no attempt to penetrate into the town.
6. An evangelical foundation for the training of priests and social workers, the education of the mentally and physically handicapped and the care of geriatrics. The complex, built in 1910, normally accommodates some 1,600 people.
7. The Napola system of schools was intended to produce leading citizens in all

walks of life. Although run by the SS and Hitler Youth organisations, the curriculum was set by the education authorities and was of grammar school equivalent standard. According to Lehmann (see Appendix IV) both the Potsdam and Spandau Napola pupils were involved in the defence of Spandau. This Napola complex was to become the first British Military Hospital in Berlin.

8. The Wald Siedlung estate off Wichernstrasse.

9. Those Volkssturm officers who had uniforms had their ranks denoted by silver pips on black collar patches in SS style.

10. This was the day that Marshal Koniev launched a massive attack across the Teltow Canal with the aim of reaching the goal of the Reichstag before his rival, Marshal Zhukov. The silence of the night noted by Altner is of significance. Despite what Marshal Zhukov wrote in his memoirs, it was a feature of the fighting in Berlin that his troops eased off the fighting at night to rest and enjoy the fruits of victory.

11. SS Gruppenführer (Major General) Heissmeyer, Inspector General of the Napolas, was in charge of the Hitler Youth Combat Group 'Heissmeyer' in Spandau but, according to Lehmann (see Appendix IV), after exhorting his charges to great deeds, he flew off to Gandau in the Alps to join his wife, Gertrud Scholtz-Klink, who was famous as head of the Bund Deutsche Mädel, the female part of the Hitler Youth. This departure was without the knowledge of Reichs Youth Leader Artur Axmann, to whom he was responsible for the combat group, and so amounted to desertion.

12. The Wald Siedlung estate again.

13. A prison for juveniles was erected on this site in 1998.

14. The scarcity of brass resulted in the Germans resorting to making cartridges out of steel and then lacquering them to prevent rusting. Once the weapons using them became hot, jamming was frequent, and machine guns would have to change barrels after every belt of ammunition used. A combination of melting lacquer and sand would be even worse.

15. The junior division of the Hitler Youth.

16. The 76th and 60th Rifle Divisions of the Soviet 47th Army attacked Spandau simultaneously from the north and west that day. Despite considerable artillery support, Soviet progress remained negligible at a heavy cost in casualties. Having failed to take the town, they withdrew again, pulling back to more secure positions for the night.

CHAPTER VIII

The End in Spandau

Thursday 26 April 1945

Somebody is shaking me by the shoulder. 'Get up! Get ready!' I get up dizzily, unable to adjust to the return to reality. I have been having a strange dream, in which I saw columns marching through the night past endless ruins. They had the faces of children, marching past with heavy tread in an endless train, and among their ranks appeared the pale faces of our dead comrades, Czech, Stangenberg, Mattern, Wiethoff, Lischka and Kranz as figures in the night marching into oblivion.

Things are coming to life in the passageway. We take our things and go forward to where the staff sergeant hands out our rations and some schnapps. Two men bring some hot coffee that wakes us up, then we sit down on benches and wait for Second Lieutenant Fricke to return with our new orders.

At last he comes back. We have to go to Spandau-West, and it is high time that we disappeared, for the enemy are already inside the factory grounds.

We pass through passages and climb some steps. The daylight hits us cruelly in the eyes and makes us blind for a second. Shots are whipping through the workshops and striking the walls, mortar bombs exploding in the gardens. We race along the streets as shells hit the administration building and shower us with debris. At last we reach the fence and slip through a gap. We are now covered from sight by the thick bushes.

Field grey figures are lying in wait in some hastily dug foxholes in the middle of the gardens. A light morning mist hangs over the paths. There is a dead man in one of the foxholes, his hands still tightly gripping his weapon. He has a small hole in his temple from a mortar splinter. We pass through.

Soldiers are moving along the street. Occasionally a pale face appears in a doorway and looks at the nearby anti-tank barrier. Noise of battle swirls all around, the infantry fire increasing in intensity. A machine gun tacks at the barrier. A tank engine roars into life somewhere. Fighting has resumed in full force.

We race across the street and reassemble under cover of the apartment blocks, then pass along streets and park areas that look as if they have died. Gradually the noise of battle recedes and we hear only the muffled sound of artillery shells bursting.

The Police School and Napola buildings appear up ahead with flame-thrower tanks of the Waffen-SS unit in front. Soldiers and civilians are being organised and there are cases of arms and ammunition stacked in the thick bushes in front of the buildings and on the other side of the street. We stop and wait for the second lieutenant, who has gone into one of the buildings. Boys in the brown Napola uniform go past carrying weapons and bits of equipment, each section being led by a soldier of the Waffen-SS. They are to be deployed as tank-hunting units.

The second lieutenant takes us to collect weapons. We file past a Waffen-SS soldier who thrusts rifles into our hands from an untidy pile, and then we have to sign for them. It is always the same with these quartermasters, it is only when we die that we can get away without signing.

We fall in again on the square and the second lieutenant counts us once more. Then we move well spread out across the grey square, which looks as if it has been swept clean. There is a wooded area a little farther on and, just before it, the charcoaled remains of buildings that have been burned to the ground. These are the huts that were reduced to ashes with our belongings still inside them. Apart from bursts of machine gun fire coming from a side street, it is quiet. We leave the buildings of the Police School behind and stop at a gate with apartment blocks in front of us. The street we have to cross is under machine gun fire.[1] The second lieutenant makes a run up and dashes across the street to stand unharmed in the cover of the buildings. But the firing has intensified, the enemy has been alerted. The bullets strike the walls, rebound and ricochet off. When it becomes a little quieter, we dash across the street one at a time. Now it is my turn. I take a run up and then dash across. The shots whistle past, but I am already over and waiting for the next man. Once he is safely across the street, the next follows with lungs gasping and his face twisted. Now it is the last man's turn. He takes a run up and starts across, but then stops short and breaks off. He turns round, slowly goes back and tries again, only to stop short again. Then the second lieutenant runs back and speaks to him. He takes him by the arm and they make a run up and race across together.

We move on down the street.[2] Thick green bushes grow in front of the tall apartment blocks, and there are allotment gardens in the gaps between them. A bird sings in the trees but apart from that it is as quiet as a dead landscape. Only the sound of our footsteps rings out on the street. The sun has broken through and is slowly driving off the scraps of mist. We move well spread out close to the walls of the buildings. Then we stop. A few soldiers, stragglers from all branches of the service, are standing on the street. The second lieutenant asks their officer, a Luftwaffe major, about the situation. The enemy are in the allotments behind the street.

We advance cautiously. An old man in a camouflage uniform is going up the staircase of an apartment block. An old rifle stands in the doorway. We go past him and open the gate to the yard behind and quickly slip through. The allotment gardens lie in front of us fresh and green with the occasional red of a summerhouse. We advance well spread out, keeping close to the bushes. The major comes with us. His men have gone back and we are alone again, just twenty-eight young men. We creep along the garden paths very cautiously. A peaceful silence reigns. All we can hear is our excited breathing. Our hearts are beating so hard we can almost hear them. When a weapon hits a fence we all stand still and listen before continuing. The enemy is hiding in the bushes in front of us, alert like us and feeling his way forward like us.

We cross another garden path. The view is limited as there are bushes in the way and there are still some wisps of mist hanging above the ground. Suddenly a bird bursts into song and flutters up, startling us to a standstill. We look around. We are in a new garden and at the far end of it is a bright red summerhouse. The second lieutenant gives a hand signal for us to stop. A bush is crackling somewhere, and we can hear light, shuffling footsteps coming from the summerhouse. The second lieutenant turns round and we go back. We leave the garden and cross another path, then lie down in some thick bushes and watch our front. The summerhouse is no longer visible.

More noise is coming from the summerhouse. Boots bang on the floorboards and steel comes gently into contact with steel. Then the bushes part and a man appears, a Russian. Our nerves are stretched to the limit, to bursting point. Our fingers are clamped to the triggerguards of our weapons. The second lieutenant whispers sharply: 'Don't shoot!' The Russian stands listening for what seems an eternity. It is quiet now in the summerhouse. Scraps of words hang in the air. The enemy looks back, then turns round and disappears into the bushes.

We go back as if we were fleeing, keeping close to the bushes, climbing over fences and going across garden paths. The mist has lifted. At last we stop. The back yards of the apartment blocks are in front of us. Somewhere a tank engine suddenly roars into life.

We lie down on the ground and wait. The second lieutenant speaks quietly to the major as we look around indifferently, all of us feeling shattered after weeks of this highly unpleasant existence. The second lieutenant calls out to us, putting an end to our brooding. We get up and go across the yard and into the street. In the building we pass through, the shocked, pale face of a child peeps out at us from the cellar. Out on the street we are assigned to the individual blocks, two men to a block. We extend from this side of the street as far as the next street across.[3]. Beyond that there is no one. We are hanging completely in the air. The second lieutenant then gives us the house number of his command post across the street. A soldier arrives and reports tanks approaching. The major's men have withdrawn back to the Police School. The major sends the runner back and stays with our combat team.

Two comrades and myself have yet to be assigned. The other two are to be employed as runners, and I am to occupy a building with the major. He sends me ahead, and I slowly climb the stairs up to a landing with windows and look out. The bushes and trees lie quiet, but sometimes I think I can make out a voice. The sun is being reflected from the wire of the garden fences. The roaring of engines comes from the distance. Tanks? A machine gun tacks in a sidestreet, stops and bursts out again.

The gardens lie peaceful in the sunlight, as if there were no war, as if the killing might not break out again at any moment. The door opens down below and the major comes up the stairs. He send me up another floor, from where I can see the summerhouse again, but there is no sign of life. But yes, there are figures slinking close to the bushes, sprinting from bush to bush like cats. I call down to the major. 'Shoot!' he calls back, and comes up the stairs. I take aim calmly as if on the range. It is so easy. A figure comes slowly into my sights and then becomes hazy. I have lost him. I stop and take a few deep breaths until I have calmed down again. Nobody seems to have noticed anything, either from the enemy side or from ours. I take aim again. Something is moving behind the summerhouse. A uniform appears in my quivering sights. My gun barrel follows it. I squeeze the trigger. The shot whips off with a bang, tearing through the peaceful silence. I squeeze again and again, the sound thundering in the narrow stairwell. Suddenly it is quiet. The roaring in my ears is even louder. But there is no one to be seen. The gardens are as if swept clean. Only the rifle shots slamming against the walls give it away that there is life down there.

I go up another floor. The gardens are now far below me. There are fields in the distance and dark spots moving forward along the street and getting bigger. Tanks!

It has quietened down, with just the odd shot whipping through the trees. I go back down one floor. The major has disappeared, so I go out into the street and into the building next door, where Barth and Staub are sitting quietly on the stairs eating. I realise that I am hungry too, and go back and eat what is in my haversack. A woman comes up the stairs and vanishes quickly into her flat. Suddenly the firing resumes and figures are running about in the gardens. Shots slam against the walls and whistle through the trees and summerhouses below. Occasionally one of the figures stops, staggers and then lies still like a dark stain in the gardens, but there is also the occasional cry from the apartment blocks.

The enemy fire is becoming more accurate, striking the windows and stairwell, and the glass splinters. We are firing almost blindly into the gardens, unable to see any of the enemy. I empty magazine after magazine, and the breech seems to be glowing. Shots are flying all around me, hitting the walls.

The woman comes down the stairs, jumping quickly past and dashes into the cellar. The empty cartridge cases leap out of the chamber, one after another, and crash to the floor. The endless din goes on.

Later on the woman comes back and asks me if we are not withdrawing soon, as there are women and children in the cellar. I tell her that I have no idea. She goes wearily back down the stairs and knocks at the cellar door, which opens with a screech and bangs shut again behind her. Time goes by and the firing stops. A dog suddenly starts barking in the gardens. Somewhere in the distance comes the dull rumbling of gunfire in the city, in that last bastion of the 'Third Reich'.

The door slams back against the wall. 'Everybody out!' I take a quick look at the gardens again and then go down the stairs to the street. The second lieutenant is standing on the street corner looking through binoculars. The major suddenly reappears. We have to occupy the buildings on the other side of the street. The comrades emerge from the buildings and cross the street to their new positions.

I too enter the building opposite and remain standing at the door. The second lieutenant leaves the street and goes through the buildings again. The street now lies dead and deserted. It has gone quiet. The sun reflects off the windows of the buildings opposite.

I close the front door. Some of the tenants hurry up the stairs to look for valuables to take down into the cellar. I go into the ground floor flat, whose door stands open. The major is sitting looking out from a small, charming bedroom, whose windows overlook the street and whose beds look freshly made. I get myself a chair from the kitchen and draw it up to the other window. Then we take the window out of its frame to stop it splintering. The wind blows the curtains out of the windows.

Then I go back into the entrance hall. We have left the front doors open across the street and closed the back doors. I take aim with my rifle and fire three shots through the back door across the way. The daylight shows up three small holes. Later I go back into the flat and appropriate a jar of jam that I find in the kitchen; soldiers' perks. We take what we want, whether it belongs to us or not.

Then I sit with the major on the beds and look out of the window. He gets himself a leather armchair and pulls it up to the other window. The clatter of tank tracks comes suddenly from a nearby street. Dull gunfire and explosions sound among the buildings. Rifle fire has also started up again, but only sporadically. A shot whistles close past my head as if it was trying to burn me. Startled, I drop my rifle and look outside. A picture that had been hanging on the wall behind me has been smashed, its glass broken. Now we are more careful. Most of the front doors of the buildings opposite are now closed, including mine, indicating that the enemy is in those apartments, only the width of the street away.

The second lieutenant suddenly enters the flat saying that several companies are supposed to be on their way to reinforce us and we will soon be relieved, but I do not believe it any more. We have been lied to too often. As always, we will have to make our own way out, and this bitter fighting will not end until death sets us free.

Once he has left the room, I go out into the back yard. Here the gardens run all the way back from the yards to the next row of apartment blocks just visible in the distance. Some children are playing in a box of yellow sand in a corner of the yard and several of the tenants are standing around snatching a quick breath of fresh air after hours in the stuffy cellar. They are conjecturing about how the Russians will behave. The women are frightened, and they are all worried about the horrors the next few hours will inevitably bring. But it will be a new experience, and the end of what they have been going through. Better an uncertain future than the deadly present.

Shells explode in the gardens, the gunfire coming from quite close. Startled, they all dash for the cellar, the children crying. I dive into the building, dragging a youngster with me. I go to the front door, open it and look out at the street. Some of the comrades are standing in the other doorways firing at the entrance to a sidestreet, from where Russians are running into the buildings. The others are firing at the buildings opposite, keeping the enemies' heads down. Suddenly a tank rolls into the street and stops at the crossroads. A bright flash comes from its barrel, the din sounding like an artillery barrage. The shell explodes sending thick smoke, rubble and debris flying around, and taking our breath away. Figures run across the street from the corner and vanish. Then the tank turns and rolls along the street, disappearing behind our row of buildings.

I go back inside, closing the front door again. The major is sitting quietly at the window looking out. I go up and look at him. At once I can see that he is dead. There is a small wound in his head dripping blood and a slimy, white mush. His weapon is still lying across his knees. His death suddenly hits me, and I could scream out aloud. This is not my first dead man, but there is nothing worse than seeing one looking as if he were still alive. It is such a small wound too.

The curtains flutter wildly. I am suddenly terrified and run out of the room, slamming the door behind me. Then I calm down, but I am not going back into that room, not at any price. A man standing at the cellar door asks for the major, but I do not answer him. A few comrades are now standing in the back yard and suddenly go into the gardens. The second lieutenant comes out of the building next door and says: 'Withdraw in five minutes! Back to the next row of buildings, and regroup there!' I stay by the back door and wait. Civilians are running out of the adjacent buildings and disappearing between the trees, some soldiers among them. Then I do not see any more. Am I alone? I too run back.

Solga dashes out of one of the buildings carrying a woman's suitcase. Then I lose them both from my sight and go on alone through the gardens, leaving the buildings behind. The little gardens are empty. I cross vegetable plots and climb over garden fences with only one thought: get back!

My foot hits something. A dead man is lying in front of me, and I had nearly fallen over him. There is a fresh hole in the ground next to him. He has been killed by splinters in his head and body, and is lying on his back staring into the sun. I try to get his paybook from him, but the dead man is heavy and his tunic full of blood, so I leave him and hurry on until a garden path leads me to the buildings up ahead.

Sergeant Richter is lying stark naked in a hallway being bandaged by some women, his body riddled through with splinters, and he stands no chance of survival.

The staff sergeant is standing in the street. When I tell him about the dead man in the garden, he orders me to go back and get his paybook. I go back through the gardens and find the dead man at last. I roll him over, my fingers wet with running blood, looking through his pockets for his papers and removing the wallet from his tunic. The dead man rolls back, blood spurting from his mouth and nose. I am suddenly filled with an irrational fear that he will wake up and demand his legal rights, making me responsible. I rush away from him, not daring to look back. The second lieutenant is standing on a garden path and I hand over the wallet to him. I slowly calm down. The second lieutenant looks up from the paybook in astonishment. The dead man lived quite close, only three streets away. I look at the paybook. That is quite correct; his address was No.5 YXZ-Strasse, Berlin–Spandau. His passport photograph shows a smiling face. He was married and had two children. Now he lies in the gardens only a few steps from his home and family, steps that he had dared not take.

Suddenly a woman rushes past us with her hair unfastened, wailing and calling out, and runs into the gardens. She disappears among the bushes. I go with the second lieutenant through the big archway leading under the building.[4] Two suitcases have been left on the street and Solga is standing nearby. These belong to the woman who ran back past us because she had forgotten her pearls.

Then we all stand around together before the staff sergeant takes us into the buildings and shows us where we have to take up our positions. Some of us are missing, but hopefully will rejoin before long. There are colourful stained glass windows on the landings of the buildings here. I smash two pieces out of the lead frames with my rifle butt and look out. The buildings that we have just left lie bright in the sunlight and will long have been occupied by the enemy. On the left runs the bright ribbon of a street.[5] The gardens are divided by a broad track. The sun shines warm and peaceful on the whole scene, on the buildings, gardens and streets.

Then suddenly firing breaks out again. Russians are running forward through the gardens from tree to tree and firing breaks out from all the windows into the gardens. But the volume of fire is not as strong as it was when there were many more of us. Now the enemy has changed tactics. He is digging in, the flashing spades betraying the positions of his men. A pile of earth is growing slowly next to a summerhouse, and a Russian is shovelling away half lying down. I take aim quite calmly, squeeze slowly and then again. His arm shudders suddenly and drops the spade. I take aim once more, and he collapses and lies still. But the enemy is working his way forward. It is only a question of hours before he will be in the buildings.

Then suddenly tank tracks rattle on the street and an engine roars. Unnoticed by us a tank has pushed forward close alongside the gardens. The engine is switched off. It has stopped. The shooting has eased off. Everyone is staring as if bewitched at the tank, whose turret is slowly turning and aiming towards us, at the buildings. The gun muzzle points threateningly at us, then a tongue of fire spurts from the barrel and the shell strikes with a roar. A hail of steel, masonry and iron showers over us. Walls crack and collapse. A cloud of dust drifts slowly and sluggishly over the gardens. I go down the stairs and into the house next door, where Solga is standing at a window. I look out. The tank is still standing quietly in the sun, as if lifeless. Then its turret turns again, just a centimetre. I cannot watch any more. I go slowly down the stairs to the front door. The shell strikes deafeningly behind me. The walls seem about to burst. Behind me masonry and glass splinters crash down the stairs. A big hole has been cleft in the wall and a window has vanished with the entire wall.

We stand despondently in the street, not knowing what to do. It is pointless wanting to attack the enemy any more, but the second lieutenant gives us the order to go back into the buildings. We go back, but the doors have been closed behind us. We knock on the doors with our rifle butts and smash them in. Then we slowly climb the stairs. It really is too much that we have to fight not only against the enemy but also against our own countrymen in this meaningless defence.

We sit at the windows again and look out. The tank is still standing motionless on the street. We shoot into the trees and bushes. Then the tank moves forward again with rattling tracks and roaring engine, and more shellbursts demolish walls. Building after building is hit, wall after wall collapses and homes are destroyed. It is all pointless.

We go back into the street and cross over to the other side. Are we going to have to go over the whole thing again from building to building? Are we going to be the birds of death, bringing death and destruction to these homes and their occupants?

No, we are not going inside, we are staying in the street. We press ourselves close to the bushes that line the front of the buildings. When we hear the sound of a tank engine, we run back into the doorways and see five Russian tanks, like large toys, go through the crossroads and disappear behind the buildings.

Just behind us the street bends to the right in a curve and is lined by a light-coloured wooden fence. Some Russians are running across the street. We stand behind the trees and shoot, but without success, it is too far. Now the enemy is trying to get across to the other side of the street from a sidestreet. One is almost across. We aim and squeeze, and the Russian staggers and collapses in the gutter. Then someone waves a white cloth and a couple of civilians run across the street and drag the hit man away.

A couple of residents are standing in a hallway looking out through the glass door. A woman comes out and gives us coffee and bread, real bean coffee. She returns with some sugar and presses it on us. Something dark suddenly slides forward behind the enemy on the other side of the street and comes closer. A gun! There is hardly time to take cover before it fires, sending masonry and steel whirling through the air. A large hole appears in front of the foremost building, and a wounded man lies in the street calling loudly for help. It is Solga. The comrades are running along the street. We are going back. We stop at the next corner and the staff sergeant finds a handcart in one of the buildings. Suddenly a machine gun starts tacking again. The Police School is just across the way, only separated from the street by a wire fence, but the machine gun is blocking the return route for us again.

We press close to the buildings as we race back, pushing, straining and pulling the handcart over lumps of masonry, kerbs and stones, causing the wounded man to scream out madly with pain. But at last we have made it and come to a halt. The apartment blocks are behind us.

We go up the broad steps of the Police School, a grandiose construction of light sandstone blocks, pass through a door and into a long passage where policemen in steel helmets are walking around as young lads from the Napola and Waffen-SS men hasten by. The staff sergeant gets hold of some medical orderlies who put Solga on a stretcher and carry him away.

At last the second lieutenant, who had disappeared into the police commandant's office, comes back with him. We must wait while something is found for us to eat, for we are no longer on the muster list, as our combat team was reported to have been lost. We sit on the floor and wait, stretching our tired legs out in front of us. Police officials are taking typewriters and files down into the cellar, and two girls of the Waffen-SS combat team go past. Later the second lieutenant returns and tells us we can collect our food. The staff sergeant issues the rations in front of the

Napola. There is a warm pea soup with bacon in it, some tins of meat and lots of cigarettes. The clock on the Napola shows that it is already three o'clock in the afternoon. We are surprised, having lost all sense of time during the fighting.

We sit down on the grass and eat our rations, and smoke. Then we stretch out and stare into the sky that looks almost summer-like with its shining blue canopy above us.

The flame-throwing tanks of the Waffen-SS are on the street outside, and Hitler Youths, policemen, Volkssturm and Waffen-SS are going past. I stand up, go along past the buildings and enter the Napola and go down into the cellar. We have run out of ammunition as the day has demanded practically our last round from us. The names of the Waffen-SS NCOs are fastened to the cellar doors where they can rest safe from the tanks and mortars. One of them asks me what I am looking for, and when I tell him ammunition, he directs me to the next building. I find what I am looking for in a corner of the yard and come away with two boxes. The staff sergeant then hands out the ammunition – one hundred rounds each.

Then I lie down in the grass again. The sun shines peacefully from the heavens, undisturbed by war and death. A few birds are twittering in the trees along the street, and some stalks of grass wave above my head. The sound of voices is sometimes interrupted by the sound of marching feet from a returning column.

I stand up. The second lieutenant is going round collecting the paybooks from everyone. The commandant, a Waffen-SS officer, has ordered company commanders to take the paybooks so that the enemy cannot tell what unit we belong to. As if we could believe that. Here, where everything is topsy-turvy, I believe that they have only taken them off us to stop us deserting. Then a Waffen-SS man tells us that the Russians shoot all soldiers they capture who do not have paybooks. So this is just another means of putting pressure on us. And if it is as we have been told, then it is that much worse, for those who fall will have no papers and no one will know their names. Also virtually all our private papers were lost when the huts with our belongings in them were set alight.

A mixed column goes past with soldiers of every arm of the service, civilians and Volkssturm, an emergency company apparently of all age groups. At their rear march a couple of Deutsche Jungvolk in brown shirts and short trousers carrying Panzerfausts and weapons. Then they halt and stand around, a discouraged, half-hearted lot who can no longer expect to survive and do not know which of them will fall within the next few hours.

The leader of this outfit, a political leader with an armband worked in gold, lets them fall out. A couple of the youngsters lie down near us. A small lad looks at our cigarettes with eyes full of longing and we call him over. He comes across slowly and sits down beside us. We ask him his age.

'Thirteen', he replies. He is from Oranienburg, and has been passed from one emergency company to another here in Spandau. They are really not Volkssturm, he says, since they belong to the newly-formed '30th January' Regiment.[6]

We ask him how he managed to land up here fighting with us at the age of 13, and he points to his comrades, some of whom are also from Oranienburg. 'We were taken from our homes by the police on the orders of SS Captain Frischessky and had to parade in the SS barracks and on the castle square. Then we were divided up by our Hitler Youth units and attached to SS and Volkssturm sections. Our sections were sent into action in the northern and eastern parts of the town. Most of us were killed by infantry fire while having to attack across open fields. Later, for two days, the fighting raged in the town. In two days and two nights the town changed hands four times, and that accounted for nearly all of the rest of us. Then the Russians started firing into the town with Stalin-organs.[7] When we wanted to pack up and go home, we were stopped and made to join the flight over the canal to Eden. My platoon commander, who refused, was hung from the nearest tree by two SS men and an SA man, but he was already 15. Then the remains of our Hitler Youth unit, eight of us – and we had been 120 – went along. We had a break after the canal bridge was blown, and I met up with two schoolfriends, who told me that the SS Captain with his girlfriend and Lieutenant Schiller from the Aeromechanics School had already made off to the west on bicycles two days earlier. I then made my way to Velten, wanting to go to Hennigsdorg, where I have an aunt, but I was caught just short of there. I then fought in Reinickensdorf on the street leading to Spandau. Then we withdrew, and this morning we were remustered and sent here.'

The youngster spoke quietly, the words falling from his lips impassionately and drily, as if it was all unreal. He too is already burnt out, at 13 a victim of his time. He asks me: 'Give me another cigarette.' I press the packet into his hand. He calmly lights a cigarette and draws in the smoke deeply, then gets up and rejoins his comrades.

The leader in the light brown uniform returns and blows his whistle as if he were on a barrack square. The men converge on him from all quarters – civilians, Hitler Youths in short trousers, a few soldiers. They fall in and count off. Then they march past to enter the building in single file. The little youngster follows behind in an overlarge jacket that he has put on over his brown shirt. The door swings slowly shut on its hinges.

Our second lieutenant comes along and we stand up. We have to go forward again. The staff sergeant gives us a can of meat each. Then we move off wearily, all heavily laden with ammunition. Shots are whipping out from a wood nearby. We go across the Napola yard and then turn into the yard of the Police School. Various groups of policemen, firemen, Volkssturm and Waffen-SS are moving forward across the yard. Suddenly explosions break out and a fountain of dirt and steel erupts in front of us. We scatter and throw ourselves down. I drop close to a pile of bricks and claw the ground. Explosions are going off all around us, each explosion being indistinguishable from the next. We cannot hear any incoming whistle from shell fire, only a gurgling, which means they are mortars. Between the explosions we hear an occasional scream, shrill and loud. Then it stops and only the sound of the explosions can be heard.

The fire breaks off as suddenly as it had begun. I stand up dazed. Here and there a figure gets up from a crater left over from this morning's shelling or from behind a fold in the ground. Only now in the sudden silence can one hear the whimpering of those who have been hit. I look at my rifle and cannot believe my eyes. The chamber has been destroyed by a splinter, the intricate chamber of this assault rifle. The weapon is unusable, but better the weapon than myself.

The second lieutenant gives us the order to advance to the trenches by bounds. When I show him my weapon, he tells me to get a new one and come back.

A wounded man is lying in a deep slit trench calling loudly for help. It is Heinrich Jakob, our oldest member. He was wounded in the arm and dived into the trench mad with pain. I drop my useless weapon and with Blaczeck's help try to extricate the whimpering man from his predicament, but it is not possible. We can only pull him out of the trench by his wounded arm. By the time we get him out, he is unconscious. We take him over to the cellars of the Police School.

I go back again. A Waffen-SS staff sergeant with a splinter in his leg calls to me. I lift him up. He his heavy, and biting back the pain. With difficulty I get him to the cellars, where a field hospital has been set up in the air raid shelter. I sit him down on a small bench and get a nurse. As he is about to go off with her, she says that he must leave his weapon behind. The SS man unfastens his belt and slips off the pistol holster. Then he presses it into my hand and empties his pockets of ammunition. He hops off slowly down the dark passageway with the nurse.

I carefully remove the pistol from its holster. The steel has a bluish sheen to it. It is a 7.65 Mauser. I suddenly remember that it once was a dream of mine to hold a pistol in my hand, but now I am not so keen. I slip the pistol slowly back into the holster and slide it over my belt buckle.

Nurses and orderlies go past carrying the wounded. Injured men are hobbling with difficulty into the dressing room, or holding some piece of material or other pressed tight against the wounds in their head, foot or arm. A few policemen and firemen wearing steel helmets are standing on the steps at the cellar entrance. A fat fire officer looks me up and down and asks me what I want here. As he turns around, I vanish quickly up a side passage. I go though the cellar and look into the individual rooms. Clouds of pus, sweat and carbolic billow from the crowded rooms into the

1. & 2.   Remaining buildings of the former Alexander Barracks
(now the Berlin Police School)

3. Ruhleben U-Bahn Station

4. The Supply Bunker with the Film Studios behind

5. The Olympic Stadium battleground

6. The Deutsche-Industrie-Werke, Ruhleben Racecourse and workers' barracks

7. The western entrance to the above-ground factory with the main road on the right

8. A laboratory building on the main road with a Soviet Guard Post built on the platform

9. Railway junction on the main road with the German guard barracks
and a laboratory behind

10. The road out to the north with the Electrolysis Building beyond

11. Two of the Bunker's ventilation towers

12. The eastern entrance to the Bunker flanked by laboratories

13. The Hotel in front with the Accommodation Block on the right and the hump of the Bunker on the left

14. Flanked by the German Electrolysis Building and Workshop, the Soviet Dining Hall, Accommodation Block and Guard Post with the Hotel behind

15. The Soviet nuclear-proof door at the eastern entrance to the Bunker

16. The Soviet House of Culture south of the main road

17.   The pond and dam

18.   The village pub

19.	The site of the windmill

20.	The Military Cemetery with its many 'Unknown Soldiers'

21. Komturei Lietzen from the valley

22. The pump at the entrance to the Komturei

23. The Hakenfelde Aircraft Instrument Factory

24. The meadow with the factory chimney showing behind the trees

25. The apartment blocks on Zeppelinstrasse

26. The archway on Zweibrücker Strasse

27. The Police School buildings

28. The former NAPOLA buildings

THE CHARLOTTEN BRIDGE

29. The steps to the bridge with the air raid shelters on either side
as seen shortly after the war

30. Above at the entrance to the bridge

31. Spandau town hall tower from under the bridge

32. The bridge, Stresow and the Deutsche-Industrie-Werke
(view from Spandau town hall tower)

passageway, making it difficult to breathe. Pale-faced nurses are rushing from place to place. The wounded are groaning aloud and whimpering. A table stands in the middle of a room under a bright lamp, a doctor standing beside it like a rock in the sea, operating and amputating. His white overalls are speckled with blood like a butcher's. The orderlies are carrying buckets filled with torn limbs, blood and pus. It is like a butcher's shop but, instead of animals, the victims here are human beings.

The corners of the passages are filled with refugees with the last of their belongings – suitcases, trunks, baskets and children. Whenever an officer appears they cringe in the dark and breathe easy again when he has gone. A few 14-year-olds are hidden under these peoples' things to escape being taken away. I go back. The policemen and firemen are still standing at the cellar entrance. I go past them and climb the steps slowly. Individual soldiers and civilians are making their way back to the apartment blocks as rifle fire whips over the yard and strikes the walls. I stop behind a pile of bricks in front of the fire brigade shed, from where I can hear loud voices. I go round the pile. Several soldiers are standing against the wall of the shed. 'Watch out, snipers!' says a sergeant who seems to be in charge of them. I look carefully round the corner. A stretch of about a hundred metres has to be crawled across, and there are a few dead bodies lying around. The soldiers disappear one by one and crawl forward. I am alone again.

I go to the corner of the shed and lie down and crawl, the way I had to learn on the barrack square, and soon come to the first of the bodies. There are civilians and Hitler Youths among them, traces of the '30th January' Regiment who have found their rest here, mostly killed by shots to the head. The journey seems endless. The sounds of battle from the forward trenches do not appear to come any closer. I stop suddenly. I have had enough. I would like the earth to open up and swallow me. I swivel around very carefully on my belt buckle, millimetre by millimetre. The sweat is running down my face, my skull is throbbing and my left eyelid has started to twitch, as it always does when I am agitated. I must calm down. At last I have done it and I start to slip back. I pass the dead and the shed is growing in front of me like life itself. I stumble to my feet and run on a few metres then sit down and calm myself again.

It is gradually getting dark. The evening sky is a rich violet-red. Even it seems to be on fire as the earth has been for years now. Two bright stripes roar through the night from a window in the Police School. The firing of a twin-barrelled flak gun thunders loudly as the tracers fly in the direction of the enemy in an endless silver stream. Mortars answer with a bombardment. Sudden fountains shoot up in the darkness, hang in the air for a few seconds, and then slowly sink back. Night hovers over it all, sympathetically and compassionately covering the dead and the living like the huge dome of a dark temple. The stream of tracer bullets is torn apart as the mortar bombs explode in the yard and strike the buildings. Walls collapse and windows shatter. One does not hear the cries of those hit any longer, only a dull thunder roaring in one's ears. Then the fire dies down. Even in the trenches the sound of battle has abated.

I go across the yard to the gate that gives on to the street. Faint candlelight glows in a corrugated iron shed. A horse whinnies. I look in through a crack. Our cook Erich is standing talking with gentle, almost soft, words to a skinny nag. Blaczeck is sitting on a ration box and is looking at the ground. As I open the door, they both look up briefly. Even the nag turns his eyes in my direction, then slowly lowers his head again. There is a stable smell and warmth in the room. I sit down next to Blaczeck, who silently makes a space for me. Gradually my eyes become accustomed to the light. The shape of a wagon can just be made out in the long garage. Whenever the horse swishes his tail, the candle flickers and threatens to go out. Erich goes on speaking gently to the horse. Blaczeck sits still, seemingly preoccupied. Occasionally a shell explodes and makes the ground shake. The candle has burnt itself down and flickers briefly before finally going out. The night hangs over us like lead. Only the grinding of the nag's hard jaws and the stamping of its hooves hang in the air along with the cracking and banging outside. Occasionally masonry and splinters strike the tin walls and make them shake, causing the horse to whinny and stamp with fear. Suddenly the door opens and Erich is standing there like a dark shadow against the lighter night. A match flares, ripping through the dark. The nag pulls whinnying at his master, seeking protection from destruction's rage. A fresh candle is lit.

I stand up. My feet have gone to sleep. Erich lends me his assault rifle, and I go outside and cross the dark square which is still under mortar fire. Across the way an apartment block is burning orange, throwing showers of sparks into the air. The night is full of noise and disruption. I stop at the fire brigade hut. Only the odd rifle shot whistles past.

Voices can be heard in the darkness. Soldiers are returning with exhausted, heavy steps. Between them, as if lost, are children with grey helmets and heavy weapons. They stagger past exhaustedly. The front line is being pulled back. I go along with the troops to the garage, where the second lieutenant and some of the comrades have already found their way and are sitting on the straw. The second lieutenant tells us that western Spandau is to be given up tonight. But thousands of dead will be remaining behind.

Suddenly infantry fire flares up again. We grab our weapons and dive outside, firing a few shots aimlessly into the dark. Then we hear: 'Don't shoot! Germans!' but only slowly does the firing die down. A pocket torch flashes on field grey figures, men of our company. Those in front are standing around something – a dead man. It is Steinszeufer, his widowed mother's only son. How will I be able to break it to her, whom I know so well? She will not be able to cope with life any more, for this single blow will make it lose all its meaning for her. Apparently, as they were coming back from the trenches, he still had a round in the chamber, which in his overtired state he let off into the air, not thinking that they could be mistaken for Russians.

One by one the figures hurry back. A runner comes from the command post of the Spandau-West Battle Group to summon the men back. Spandau has to be evacuated by midnight. I look at the time. It is now nearly eleven o'clock. We then go back to the street together and stand in front of the Napola buildings, where the last to leave are emerging – boys, policemen and firemen, and women in SS uniform.

Our combat team, i.e. our company, is holding the last position. We have to cover the withdrawal and may only leave the Napola bang on midnight. The stream of refugees gradually ebbs and then is gone. We are alone.

The fire from a burning building is throwing flickering light over the street, exaggerating the shadows of the trees and the ruins, as if they were coming to life. The minutes drag past, time seems to be standing still, only the beating of our hearts signals its passing. We are gradually growing uneasy, for it is scary in the night with its fires and secret life breathing and pulsing. We squat down like lost souls, tired and empty, and wait.

Then we leave the Napola buildings behind to move about 300 metres back along our line of retreat. Here we stop and spread out across the street. The second lieutenant comes to each of us in turn and hands back our paybooks. But not everyone he collected them from at midday is still here. Our little gang has dwindled yet again. More lives have been lost during the course of the day, and we who remain and are still alive regard it as a punishment, not as a miracle.

A call comes from somewhere, making a hollow echo. A shot thunders in the distance. Once an aircraft flies over us with a tacking engine. Time drags slowly by. The figures and hands of my watch show up faintly, barely discernable.

The second lieutenant comes along. 'Get ready!' Figures emerge from the shadows of the trees and buildings, and we gather round the second lieutenant, looking at our watches. We stand and wait. Then from far off across the town come four light chimes followed by twelve heavy ones – the sound hangs in the night air.

We move off, pushing open again the door of life that we thought had already closed behind us.

Friday 27 April 1945

We leave behind the buildings, the trees, the ruins and the dead. Night closes down spreading its cloak over men and earth. We go through the streets sticking tightly together. Moonlight lies on the ruins whose bizarre shapes stand out. White bands of cloud hang low in the sky, seemingly pulling at the dead fingers of the ruins. We are alone in this landscape of rubble. We stop at every corner and peer into the darkness before quickly crossing the street. Our tired, harassed footsteps echo from the ruins. There is no sign of life, no human being still alive in this dead landscape. Occasionally bitter smoke and the smell of corruption pours out from the burning debris of those buildings set alight in the retreat.

The shattered town goes past like a film strip, building after building, ruin after ruin. No living thing disturbs the sleep of the dead. We stop at ever shorter intervals, look back, go down sidestreets and make diversions. Far off, but then nearer and finally almost palpably close, the sound of Russian voices comes from the dark sidestreets, the enemies' footsteps following close on our heels. They are probably watching us from a side street now. Occasionally a shot rings out, causing us to draw closer together.

We hurry on, feeling our way through the maze of buildings. Then a square appears out of the darkness. The tall towers of a big church rise into the night, standing intact alone among the ruins surrounding the square.[8] The second lieutenant and the staff sergeant search the town map for our location and to find a way out. Voices suddenly come from the church and the door slowly opens, inch by inch. Some soldiers emerge, also Germans, and look at the second lieutenant in astonishment. Then they come up to us. They belong to a clothing depot for naval officers and got lost among the maze of streets and ruins. The second lieutenant orders us to go into the church and wait. We file slowly into the nave. The wind is whistling through the broken windows. The organ pipes shine like gold and seem to be whispering and muttering to themselves high above the nave. We hardly dare breathe so as not to break the silence. The second lieutenant comes back along the aisle and calls to us. We quietly slip off the pews and tiptoe over the carpet that lines the aisle. Then we close the door behind us and go back out into the night.

We move on. The men from the clothing depot have linked up with us. On our left there is a small river in a ditch.[9] The bridges across it have been blown. A barricade made of trams and vehicles driven together blocks the street. We pass through a tram one at a time, our footsteps echoing loudly. A Waffen-SS flame-thrower tank is on fire in the street and a dead man is lying nearby, but he isn't dead, his lips are trying to form words. I bend down and then I find out what is wrong with him. He is not dead, just dead drunk. He is still holding a bottle in his hand with its neck broken and he has spilt half its contents on the street, the wine lying as dark as blood on the cobbles, and a penetrating smell of schnapps and alcohol overrides even that of the burning oil coming from the tank. We go on slowly, leaving the ruins behind us. We pass buildings still untouched by war. The streets become narrower, and the buildings and apartment blocks become bigger.

On the street are lying a lot of dead who look as if they had been suddenly mown down. Torn bodies, burnt corpses, women, civilians, and bits of baggage are strewn around. A policeman in his pale green uniform lies in the gutter, his face a smashed-in mess. Dead children look as if they are asleep, their wounds hardly discernable. Women, girls and men. Between and over them lie the remains of the cables and wiring from the street lighting. A solitary soldier's boot shows a bloody stump in the leg. A dead man leans against a dark doorway as if he has simply fallen asleep. We go past, stepping over the dead, stumbling against bits of bodies many of which are burnt. A nauseating smell of burnt flesh hangs in the air. We take out our handkerchiefs and flee.

In one corner a building is burning like a torch. We turn into a side street with an anti-tank barrier right across it, blocking the road. A challenge rings out in the night and we stand still. A soldier appears at the barrier and asks for the password, but we have not been given it, so he goes away again. We stand in front of the barrier and wait. At last a narrow gap opens up and we slip through and are counted. A runner shows us the way.

We slowly leave the barrier behind. Soldiers are lying asleep in the dark corners of the buildings. A woman is moaning in the middle of the street. Faint glimmerings of light leak from the cracks at several windows. Our footsteps throw back a hard echo from the walls as we go on wearily, hardly able to stay on our feet. The town centre of Spandau has been cleared and we were the last ones out.

A big square with grass, bushes and trees appears. Spandau town hall stands out dark against the sky. Civilians and soldiers are lying around on the grass, in the streets and in doorways. We go up the town hall steps and sit down.

Machine gun bursts startle us. Fleeing people run around wildly on the street calling out. Nobody knows what is going on. A Waffen-SS flame-thrower tank is called forward and pushes past us in the dark. Suddenly a bright tongue of fire flashes from its thin barrel and strikes the wall of a building. Men cry out in animal fear, then it is silent again. A faint tongue licks sootily around the tank's gunbarrel. Then it turns round, comes back and stops. The crew climb out. 'They were Germans,' one of them says.

I have lain down on the grass and am staring up at the sky. There is a lot of activity going on in the street and the doorways as individual combat teams form up and move off to cross the Havel. Spandau is to be completely evacuated. The distant sound of an aircraft engine sends everyone diving for cover before it glides like a great bird over us.

Voices call out to one another as everyone start looking for their combat teams. I stand up and walk around, finding my comrades at last. Then we too are called. We go into an entrance hall and wait. The second lieutenant and the staff sergeant are standing near a candle being briefed by a captain and given the places now to be occupied. Our company, now reduced to eighteen men, is to go to the Deutsche-Industrie-Werke on the other side of the Havel, where we are to spend the night at the commandant's command post. With immediate effect, we now belong to Captain Pavelick's combat team.

We go back out into the street. The doorways are almost all empty. The remains of companies, now reduced to section strength, are drawing past as we form up. We have already marched past this town hall, but as a company of 150 young soldiers wearing their field grey uniforms for the first time. We move off. On the right the Havel flows in its river bed, and on the left the trees cling to the buildings. A light-coloured concrete block, an air raid shelter, stands close to the water and, close behind it, the bridge[10] spans the murky river. We are about to turn into the street leading to the bridge when there is a roar and banging against the bridge superstructure. Scared to death, we run back. Are the Russians laying a barrage on the bridge? Is our line of retreat blocked?

We go back into an entrance hall, sit down on the cold floor and fall asleep. A narrow ray of light comes through the darkness from a window in the passage and falls on the faces of the sleepers. Music is playing gently from a loudspeaker.

I am getting cold from sitting. I get up and stretch my legs, then go back down the passage. A door opens and light spills out into the stairwell. I go into the room, where the second lieutenant is turning the knob on the loudspeaker, and sit down at the table. Two children are lying asleep on the sofa. I stretch my legs out under the table and snuggle down in the chair. On the table is one of Goebbels' leaflets, in which I read: 'Whoever is capable of bearing weapons should report immediately to the Berlin Kommandatura. Even the wounded are of value for their experience and skill in leadership!' Signed: Joseph Goebbels, Defence Commissar of Berlin.

The gentle music on the radio suddenly breaks off and a voice announces: 'This is the Greater Germany Radio. We will read to you an appeal by the Reichsminister and Defence Commissar for Berlin which he has had published in the battle newspaper for Berlin, the *Panzerbär*.[11]

'Berlin will not be given up to the Bolsheviks. New forces will shortly be engaged in our battle. The Russian onslaught must be smashed in a sea of blood. Those traitors who hoist the white flag on their homes and buildings no longer have a right to the protection of the community. All the occupants of such buildings, not just the traitors themselves, will be regarded as traitors. As against the treacherous Westmark[12] that is not worthy of being called part of Germany, the whole weight of retribution will be brought down on traitors in the battle for Berlin. Berliners, the whole German nation is looking at you. Think about it! The hour before the dawn is the darkest, and our victory eagle will rise up into the sun of the new day radiant and magnificent!'

The voice breaks off and the German national anthem comes from the loudspeaker, followed by the Horst Wessel Song.[13] Then the second lieutenant abruptly switches off the set and leaves the room. A soldier plays with the dial and suddenly the words come through the room and make us jump: 'This is Radio Free Germany.' The staff sergeant wants to switch it off at first, but lets it play on. He takes his map and spreads it out on the table and then marks in red pencil the places that the radio says have been taken. The outer towns and villages of Velten, Oranienburg, Bernau, Erkner, Teltow, Potsdam and Staaken have been lost. The city districts of Köpenick, Lichtenberg, Weissensee, Pankow and Reinickendorf have been lost. Fighting is taking place in other parts of the city. Spandau-West was cleared up to the Havel this evening. Only a few German troops still remain, waiting for a suitable moment to cross the bridge. The ring around Berlin has been closed and within the city districts themselves the enemy is trying to cut off small pockets and isolate individual bits to finish them off. The 9th Army has been surrounded and defeated at the gates of Berlin south-east of the city. The ring around Berlin is being drawn tighter and tighter until it cannot breathe any more.

The staff sergeant folds up the map and looks at the time. It has gone three o'clock. We stand up, go out into the yard and wake up the comrades, who are all huddled up against one another against the cold. Then we stand on the street and look at the bridge, where it is quiet and calm. There is a soldier asleep here and there in the doorways, but everyone else seems to have crossed the river.

We go up to the bridge, where a closed anti-tank barrier blocks the street. We go on to the bridge and cross over quickly. There is a dead man almost in the middle of the bridge, and the superstructure has been damaged by the shelling. At last we come to the other end and stop. On the right there is half a corner building next to the river and on the left a light-coloured concrete block, an air raid shelter. We go past them and turn left. There is a half destroyed building on the street and the second lieutenant orders us to go into its cellar, so we jump into the slit trench that runs under the building and go into a cellar room, where the floor is damp and slippery. Someone lights a Hindenburg-Light[14] and puts it on the ground. The cellar is empty. There are slit trenches stretching towards the river, covered over with railway sleepers and with just some small loopholes in them like in a bunker. Masonry and stones are lying about on the floor. I sit down on a block of stone and brood. The staff sergeant and the second lieutenant have gone to the factory to find our accommodation for the night.

We sit here staring at the light, asleep with our eyes open. The day goes past like a film strip. The ruins of Spandau and the dead. Spandau has been abandoned by German troops, and our dead lie in the buildings of the town, in the Napola, in the Police School, at the Nordhafen and in the woods. In Siemensstadt and elsewhere the companies are being burnt to cinders in no time at all. A straggler told us that eighty-five percent of his company was lost at the Nordhafen, either dead or captured, and that is the scale of casualties in virtually all the critical points in the fighting. Women, children, old men, Volkssturm and other civilians have suffered casualties that no one knows about, and which no one cares about.

The second lieutenant comes back into the room and stands near the candle. Then he says suddenly: 'It will soon be over. No one can go on taking it much longer.' Someone puts out the candle and we climb out of the trench. We go past some sheds and then through a gate that closes behind us. The staff sergeant stands in front of us. A wood shed appears and we stream inside and sit down on the logs. Then we go on again past workshops and along dark streets, one workshop looking exactly like all the others. We are going through an enormous labyrinth as if we are never going to reach our destination. At last we see a faint light that we had nearly overlooked. Steps lead steeply down into a cellar. We rush for the entrance, everyone wanting to be first inside. We slowly climb down the steps and open a door. Bright light streams out, blinding us as we enter.

There are some camp beds in the room. We fall on them, unfasten our greatcoats and sleep overcomes us.

NOTES

1. Pionierstrasse.
2. Zweibrücker Strasse and Falkenseer Chaussee.
3. Zeppelinstrasse to the corner of Falkenseer Chaussee.
4. Nos. 83–85, Zweibrücker Strasse.
5. Falkenseer Chaussee.
6. Named after the date the Nazis came to power in 1933.
7. The troops that attacked Oranienburg were in fact mainly of the 1st Polish Army, raised by the Russians from those prisoners of war who had not been fit enough to go to the British-sponsored Polish Army, and recruits from the newly conquered homeland.
8. The Marienkirche.
9. The moat of the old town.
10. The Charlotten Bridge again.
11. The bear is the city emblem, so *Panzerbär* (Armoured Bear) was an apt title for this one-page newspaper.
12. The Westmark comprised the provinces of the Saar and Rhineland Palatinate that had recently fallen to American and French forces and resumed their French identity.
13. The Horst Wessel Song, named after a Nazi thug murdered by Communists in Berlin during the days of the Weimar Republic, had been given the status of a second national anthem by the Nazi Party.
14. A development from the First World War consisting of a small paper cup containing candlewax and a wick, rather like a night-light.

CHAPTER IX
Stresow & Ruhleben

Later, 27 April 1945

When we are woken up again it is bright daylight. We stand around with heavy limbs. There is a busy coming and going with officers and runners going into the next room, where the battle group commander has his command post. Loud voices assault our ears. A fire brigade officer, a portly gentleman in the silver epaulettes of a major, is standing beside Second Lieutenant Fricke and talking animatedly to him. Then both of them come up to our section who stand there tired and uninterested, and inform us that we are to come under the command of the fireman for the day.[1] The latter tells us that the Führer has ordered that the Deutsche-Industrie-Werke, in which assault guns and tanks are assembled, is to be defended to the last bullet and the last man against the Russian onslaught. It may only fall into enemy hands as a heap of rubble over our dead bodies.

We pick up our weapons. The fireman in his highly polished boots and blue uniform covered in medals takes over command and we leave the room. We slowly climb the steps up to the world above and go along the silent factory streets. The workshops lie as if dead, staring with empty windows at the day. Begun and half-finished giant tanks and assault guns stand lost in the big workshops like mammoths, against which human beings look like dwarfs. Our footsteps pound hard on the concrete as we go through the workshops, throwing back a ringing echo. The factory streets are strewn with long-life bread and chocolate wrappings, the colourful paper looking like confetti on New Year's Eve in its variety of colour and shapes. The big chestnut trees are waiting for warm sunshine to open their buds. Empty handcarts and broken packing cases are lying on a trampled lawn among the trees.

We open the gate leading to the street, which screeches on its hinges and falls back heavily. Our section is split up, a Waffen-SS sergeant taking over part and the others going with the fire brigade officer. We have to occupy the river bank and defend the bridge against enemy attack.[2]

The Waffen-SS man's section disappears down a side street as we head for the bridge. There are some large lumps of masonry in the street from the surounding buildings, most of which have been smashed down to single-storey height. The street-lighting cables are partly hanging from the remains of walls or lying like coils in the roadway and a thick carpet of broken glass covers both street and pavement. There is the odd, almost undamaged building among the ruins and one can only wonder at it, the destroyed and the intact standing side by side. The streets are empty with no human beings to be seen apart from ourselves as we stumble over the rubble landscape. Then we turn down a side street, whose buildings, with a few exceptions, are still intact. We turn left and come on to the Havel embankment. Slit trenches have been cut into the asphalt along the quay and the pavement, even under destroyed buildings. The Havel flows past sluggishly, murmuring gently.

We stop under the bridge. I have to stay here, as I am the only one with an assault rifle, to keep an eye on the bridge that hangs over us, leading to the other bank. The comrades then move on and disappear down a side street. I sit down on the steps leading up to the roadway above and stare at the opposite bank. In front of me a strong wire fence separates the embankment from the river, on which small combs of foam and grey-green waves are dancing. On the left the blown superstructure of a bridge lies in the river – presumably the S-Bahn bridge. Across the way the grey, square tower of the Spandau town hall rises menacingly in the morning sunshine. There is no one to be seen on the street that runs along the front of the buildings.

The grey concrete block of a deep bunker lies in the golden sand between the street and the river. A few people are standing around. There is the occasional whinny of a horse roaming freely and nibbling at the fresh greenery of the trees showing brightly over the river. To the right of the bridge the buildings stand close to the river bank. White pieces of cloth are hanging from the open windows and fluttering in the wind, and a thin cloud of smoke is rising from a burnt-out apartment block. After a few hundred metres the river disappears round a right-hand bend between the buildings and the redbrick structures of the Deutsche-Industrie-Werke on this bank.

It is calm and quiet. No shot disturbs the wonderful peace that lies over the buildings and ruins. Occasionally a civilian hurries by pressed to the walls and disappears up a side street, or hastens to the air raid shelter laden with bags and suitcases. The narrow path running under the bridge, where it is separated from the river by a grill, has been ripped up and two foxholes dug into the pavement. There is a weathered plank door laid over one of them, and a few stones lying around.

I stand up and move up to the grill, looking at the dark flood with its gently chuckling waves, and let my thoughts wander and drift along with them. One can forget the war at such a moment, when only the ruins serve as a reminder and there are no sounds of battle coming from the streets, while the sun shines brightly. After days of distress and death, one can take the silence and peace of this moment as a gift, but it can erupt again at any moment and shower down the fury of destruction.

The bridge curves above me, reaching across to the opposite bank. Thick water and gas mains run suspended beneath it along with electricity cables as thick as one's arm. Occasionally a seagull flies past with a gentle flap of its wings and skims low over the water.

Suddenly a shot rings out shattering the silence of this heavenly spring morning and smashing into the wall behind me. I throw myself down, haul the door from the foxhole aside, and roll in. Then I carefully raise my head and look at the bank opposite. Another shot whips out and strikes the bridge. A figure is leaning out of a window in the town hall tower, only becoming noticeable just as it disappears. I carefully take my assault rifle from the foxhole and prop it against the mesh of the wire fence. I set the range and switch to automatic fire. Then I calmly aim at the window and wait until the figure reappears and squeeze the trigger. The shots whip out from the barrel like a single blast. The figure has disappeared. I wait a while without moving my weapon, and only ease off when everything remains silent and nothing shows itself. Then I climb out of the foxhole and push the door back.

It is all quiet again, so quiet that one can scarcely believe that people are still alive and breathing under the landscape of ruins. I suddenly think of my comrades now out of sight. Am I alone and have they already been deployed to another location? Have they forgotten me? I slowly climb up the steps to the bridge. A machine gun stands unmanned in the street. There is no one to be seen. But yes, behind one of the superstructure uprights I can see a pair of typical issue boots. The soldier looks up briefly as I approach him and then goes back to watching the opposite bank. I ask him if he has seen my section with the fireman. He says not. He says that he is the only man on the bridge and that he has to prevent all enemy attacks and any attempts to cross.

With hasty steps a civilian comes across the bridge and stops beside us. Civilians are not being stopped by the Russians and can cross freely; only soldiers are fired at. The civilian says that the enemy has not occupied the buildings opposite. His troops, including female battalions, are only in the town hall and the buildings by the railway bridge.

A soldier appears at the barrier that blocks the far end of the bridge and rushes across in quick bounds without mishap. Occasionally a solitary woman comes along holding a child by the hand and some bags, and disappears up a side street or into one of the air raid shelters located close to the bridge on either side of the Havel. There is a propaganda slogan in bright white paint on the shelter on this side. On the corner building on the other side, whose upper storey has been burnt out, a balcony hangs half out of the wall as if about to fall at any moment. A tin pub sign that has lost its enamelling is swinging in the wind and banging against the wall like a dull bell. The big square leading on to the bridge lies dead and empty, surrounded only by ruins, the symbols of our time, two intact buildings standing out alone amid the piles of rubble.

Another soldier appears at the other end of the bridge and rushes across with long strides, pausing behind the uprights of the superstructure. Then a machine gun opens up and sends bursts of fire against the iron uprights and bracings. I run across the street and down to the entrance to the air raid shelter, going down a few steps and take up my position there. The civilian who had been standing beside us scrambles in beside me on the steps. Then we stand up and look cautiously out at the bridge. The machine gun has not stopped firing. Behind me the steps go down steeply into the earth. A faint light burns below and dark figures are looking up. A nurse with a white face slowly climbs up the steps and stands beside us. 'Please go,' she says, 'there are women and children down there who have not been out in the air for days and have hardly anything left to eat. Go out on to the street. If the Russians come and find soldiers in this bunker, they will blow it up.' But we do not pay any attention to what she says, and remain silent, although I dare not look around. The machine gun is still firing on the street, and it would be pointless to leave the shelter of the entrance, and as for the people sitting down there in the cellar – out of sight, out of mind.

The machine gun has stopped firing and peace reigns once more, so we go back up to the street. The nurse remains standing in the doorway with her pale face, as if she wanted to provide for all those hungering after peace and to protect them against all the dangers that war can bring. The soldier who had been running towards us is lying peacefully on the bridge. One more bound and he would have made it. His rifle lies flung out in the road. The machine gun at the entrance to the bridge stands threateningly, like a multi-death machine just waiting to be released to attack people, but the soldier who had been guarding and defending the bridge with it is also dead. He is lying turned over, half on the steps, his head looking as if it has been smashed with a hammer.

Some seagulls fly over us with gentle flaps of their wings and sail away, following the course of the river. The waves of the Havel slap gently against the embankment, and white combs of foam play on the grey-green flood. The ruins lie silent in the sunshine and the pub sign keeps banging regularly against the wall like a dull bell. The sun shines on the quiet buildings and streets on the opposite bank and is reflected from the few remaining windows as the white pieces of cloth wave gently in the wind.

I go slowly back down the steps to the quay. The steps are shattered from splinters and shellfire. On the right the trenches extend along the quay to the walls of the Deutsche-Industrie-Werke, where the river disappears round the bend. The building with the cellar we stopped in for a while last night stands alone in the rubble between the bridge and the factory. Its upper storey has fallen in, leaving it looking like a tree stump. There, where the upper storey used to be, a burnt-out boiler stands insecure, threatening to fall at any moment and pull the wall down with it. Of the other buildings that once stood here, one can only make out their rectangular bases and the outlines of their rubble-filled cellars. Slit trenches have been dug into the earth in zigzags through the desert of rubble and pass right through under the building.

I stand beside the water again, mesmerised by the play of the waves gently bobbing. The quiet and the sunshine bewitch me into feeling that it is a Sunday morning and that there is no war. The river bank is quiet, peaceful and silent. The sight of the ruins does not spoil the picture, for they have become an everyday part of life, and over there on the other bank the war has come to an end. The river is a narrow no man's land. Over there they can breathe freely again after the horrors of war, even if it is still so close. The white scraps hanging from the buildings symbolise this.

And here? The inhabitants of this unfortunate city still crowd the catacombs and cellars and carry on hoping for the peace that is almost unattainable. For them the future threatens, sinister and menacing, as a black, incomprehensible void.

Two people emerge from the air raid shelter on the opposite bank and approach the river. I watch them with interest as if they were aliens, no longer humans. They slowly come closer, a man and a woman, sticking together. The nearer they come, the more clearly I can see their faces. They are old, with silver-grey hair. The woman is carrying an old black handbag and is wearing an old-fashioned hat. The man is bareheaded and has silvery hair. Then they stop right opposite me under the bridge. To their right a few steps lead down to the water, ending in a small platform for mooring boats. They look across at me, but seem not to notice me. We stand opposite each other, two civilians and a soldier, and the river separating us into two different worlds. Then they move. The man opens a gate in the grill that is scarcely visible. Between the water and the grill there is now only a short step. I think suddenly that they must be making their way to a hidden bunker that I can't see. Then the woman steps through the gate. The man follows slowly and closes the gate carefully. They stand on the water's edge, on the stone wall that drops abruptly to the river. They hold hands and kiss. I am still standing there with no idea what all this means. Then suddenly they jump, their faces quite calm, quite without fear, as if they were no longer of this earth. The man's hand lets go. He dives deep into the water. The woman dives in and sinks. A few air bubbles rise to the surface. A lonely hat turns round in midstream and floats away, then the man's back appears stiff as a board, as if he is forcing his face down under water. The woman moves away, still touching the man. They remain in the middle of the river turning and going slowly down to dance as dark spots beneath the grey-green stream. Then they can be seen no longer. The water murmurs gently past as if nothing has happened. I rub my eyes as if I had seen a ghost. In the distance a hat with a white veil moves along like a dark spot, turning and moving on.

I stand as if petrified. My first thoughts are to dive in and save them, but they did not want to go on living, and it would be senseless to do so. Then I slowly recall what a soldier told us yesterday about the bridge by the Nordhafen that was going to be blown up. When this became known, people went and stood on it, women with babies in their arms, mothers holding crying children by the hand, old men and youngsters of both sexes, even soldiers, and they would not let themselves be driven away, by threats or by force. They stood there quietly, not listening, just looking at the water and staying silent until the bridge was blown as the first tank appeared on the bank. A dark cloud rose slowly and flames shot upwards, and the people fell into the river in a cloud of fire and lightning. Yesterday I did not want to believe it, but today I do.

I tear myself away from these thoughts and go along the embankment. I just need to see someone. I go up the steps to the bridge and look at the dead men, then I go along the street past the bunker. There are slit trenches here dug into the ground right up against the walls, where the slogan: 'We dig for victory!' appears in luminous paint.

I keep going along the street and turn the corner. In front of me is the gate to the Deutsche-Industrie-Werke. An old watchman is sitting on a bench at the gate outside the porter's lodge and looks up when he hears my footsteps. I ask him if he knows where my combat team has got to, if he has seen my comrades. But he says not. He has no idea where they might be. Then his eyes fall on my full knapsack and he asks me for something to eat, for he has been unable to leave the factory for two days now and has had hardly anything to eat. I take a can of meat from my pocket and press it into his hand. Who knows whether I will ever need it. He feels in his pockets and gives me a few black cheroots. Then I go along the street I had already been in today with my comrades. A man wearing dirty work clothes is standing in the doorway of one of the buildings. I ask him for a light and he gives me his box of matches. I smoke slowly, drawing the smoke deep into my lungs. A woman then comes out with two men and we all stand together. With few exceptions, the buildings on this street have only sustained a little damage. A roaring starts up somewhere quite far off like a strong wind, almost a hurricane, then there is a sudden hissing and a howling in the air. I dive into the building and draw my pistol, as if that could help against what is coming. I throw myself down on the floor. Suddenly it is dark and I can see nothing. There is only the hissing and howling in the air and a bursting and banging. The earth shudders and shakes as if it wanted to open. Sand and stones fall around, hitting my body and banging lightly on my steel helmet. There is a roaring in my ears and I am unable to think. I just lie there waiting for my end.

It slowly gets lighter, and suddenly it is quiet. I stand up. My clothes are grey with sand and dust, my oiled pistol filthy. Behind me someone gets up out of the dirt, and others emerge here and there out of the piles of masonry and plaster. The panes in the front door are broken, there are big holes in the ceiling and chunks of wall have fallen out. The back door is half split in two. I go out into the sunshine through the back door and come into a typical city back yard with its thin strip of yellowish grass. There is a carpet beating rack and in the corner an overfilled rubbish bin. Behind them are the remains of the back building, now a ruin. What is left of a tree lies around in splinters. Then someone taps me on the shoulder. I turn round. It is the woman from before, her hair all covered in dirt as if it had been sugared. 'Come down into the cellar with me and take a rest for a while,' she says. I follow her without thinking and let her lead me down into the cellar.

We go down a few steps and open an iron air raid shelter door, close it again and are suddenly standing in deep night. The eyes accustom themselves slowly to the almost complete darkness, which is only broken by the feeble light of a flickering candle. People turn their heads towards us and look at us without saying a word. Then someone pushes a chair up towards me and I sit down.

The cellar is stuffed full of baskets and household stuff. Children are sleeping on bundles of bedding, while the residents sit silently on chairs and boxes listening to the noises coming from the street, which only sound very faint from the room. Occasionally something is said quietly. The cellar is big and filled to the last corner. Wooden beams provide improvised support for the ceiling and give an impression of safety, but would be worthless in the event of an attack. Occasionally someone gets up and opens the door to go outside, or to their apartment to quickly make some coffee or porridge for the children. The women wait anxiously and only breathe again when the man returns safely to the room. The peoples' faces are as pale as death masks. Sometimes a child starts crying and a tired voice murmurs comforting words, then everyone falls silent again. An old man comes into the cellar holding his head, blood oozing between his fingers and dropping on to the ground. A woman shrieks, moans, cries and complains, all in one breath. A few other women rush up and press the wounded man down on a chair. They wrap his head in a thick bandage, which is soon soaked in blood, until only his nose and eyes are visible. The moaning woman has finally calmed down and is now scolding her husband for having left the cellar.

I am gradually becoming sleepy, not being able to see anything except the anxious people around me. I am still wearing uniform and therefore feel as much a stranger as one can today in the relationship between soldiers and civilians, even when sitting among them. For them it will soon be over, but who knows how long it will be before I find peace...

I push back the chair and stand up slowly. A woman offers me a piece of bread, but I turn it down. I am not hungry, although I have not eaten all day, but she insists politely and I take a bite of it and suddenly I am overcome with almost unbearable hunger. The man with the bandage groans aloud, the pain now beginning as his body relaxes, as it does with all injuries. The woman beside him is still crying and holding his hand. The candle stands on a table in a porcelain dish with a gold band into which the running wax is dropping. The occupants sit silently as if sleeping. Only their burning eyes betray that they are still alive. Sometimes the voice of a child asks for bread and gets a tired response.

I go up to the door, open the bolt and push it open. The daylight suddenly floods in making me close my eyes with blindness. Then I close the door, pull the bolt, and slowly climb the steps. The front door opens with difficulty, as it is blocked with fallen masonry and rubble. Big lumps of masonry and glass splinters are lying in the street and smashed furniture blocks the way. Exploded rocket cases are lying around like big steel bottles. There is a noticeable crackling and sighing in the air. I look around and up at the next building, where a rocket has come through the attic and ripped a wide hole all the way down to the first floor. The building is on fire and is burning like a torch, crackling and spewing out a rain of ashes over the glass and masonry covered earth. Attics are on fire here and there among the hitherto undamaged buildings, and at every corner the roofs of burning houses are in flames. Grey smoke clouds billow up and dusty draughts blow along the streets.

I go back down the street to the factory. Here too I encounter dark smoke. The porter's lodge at the entrance has been crushed by the collapsing building behind it and some big oil barrels have rolled around and are burning. The watchman is lying in the burning oil, and exploded rocket cases are lying around like compressed air bottles, but smaller and narrower. I have already been under fire in the open field from these weapons we call 'Stalin-organs'. The burning oil produces a dense smoke that makes the eyes water. There is no way through here, as the whole street is on fire and even the tarmac is beginning to glow.

I turn back to find another way into the factory. The residents are standing in front of their burning buildings, senselessly dragging bits of furniture and equipment into the street, where they block the way. The face of a man appears for a few seconds through the flames in one building where he is apparently trying to rescue things from the fire that has burst into his first floor flat. I find another entrance to the factory just round the corner. The gate is open and I go in. Here too rocket cases are lying around, some stuck in the ground, and patches of grass and asphalt are on fire here and there. In a crater in the middle of a piece of grass are some colourful cartons looking like a paintbox. I go past the trees and look for the entrance to the dugout under the workshops where we spent last night. I go through the dirty workshops to make a short cut, passing through workshop after workshop, searching and searching, but they all look alike in their miserable dreariness with their blind or broken windows. I cross their stone floors as if I am in a labyrinth, unable to find my way out.

In some of the workshops there are mammoth presses and chemical baths in which the salts are solidifying, and furnaces with open doors. Everywhere is dead and empty, and it is quite scary among all this gigantic machinery and equipment. The metal sheets covering the floors echo my footsteps loudly and throw them against the walls, echoing them on and on. One building is much like another from the outside and most now also inside. Then I give up my search and turn to go back, but finding the way back is no easier. The factory is like a town of its own within the framework of Berlin.

It is the smell of smoke from the fires that eventually gets me out of the maze of streets, to the burning barrels and the blocked exit which I bypass. I go back on to still dead and empty street. The abandoned machine gun still stands on the bridge, but no soldier has been assigned to it. Everything seems to be left hanging in the air.

I stand on the bridge. A few shots ring out on the other bank. I go into the corner building with the pub sign and duck hesitantly under the balcony, afraid that it will fall on top of me, then go through the rubble into the cellar, where the ceiling has partly fallen in. The cellar next to the Havel bank has been turned into a proper fortress with loopholes knocked into the walls, railway sleepers and wooden beams supporting the walls. There is a Panzerfaust and a bowl on the floor, and a wooden bench with some filthy cushions that also seem to have some drops of blood on them. The loopholes that overlook the approach to the bridge are big enough to fire a Panzerfaust through from the cellar. Only a little daylight penetrates, lighting the room with a faint twilight, and there is no view of any size. One can only see the approach to the bridge, the concrete block of the air raid shelter on the opposite bank, and part of the barrier at the far end of the bridge.

One could fall asleep in this unaccustomed quiet. I take the cloths I use for weapon cleaning out of my haversack and clean my rifle and filthy pistol. Occasionally a shot rings out across the way, but this does not bother me. Then a roaring begins somewhere not too far away, the Stalin-organs again for sure. The enemy seems to be firing from Spandau. Flames suddenly leap up on the quay, race against the walls and threaten to come through the loopholes. There is a roaring in the air again, like a hurricane raging over the rooftops, and suddenly there is an explosion that drives me back in shock. Then it is dark and I can only sense that my feet are hurting up to the knees as if they were on fire, and something hits me on the head. I can hardly breathe, I can only taste sand on my tongue, and my skull is aching as if about to burst. An iron clamp forms round my heart and robs me of consciousness.

I come to again. I can feel a stabbing pain in my feet and have a piercing roaring in my head. I slowly feel my legs and try to move them, coming up against stones and rubble. My legs are buried up to the knees. I try to prise myself free from the pile of stones, but it does not give. The room is dark and I do not know whether I can get out of here. Perhaps the door has been destroyed and buried in masonry. I slowly bend down and remove the stones one by one, making a loud noise in the room. My legs gradually become free enough for me to move them, and at last I am out. My legs hurt with every step as I climb over the debris. It is completely dark and I do not have a single match left in my pocket. I grope my way slowly in one direction and come up against a wall. I feel my way along and meet a pile of debris. I feel my way farther like a blind man. My terrific headache seems about to blow my head open. I calm myself and sit down to rest. Then I get up again and carry on. My hand goes into nothing. The wall must surely end somewhere? Then I suddenly come up against a door and throw myself at it, but it seems to be locked. A little light is coming through some cracks. I go up to the door with my hands outstretched, find a bolt and pull. The door suddenly gives way and I fall back. Light breaks through the ceiling of the cellar next door. The eyes only dare accustom themselves to it slowly, but the light is still there. I slowly get up and look down at my legs. My trousers have been ripped through in several places and the white of my underpants is showing. I feel my head and find a wound in my hair wet with blood. My hair is filthy with dust.

I go back to find my rifle and pull it out from under the rubble. The ceiling has partly fallen in and the walls have collapsed into the cellar. I was lucky not to have been sitting at the loopholes or they would have fallen on me. But my feet and head are hurting almost unbearably, and I have a light veil in front of my eyes. I climb up a fallen iron girder with difficulty and fall to the ground.

I slowly get up again and go to the bridge. The world seems to have changed noticeably, the sun is no longer shining as brightly as it was this morning. A mist with red crosses and stars is swimming in front of my eyes, and my feet are as heavy as lead. The streets are devoid of people, with only a nurse standing at the bunker entrance looking at the bridge. I turn down the street leading to the factory and cross the big square. Dull fatigue fills my brain as I stagger forward like a drunk, my feet behaving as if I were a child learning how to walk. Once I stumble and fall to my knees, groaning from the maddening pain.

The factory gate appears as if from behind a white wall of mist. I go up to it and stop. I slowly calm down, then go through the factory with short, careful steps. Once I see a soldier looking at me strangely, then he disappears again in the maze of streets. Then at last I see a soldier I recognise coming towards me. He looks at me. I approach him cautiously and stop. 'What do you look like?' is all he says. Then we go on together. It is Blaczeck, the company runner.

He tells me that the command post has been completely destroyed and the workshop above has collapsed. He was with the factory's defence officer when the Stalin-organs and artillery opened up simultaneously. When he came back he saw that our comrades, who had been withdrawn from the bridge by sections, forgetting me, were all dead.

We go on and come to the boilerhouse. Railway tracks run across the road to a big heap of slack. Several railway wagons full of coal are standing around and a large crane with giant rollers rears over our heads. The gate leading out to the railway tracks opens only with difficulty. We go across the tracks and in front of us the S-Bahn embankment runs to Spandau-West station. Between the industrial railway tracks and those of the S-Bahn there is a narrow strip of grass, which we follow towards Ruhleben. I suddenly pull the trigger of my assault rifle, but it does not move. I examine my weapon. There is a cartridge in the breech but the chamber is bent. I could really throw it away, as it has become useless.

Suddenly some figures in brownish uniforms appear on the embankment, shocking us into colliding with each other and throwing ourselves down. But it is too late, they have already seen us and are coming towards us. Then they put their hands up. We stand up and they let their hands fall again. They are Germans.

When they get to us they say that they had taken us for Russians, just as we had them. We go on together through an underpass that leads under the S-Bahn. A tank is standing across the street. We go carefully along the embankment toward a hutted camp. The others, mainly young boys, want to try and get to Spandau somehow to get civilian clothing and shelter from relatives there. They are confident that it will all work out and are quite happy to be getting out of the mess this way.

Then our ways part. On our left lie the huts of the foreign workers' camp, in front of which men with dark faces and with their hands in their pockets are watching us. Some foreigners carrying big loads of bedding and furniture are coming along the allotment garden paths from behind the huts. The others say goodbye to us and disappear chatting away loudly in the tunnel that goes under the S-Bahn here too.

At first we do not know what to do, and then decide to go into the allotment gardens. There are summerhouses in bright colours on either side. We open a gate and go through into a garden. A woman comes out from behind a shed and looks at us in startled surprise. A boy and a girl are standing in front of a hole that they have dug in the ground. They are packing clothes and food into a box to bury them. Blaczeck takes off his pack and we ask them what the situation is, but they do not know. According to some factory guards who live on the allotments and returned this morning, the Russians are in the Deutsche-Industrie-Werke. When we tell them that we have just come from there, they look astonished. They say that the Russians have occupied Spandau-West station and have been mortaring the allotments from there from time to time. This morning the SS combed the gardens and promptly executed some soldiers they found hiding there, as well as the garden owners who had hidden them.

Then they go into their summerhouse and come back and press some civilian clothing into our hands. We go into a shed used for storing firewood, roll our uniforms into a bundle and stick our weapons inside it, but I put the pistol in my pocket for emergencies, in case the SS discover us. We give the uniforms to the woman to bury in the garden.

The trousers I have put on are far too big, as is the jacket, and so dirty that I cannot feel right in them. Perhaps this is only because I have not worn civilian clothes for almost four years.[3] Blaczeck is a little better off and at ten paces might perhaps not be taken for a soldier. He digs into his pack and gives the children some biscuits and sweets from the front line packets with which his pack is crammed. These were intended for the whole company and have been saved because he always takes his pack with him wherever he goes in case he should suddenly get new orders to go into action. Later we hide his pack behind some old sacks and go into the summerhouse, where the woman has prepared some coffee on a little spirit stove and we eat some biscuits. Then she warms up some water and I carefully wash my face. The wound above my eye has reopened and a dirty stripe runs down to my eyes. Blaczeck carefully washes my wound and then cuts the hair away from my head wound and deals with it too. 'You are lucky that your skull wasn't broken,' he says. Finally the woman gets a plaster and applies it to the wound.

A man advises us to go into the garden next door, where the owner has fled, and a home-made air raid shelter will keep us safe from surprises.

We get up slowly. Our army boots do not go so well with our civilian clothing and we feel decidedly uncomfortable. We climb over the fence into the next door garden, open the door to the shelter and close it securely from inside. Blaczeck strikes a match and we open the second door and go down the steep steps. The shelter is stuffed full of clothing and bedding, with trunks and large travelling baskets standing on the floor. We push these things to one side and lie between the clothing so that we cannot be discovered easily. Then we stick cigarettes in our mouths and two points begin to shine like glowworms. We have rolled ourselves in blankets and try to sleep, but our experiences are too fresh in the mind to allow us to rest. Somebody knocks on the door. I get up with the pistol in my hand and open the door, but it is only the woman, who has brought us something to eat and the stump of a candle. I close it again and go down carefully so as not to spill the soup, then we put the candle on a box and eat.

Muffled voices come from outside, sometimes close, sometimes distant. I get up carefully, not wanting to wake my friend, and climb the steps. Then I leave the shelter. Some soldiers are lying on the embankment looking across at the station. Not wanting to be seen, I hardly dare leave the cover of the shelter. The woman says that the soldiers would like to disappear themselves. They have to occupy the station, which the Russians have abandoned. I go back inside again. Blaczeck has woken up and listens as I tell him what has been happening. Then we discuss what we should do next. A friend of his father's lives in the Tiergarten District. We could make our way there and hide. We can put our uniforms on over our civilian clothes so as to get past the Wehrmacht and SS sentries.

When it is dark we leave our hiding place. The soldiers have disappeared in the direction of the station. We put our uniforms on again. I put my civilian clothes aside because they would bulge out under my uniform. Then we quickly shake the woman's hand, leave the garden and quietly close the gate.

We go along the path between the allotments. I have my pistol in my hand as we strain to see in the darkness. Then we turn right towards the apartment blocks we saw this morning. On the left are the huts of the foreigners' camp and on the right the Schlagengraben allotment gardens. At last we reach the street and breathe out. We then go along cautiously in the shadow of the trees. Once footsteps can be heard coming along the pavement and two shadows pass on the other side of the street, one big and one small, a woman and a child. The woman, leaning forward wearily, is huddled shivering in a big wrap. They go past us without seeing us. The child's voice sounds tired. Their voices fade away.

We go on slowly. Suddenly there is the sound of a tank on the street. We quickly hide behind an advertising column[4] and hold our breath. It gradually gets closer, frightening and threatening. There are also footsteps and voices hanging in the air. Now it is quite close. An assault gun rolls past. The figures of soldiers go past like an army of ghosts. The tank tracks sound farther and farther off until they vanish altogether.

We are now in Ruhleben. The trees stand dark on both sides of the street with shot off branches and broken twigs scattered all over the road. Nearly all these big thick trees have been half sawn through in a wedge so that they can be quickly dropped to block the road in an emergency. A high stone wall appears on our right and then the barrack gates. A soldier

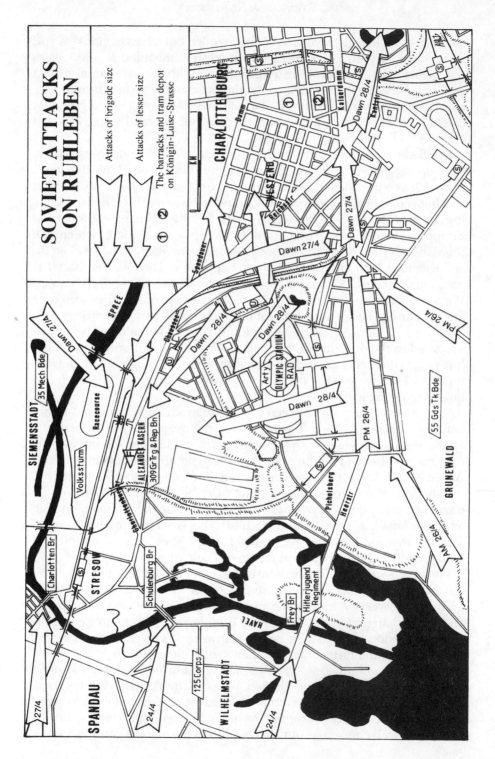

SOVIET ATTACKS
ON RUHLEBEN

Attacks of brigade size

Attacks of lesser size

① ② The barracks and tram depot
on Königin-Luise-Strasse

KM

CHARLOTTENBURG

WESTEND

Damm

Kaiserdamm

Knobstr

Dawn 28/4

Reichstr

Dawn 27/4

Dawn 27/4

Spandauer

SPREE

Dawn 27/4

35 Mech Bde

SIEMENSSTADT

Racecourse

Chaussee

Dawn 28/4

Dawn 28/4

PM 26/4

Volkssturm

ALEXANDER KASERN

309 Gr Trg & Rep Bn

Arty

OLYMPIC STADIUM

RAD

Dawn 28/4

55 Gds Tk Bde

GRUNEWALD

PM 26/4

Pichelsberg

Heerstr

AM 26/4

Charlotten Br

STRESOW

Schulenburg Br

Charlottenburger Chaussee

HAVEL

Frey Br

Hitlerjugend
Regiment

SPANDAU

27/4

24/4

125 Corps

24/4

WILHELMSTADT

142

standing in the shadows stops us. We show him our paybooks. Then he calls the guard commander, who is Sergeant Eckert. We go with him through the barrack gates towards the dark buildings. There is a sentry outside the Convalescent Company block, who asks us brusquely where we are going. When we tell him that we belong there, he tells us where to look for somewhere to sleep.

We enter the building and climb the stairs looking for somewhere to sleep. We go exhaustedly from room to room, all of which are crammed full of stragglers. There is an acrid smell in these rooms that takes our breath away. We go back down to the cellar, and into the company commander's command post, where Lieutenant Stichler is sitting at a table. He looks up at us in astonishment. We report in. He then takes us across to the runners' room where there are some palliasses on the floor and a few sleepers are breathing gently. We put our things down and get a blanket and then lie down with the others. I have a sudden longing for a cigarette. Then a leaden fatigue falls over me, the room and everything in it seem to be spinning, red flames dance before my eyes and my head suddenly aches unbearably. Then everything calms down again and I drift off to sleep.

Saturday 28 April 1945

I wake with a start to the pounding of nailed boots, loud shouts and explosions that seem to make the earth quake. Around me people are pulling on greatcoats, putting on their steel helmets and dashing outside. Now I am fully awake. Blaczeck dashes into the room and shouts in my ear that the Russians have broken through and are in front of the barracks.

I throw on my greatcoat, grab a rifle and a few belts of ammunition, and dive outside. The night has woken up to frightening activity. The thundering of guns and exploding shells, with the roaring of collapsing walls, the splintering of windowpanes and the hammering of machine gun fire, has become one single noise that paralyses the senses and makes one's eardrums vibrate. The din has become a constant thunder, above which it is almost impossible to distinguish the individual gunshots and explosions. It penetrates and consumes one like an inevitable disaster. The earth shakes until one expects it to open up at any moment and swallow everything up in the darkness. Figures running across the square show up like ghosts whenever an exploding shell spreads its bright flash of light for a few seconds. I stand in the cellar entrance waiting for something to join on to. Then some figures dash by racing toward the barrack gates, so I run with them.

Nobody knows what is really happening, where the enemy is, or in what strength he is attacking. Fire is coming from all sides, and is closing in on the barracks. The firing appears to have started from the racecourse.

The enemy occupied Siemensstadt yesterday after some hard fighting and has pushed forward slowly from there, apparently crossing the Spree by his own emergency bridges, as all the bridges had been blown. He also appears to be attacking from Charlottenburg, and from the Heerstrasse. Only one direction seems secure, and that is towards Spandau-West, where the Havel forms an uncrossable obstruction.[5] We are surrounded and do not know whether there is any way out.

The barrack gates are closed and we slide some trees and Spanish Riders[6] that were lying on the grass against them to have at least the minimum of protection. A truck that was standing on one of the barrack streets races round the corner, blinding us and making our eyes hurt. The truck is driven up against the gates, while we lie on the ground and keep a look out. I have landed in the right group with Sergeant Rytn, Wegner, Bräuer and another three I do not know.

In the distance on the right one can see the fire of tank guns that must be on a level with the U-Bahn station. The shells explode in the walls above our heads, knocking down trees and sending splinters whistling through the air. The tanks are rolling slowly forward with frightening regularity, tongues of fire licking the night. We fire like mad at the tanks to prevent any accompanying infantry advancing. Then there is a sudden explosion in the wall above, showering us with bits of stone. I clasp my head, for I have no steel helmet on, only my field cap.

There is no point in staying here by the gates any longer. The tanks will be here within minutes. A tank destroyer team remains behind as we run across the street. The lieutenant, wearing a steel helmet, stops us. We have to go behind the barracks as quickly as possible, where the enemy has already occupied the Reichssportfeld and is now advancing on the barracks. Apparently the T-34s[7] on the street in front of the barracks have no infantry support.

We run along the barrack streets in which the shocked refugees who had sought shelter in the barracks are now desperately looking for the air raid shelters. Lost children are running around looking for their parents. A few dead struck down by falling masonry or killed by artillery splinters are lying around. Some wounded are making their way back to find shelter in the barrack block cellars. The night is by no means over. Only the lightning flashes of the guns and the exploding shells, and the dazzling streams of fire from tracer bullets rip through the darkness. Will day never succeed this night?

Shots are whipping through the barrack streets from the Reichssportfeld. One can see the muzzle flashes and hear the roaring afterwards as the shells strike everywhere, ripping the earth up into a field of craters. We run across the barrack training area, stumbling over the trenches and craters there. It is so dark that one can hardly make out where one is, where our positions and those of the enemy are. At last we hear German voices quite close, just as we were about to rush past them and go on. Then we split up among the individual foxholes once used for training recruits, firing into the night in front of us, not knowing where the enemy is. He could appear at any moment and jump into our trenches. Somebody goes past crouched down. 'Advance one hundred metres and occupy the trench!' We jump out of our holes and race forward, firing as we go. We fall into foxholes and over tripwires, gather ourselves up again and at last reach the trench. We let ourselves fall into it and resume firing. There is no letting up. It is really desperate when one has to shoot not knowing where the enemy is.

The trench seems to be densely filled. Apparently all the emergency companies housed in the barracks have been thrown into the fight. I go along the trench, squeezing past the riflemen, looking for Sergeant Rytn and the remaining comrades who were called up with me and have only the bombing attack on the tractor and trailer to thank for their still being in the barracks. At last I run into Wegner, who points to his left where the others are firing. Then I stand beside him and fire into the night.

Once it has quietened down a bit, Sergeant Rytn comes along the trench. He says that the enemy made a surprise attack on the Reichssportfeld from the Heerstrasse and captured the entire crews of the artillery positions deployed on the field. Even the heavy guns have fallen intact into their hands. There were 88, 105, 125 and 150 millimetre guns deployed there, and it makes me weak to think that the Russians can now use the guns to fire on the barracks. There would not be much left of the buildings, let alone ourselves.

The sound of battle has died down. The enemy appears to be waiting for dawn to attack the barracks, or perhaps he suspects we have some heavy weapons inside the walls? The sound of tank guns comes from Ruhleben U-Bahn station. A bright fire is burning on the far side of the barracks. Is it an accommodation block or a tank? A runner comes up from the rear and goes along the trench. We have to give the enemy no respite and keep up an uninterrupted fire, reinforcements are on their way. But what is the point when we have nearly all run out of ammunition? And the reinforcements will not be able to drive the enemy back from the ground he has already won. We have lost the Reichssportfeld and, in practical terms, the barracks too. Is there really any point in continuing the fight? If only there was not this uncertainty about one's fate as a prisoner of war.

Sergeant Rytn comes back again. 'Watch out! Deserters!' We strain our eyes but can only make out shadows in the darkness. Is everything lost now, or is there still a gleam of light?

The night gradually lifts its veil. Trees and bushes stand out sharper. The infantry fire has increased and is hitting the sand. Bursts of tracer bullets come from in front of the barracks to strike the road embankment that runs along the side of the Reichssportfeld. Now we can see it for ourselves. Here and there a figure jumps out of the trench and runs across to the enemy, disappearing between the bushes. Suddenly the sound of a tank tears through the dawn and a dark colossus runs up the road and stops by the bushes. We have thrown ourselves down, waiting for the end. Then it is suddenly silent. Even the enemy's infantry fire has stopped. We stick our heads above the parapet, and recoil. The tank is standing quite close to the trench like a dark monster, only holding its breath before it devours us. Then our eyes seem bewitched as the turret hatch opens and a head appears. 'Don't shoot!' suddenly sounds through the silence, and we hold our breath. Only the distant roaring of explosions somewhere sounds like thunder in the wings. I think it is a German tank, but I must be wrong, it can only be a Russian. Then it drops in the silence: 'Comrades, give yourselves up! There is no point in fighting on. The Russians outnumber you. The barracks are completely surrounded. Run across and report to the Russian troops on the Reichssportfeld. You will be well treated, and you will be able to go home as soon as hostilities are over. Soldiers, there is no point any more. Do you want to lose your lives in the last hours of a war already lost?' The hatch slams shut, the engine roars into life and the tank clanks away, a white cloth fluttering behind like a flag. Now I know why it was not fired at.

Soldiers are jumping out of the trench and running across the field to disappear between the bushes and then scramble up the hill to the road, where they vanish between the mostly shot up weekend houses. More and more are going, running across like an avalanche, civilians and soldiers from the emergency companies. From the distance comes a voice: 'Soldiers, give yourselves up! There is no point any more!' Now I realise that he must have been using a loudspeaker, and that he had kept his head half covered to avoid being shot.

Sergeant Rytn comes along with a chalkwhite face. 'Those swine, those swine...' he forces through his clenched teeth and holds a pistol in front of our faces. 'Are you thinking of running over, eh? Then you would get a bullet faster than you would have got over.' He orders us to fire at the deserters. I look to my right and left. The trench looks as if it had died. The next man can just be made out in the distance and a few dead are lying in the bottom like dark flecks. The last of the deserters is disappearing between the bushes, followed by a few shots. A machine gun opens up and I fire too, but aim high into the trees.

I too would like to disappear, turn my back on everything and hide myself somewhere to wait until it is all over. The oath that binds me means nothing any more. I feel myself released from it since it became clear what sort of game was being played with us. But there is something else that holds me back despite everything. The words 'obedience' and 'duty' are so deeply burned into our hearts they they smoulder on like a small spark to hold us back. We simply cannot find a way out of the maze of feelings,

146

out of the conflict between our upbringing and the commonsense that comes to us in terms that we do not recognise, as they contradict everything that we have been taught in our lives. We do not hate the enemy, we only shoot because conformity with the mass seems to spare us from taking responsibility for ourselves.

The shooting has died down. The Rytn Section, to which I also belong, is still in the trench with a few sergeants and corporals, hardly twenty men in all to defend a section of trench almost five hundred metres long. We split ourselves up along the trench so that there is a rifleman every fifty metres. There is a machine gun post on the left and some training bunkers on the right that are, however, unoccupied. Presumably the enemy will avoid those positions as he does not know the strength of the occupants.

It has become fully light and the sun breaks through from time to time and then is hidden again behind the clouds. Some birds are twittering in the trees and fluttering around. The execution posts of Execution Place No. 5 stand up against the Reichssportfeld embankment like dead fingers. They will certainly not be needed any more.

The enemy attacks, smothering us in terrific infantry fire and driving us to the ground. When the firing suddenly stops, he is already in the bushes in front of us. We have collected up the weapons of the dead and deserters and laid them loaded in front of us on the parapet, and I have got hold of a submachine gun. We fire like mad. The machine gun on the left combs through the bushes. It is all so absurd. We would like to throw the whole business aside and vanish, but nevertheless still hold on. Our youthful trust has been shamefully abused and misled, but we still hope in a miracle that can no longer save us, for the war is undoubtedly lost. But can we get through this again and escape capture? Or is it something else still? That inner voice that whispers: 'Fight on until you get a bullet.' Everything that we believed in has collapsed and we stand here empty-handed.

The enemy tries to resume his attack, concentrating on the machine gun post, and seemingly uncertain about the bunkers. We shoot like robots, aiming and firing, and again the enemy withdraws, firing on our trench and pulling his dead and wounded back. If he just knew how thinly the trench is held! The machine gun has proved its worth; we would have been lost if it had come to close-quarter fighting.

The enemy suddenly withdraws, running back across the open positions between the bushes and clambers up the embankment. We are hardly firing any more, being happy to have survived intact. Only the machine gun keeps on firing. Suddenly shots come from behind us. I look round and now understand why the enemy has abandoned his positions. Soldiers and Hitler Youths in their brown or black uniforms[8] are running across the field from the barracks. We duck our heads down in the trench, as some of their shots are whipping by dangerously close. Then the first ones are already jumping into our trench. The lieutenant is also with this group.

The Reichssportfeld is to be retaken. Reinforcements from the Deutsche-Industrie-Werke and the strong points around are hurrying in. All Hitler Youths that are not already wearing the uniforms of the Volkssturm or the Wehrmacht have been taken from their homes in Spandau and Ruhleben, so that there are about two thousand Hitler Youths and a thousand soldiers. The attack will begin promptly at ten o'clock. Meanwhile two combat teams are fighting their way forward from Ruhleben U-Bahn station towards the Reichssportfeld and could be near the Olympic Stadium by now.

The time goes by slowly. More and more soldiers and Hitler Youths come up from behind to fill the trench until we can hardly move. Many stay behind in the foxholes to wait for the attack to begin. The enemy seems insecure and is spraying the area with machine gun and quick-firing gunfire. The Hitler Youths duck down behind the trench walls in their fear. They are mainly armed with old captured German and Italian rifles with a few mainly useless rounds. The Deutsche Jungvolk have never held a weapon in their hands before and are having to make do. The recoil alone must be enough to knock most of them on their backs. Not many of them will survive when the attack begins.

It is almost ten o'clock. Suddenly a mortar starts firing on the Reichssportfeld from in front of the barracks. Punctually at ten we haul ourselves out of the trench and charge forward to be met by heavy infantry fire, but we get some cover under the embankment for a moment. Some Russians who fled ahead of us and ran into their own fire are hiding behind the buildings. Then we are over the top and the Reichssportfeld lies before us. Sounds of combat come from our left as the enemy withdraws slowly, step by step, across the field toward the Heerstrasse. Our troops have fanned out over the sports field and are moving forward with the Hitler Youths advancing between them, trying to use their weapons. Then suddenly machine gun bursts come from the sports school buildings[9], mowing down the ranks. More and more fall to the ground. We lie down behind the dead and open fire. The combat team to the left of us has become involved in some fierce fighting behind these buildings. We jump up and run on, firing at the fleeing enemy. Then soldiers come towards us from the buildings, German soldiers captured during the night. Or also deserters?

One combat team thrusts forward and tries to reach the Heerstrasse. Others occupy the sportsfield to prevent a counterattack, but we stay behind and then head back for the barracks.

The ground is strewn with dead and wounded, mainly Hitler Youths in uniform or the civilian clothes they were wearing when they were collected from their homes. The survivors of their devastated units form up and are counted. They have sustained eighty percent losses. They can now go home, a major says, until the next time.

We head for the barracks. There are Germans and Russians lying on the street between the weekend houses, here too mainly Hitler Youths killed in the attack, an expensively bought 'success'. About two thousand dead and injured is not an overestimate for the one hour of the attack, but human life has become so cheap that one cannot make a fuss about it. Whether soldiers or Hitler Youths, whether women or civilians, it is all the same who gets involved in the melting pot of war and who goes under. The orders of <u>one</u> man bring everyone to the same point, and whether it means death to them is of no consequence to him and the others. Better to be killed than to slowly die of starvation in our cellars, as one 14-year-old said beforehand.

The barrack blocks have become a vast field hospital, and the dead are being piled up in front of the East Block. The field grey of the soldiers lies next to the civilian clothing of the Volkssturm and the brown of the Hitler Youths. Even a few women who strayed into the streets during the night have been killed. The barrack blocks have been badly damaged, and a whole corner has been torn off the Convalescent Company building. There are some big holes in the walls, stuffed with sandbags, that were the work of the tank now standing burnt-out in front of the barrack gate. All the windows have been broken, and a few vehicles that stood in front of battalion headquarters have been shot into unrecognisable heaps of scrap metal. There are some dead lying around here too.

We go below into the cellar and put down our weapons. Sergeant Rytn and his section are to guard the supply bunker by the film studios, and I am to join them later. Sergeant Major Kaiser, a platoon leader in the company, has returned after being captured by the Russians. He was taken by surprise during the night and put on a Russian armoured personnel carrier, but managed to jump off while it was on the move. He then hid in the cellar of one of the little weekend houses. Another soldier from the company was also captured during the night and has now returned. He says that they were well treated. They were given schnapps and cigarettes, and even bread. He thinks, however, that this was only a ploy to get them to persuade others to desert. We still do not know where we stand.

NOTES

1. The Fire Brigade had been reorganised as part of the police forces within Himmler's extensive empire.
2. Unknown to the Germans, the Havel river here and the Spree, which flowed into it north of the factory, constituted the boundary between the 1st Byelorussian and 1st Ukrainian Fronts, and, in view of the rivalry and lack of

communication between the Soviet commanders, was highly unlikely to be crossed.

3. In his previous employment as an aircraft engineer apprentice, Altner had been obliged to wear the Air Corps uniform of the Hitler Youth.

4. These columns, to which advertising posters can be pasted, are a feature of Berlin, standing about three metres high and one metre in diameter.

5. See Appendix III. The Soviet advance through Siemensstadt by elements of the 2nd Guards Tank Army of the 1st Byelorussian Front and penetration as far as Ruhleben Racecourse had taken place on the 27th as described, but this involved a crossing of the inter-front boundary, and when Colonel Dragunsky's strongly reinforced 55th Guards Tank Brigade of the 1st Ukrainian Front advancing along the Reichsstrasse made contact that day, the former were obliged to withdraw back across the Spree again.

The attack on Ruhleben Barracks on the 28th was conducted by elements of Colonel Dragunsky's brigade, the main body of which had been ordered to launch an attack eastwards along Kantstrasse at dawn that day in support of Marshal Koniev's attempt with the 3rd Guards Tank Army to reach the Reichstag ahead of his rival, Marshal Zhukov. Colonel Dragunsky therefore decided to secure his rear with this attack on the Olympic Stadium, Reichssportfeld and Ruhleben positions by part of his force.

It was mid-morning when Koniev discovered that his route was already blocked by some of Zhukov's troops. He quit Berlin, leaving the 3rd Guards Tank Army to change course towards the Kurfürstendamm. Meanwhile Dragunsky's main force had become heavily involved in the area around Karl-August-Platz. Orders for them to return to a blocking position in the Westend took another day or so to implement, and then it seems they holed up in the barracks and tramsheds located off Königin-Elisabeth-Strasse in the Westend and let the battle finish without them.

6 Obstacles made of barbed wire on wooden trestles.

7. The Soviet T-34/85 was a medium tank of 32 tons with a top speed of 53 kilometres per hour. It was armed with an 85mm gun and two machine guns, and had a crew of five.

8. The Hitler Youth wore brown uniforms in summer and black in winter.

9. Later the British Sector headquarters complex.

CHAPTER X

The Tunnels

Saturday 28 April 1945 (Afternoon)

I feel tired and washed out. A dull pressure in my head prevents me from thinking clearly, even killing the heavy thoughts that descend upon us like the shadows of the night in the quiet hours. Our uniforms are grey and so are our forebodings about a future that gives us not a glimmer of hope. I just want to sleep, sleep and suddenly wake up to discover that it was all nothing but a bad dream, that there was no war, that there are no ruins, no dead and ripped apart bodies, but that there is peace and that the sun shines and life pulses without the threat of coming to an end at any moment. But this is only wishful thinking. We are condemned to death and do not know why, nor do we know why we are not allowed to live!

The lieutenant enters the room. It is by no means over, for all of Ruhleben has to be cleared of the enemy. Several combat teams have already set off in various directions. One combat team has gone over the Reichssportfeld towards the Heerstrasse to clear the Pichelsberg, and another is securing Ruhleben north of the S-Bahn line to the Spree. We are to follow the U-Bahn line as far as possible towards the city centre, while another combat team will thrust down the Spandauer Chaussee into Charlottenburg to strengthen the hitherto weak link with the city centre. It is even rumoured that Hitler is coming to Ruhleben.[1]

The company falls in in front of the building. Sergeant Rytn has taken over the supply bunker, so is not present, and Blaczeck is to remain behind as the company commander's runner. I am thus alone among what to me are still strange soldiers, almost all of them older than myself, but in time one becomes accustomed to being thrown around from one unit to another at a moment's notice, never getting settled down and therefore not getting worried about the big losses in dead and wounded.

Several groups come along the barrack streets to join us, mainly companies of stragglers who arrived in the barracks yesterday and had to repel the night attack. Now there is a new task to perform as pointless as all the others, as they cannot possibly make any difference to the eventual outcome. Amid this unwilling mass everyone is for himself alone, leaving aside all thoughts and feelings to make things as easy as possible for oneself, thinking about neither the future nor the present, just swimming in the mass, being simply a tiny wheel without a purpose of its own.

We close up and march through the barrack gates and turn towards Ruhleben U-Bahn station. A burnt-out T-34 is standing on the tram tracks directly in front of the gates, and the tramstop sign has been almost severed, but one can still make out the route numbers 54 and 154 on the metal. We go down the road in long files, almost five hundred strong. I have exchanged my rifle for a submachine gun, which is handier and more suitable for close combat. However, the ammunition for it is limited. What use are a hundred rounds when one does not know what lies before us?

We stop at the U-Bahn station. The interior is totally unrecognisable. Everything that was not securely fastened down has been ripped from the walls, even the light switches. The inhabitants of the foreign labourers' camp over by the race course have been helping the Russians. According to some local inhabitants who have been sheltering in the cellar under the station, the SS have raided their camp and have already shot a number of those found with weapons.

We push on along the U-Bahn line. The Russians appear to have had a machine gun nest by the bathing pool on our right, where dead soldiers and Hitler Youths are scattered around, and there is a knocked-out anti-tank gun with its dead crew at the Reichssportfeld U-Bahn station.[2] A few soldiers and civilians are digging graves in front of the cemetery and collecting the dead, most of whom are Hitler Youths. Some wounded, supported by civilians, are being brought to the dressing station set up in the U-Bahn station.

We have to be careful as we do not know how far the enemy has withdrawn. We follow the line of the U-Bahn, maintaining a broad front as we comb through the area. We cross Westendallee to the Neu-Westend station, which is unoccupied. Locals tell us that the enemy has withdrawn towards the Grunewald.[3] Just beyond the station is a big yellow BVG bus, its windows broken but otherwise apparently intact. There is still no sign of the enemy, but one can hear the sounds of combat in the distance, and it seems that the combat team that thrust down the Spandauer Chaussee into Charlottenburg has become involved in a fight.[4] We pass Preussen-allee on our right and then Kastanienallee on our left, which branches off to the Spandauer Chaussee with Branitzer Platz half way along.

Adolf-Hitler-Platz[5] is not occupied and only bits of German and Russian equipment lying scattered around and some dead bodies in the buildings reveal that fighting has taken place here. Locals tell us that the enemy has withdrawn to positions behind Eichkamp station. Our combat team leader, a Luftwaffe captain who does not appear to have much idea about infantry warfare, orders a strong section into the Exhibition

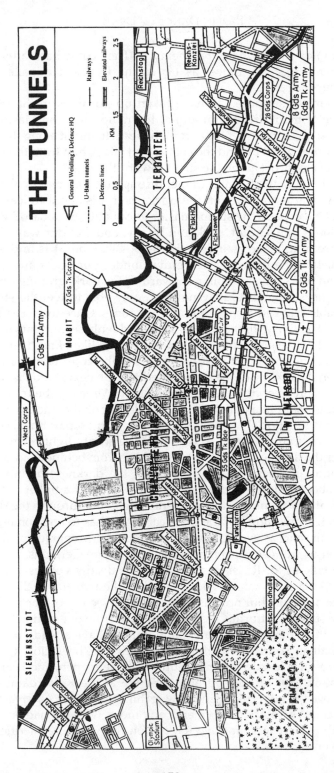

THE TUNNELS

General Weidling's Defence HQ
U-Bahn tunnels
Defence lines
Railways
Elevated railways

0   0,5   1   1,5   2   2,5
         KM

SIEMENSSTADT

MOABIT

2 Gds Tk Army

12 Gds Tk Corps

1 Mech Corps

TIERGARTEN

CHARLOTTENBURG

WILMERSDORF

Reichstag

Reichs-Kanzlei

28 Gds Corps

8 Gds Army +
1 Gds Tk Army

3 Gds Tk Army

55 Gds Tk Bde

Flak HQ

Flak-Tower

Funkturm

Deutschlandhalle

Olympic Stadium

Grounds to discover where the enemy is. They come back after a short while having reached almost as far as the Deutschlandhalle without coming under fire.

The enemy is supposed to have taken up positions in the buildings either side of the Kaiserdamm and at the radio tower on Masurenallee. The captain gives the order for part of the team to thrust along the U-Bahn tunnel in order to get behind the enemy and attack him from the rear. The other part is to thrust along the street toward the Knie[6]

We go down to the U-Bahn tunnel through the empty and abandoned station. A train is standing on the tracks as if it is about to leave at any moment. One expects the stationmaster to call out 'All aboard!' We come to what looks like a vault, dark and musty, and feel our way along the tracks, careful to make as little noise as possible, but it is impossible to move quietly. The gravel ballast moves under our boots and crunches gently, and it is scary stumbling forward in the dark, groping one's way forward and seeing absolutely nothing, only able to feel the strands of electric cable that run along the walls like ropes. Once there is a hold-up ahead and I collide with the man in front, suddenly seeing stars in front of my eyes. Then we grope our way forward again like blind men. I feel an obstruction and try to get past it. It is a U-Bahn train that has been left standing in the middle of the stretch. Perhaps the next station is not so far off? Below here everything seems so distant. We leave the train behind, then there is a shimmer of light up ahead playing on the track, which turns out to be a ventilation shaft to the street, only a grid separating us from the world above. I am reluctant to continue, the scanty light seems like life itself after the darkness, but they are pushing from behind, and we go on.

Every time we pass a ventilation shaft the darkness becomes much harder to bear and more frightening. We can expect a bullet to bring an end to us at any moment. It is nerve-racking going through the darkness unable to feel anything but the thick cable that has to end somewhere in the open air, and at every moment we must be prepared for fire to be opened on us from somewhere. Perhaps there are Germans ahead of us who will take us for Russians and can direct deadly volleys at us at any moment. At last the tunnel widens out to take two tracks that must be leading to a station, but no, it is only a double section of track. We climb up on to a station platform. One normally goes from one station to the next in two to three minutes by the U-Bahn, but we have already been under way for half an hour. The platform entrances have been closed with iron grills, but a few blows with a rifle butt break them open, and I can see the shiny station sign in the half-light. We are at the Kaiserdamm. A big cinema poster is advertising the new technicolour film 'Opfergang' (Way of Sacrifice). We do not need cinema any more, we have had enough life and death experiences, and we too are on the way to a sacrifice, but a pointless one.

Some soldiers have gone up to the street, where sounds of fighting are coming from the direction of the Knie, and tanks seem to be involved. The other part of our combat team can be seen making their way down from Adolf-Hitler-Platz. Some of us wait above for them to arrive, while others climb down again and feel our way forward through the maze of the underworld with its dark secrets that make us hold our breath and leave us feeling small and insignificant. Nobody wants sun and air more ardently than us. It is scary in a darkness that seems to watch us like a slinking animal about to spring at an unsuspecting moment and bring us down in an inferno of death and horror.

Another ventilation shaft appears, and the noise of battle sounds like a distant roaring overhead. Shots ring out from up ahead and generate a thundering echo in the narrow tunnel, increasing to an ear-deafening din, and we plunge forward, throwing ourselves into the darkness. Shots whip against the walls and send the gravel ballast flying. Suddenly the firing stops and our ears almost ache from the abrupt silence. We go on slowly and mistrustfully, unable to shoot without hitting the man in front. The tunnel widens and we come to a platform where some Hitler Youths with Panzerfausts and Waffen-SS men are standing about. They had fired at us, thinking we were Russians. This little error has cost us four dead and wounded. They tell us that the enemy has occupied the area around Richard-Wagner-Platz, and that the Westkreuz and Charlottenburg S-Bahn stations are also in their hands. The Russians have occupied Bismarckstrasse between Sophie-Charlotte-Platz and the Deutsches Opernhaus, driving a wedge between the two stations. We look down along the street. The noise of fighting in the immediate neighbourhood indicates fierce fighting. The combat team coming along the street is keeping close to the buildings.

We are split into individual combat teams to continue at intervals underground and try to get past the enemy. Some Hitler Youth combat teams specially trained for underground fighting join us. We jump back down on the tracks and advance slowly, keeping pressed close to the walls. The U-Bahn line has some gentle curves behind any of which the enemy could be lurking. We advance step by step. A ventilation shaft allows us a pause, and the battle from the streets above sounds like distant thunder and takes our breath away. It does not seem to be all that far off; we are right under the combatants. We feel our way forward step by step, pressed tight against the walls as if they could protect us from the destruction that could break out at any moment, as it surely must if the enemy has occupied the next station. We go on slowly. An occasional shaft gives its faint light and the sound of battle through the grill. Then it happens, and it comes as a relief from the uncertainty. Now we know where we stand.

I have thrown myself to the ground and put my head against the cool rail that is vibrating as if a train were approaching. A bright flash rips through the darkness and an explosion echoes back a thousand times from the walls, almost shaterring our eardrums. Then there is another explosion and a new flash of bright light in which figures can be seen running forward. We run forward as if drawn by a gigantic magnet, firing into the darkness, stumbling and falling over dead and wounded. Up ahead a 'Hurrah' rings out from young throats, high-pitched and hoarse. We rush forward firing, driven by a blind urge to kill, and not to be killed ourselves.

Shots are coming from a U-Bahn tunnel on the left and hitting the wall. We run past under withering fire. I stumble, fall and crawl along the ground out of the line of fire. Suddenly there is another flash and one can see figures running forward for an instant, the rails and the cables on the walls, and a Hitler Youth who has just fired a Panzerfaust into the adjoining tunnel. Then it is suddenly dark again. A torch flashes for a second, and one can see dark figures lying between the rails. Then I run on, thrusting forwards and firing like mad into the darkness in front of me. Then the gun stops, the magazine empty, as is the second one that I used up just before. We stumble over more and more dead, many of them Hitler Youths who had previously been up in the lead with their Waffen-SS men. Then another ventilation shaft appears. The firing is going on behind us without respite. We do not know if we are running straight into the hands of the enemy, or whether he is only attacking from the side tunnel.

At last a new station, Deutsches Opernhaus. One can hardly imagine that life once pulsed through these dead tunnels at its fastest, that brightly coloured trains used to tear along disgorging thousands of people at these stations and taking on more into their carriages. One certainly cannot imagine that there is now anything other than this constant race with death. But better to fight above ground in the light and sunshine, where one can see one's fate in the form of giant tanks and the enemy, than under here in the city's burial chambers, which have now truly become graves for those dead lying between the railway tracks and the stations. I suddenly think about how we are going to get back to Ruhleben, as the enemy will have blocked this stretch and the underground route is as shot up as that above on the street. But we have no time to think now, only to press forward out of these catacombs into the light and life again.

We feel our way forward again. This darkness has no end to it. We go along the walls like shadows of the night, worrying about the next incident that will surely befall us. It has not quietened down. Behind us comes a thundering like a storm, roaring and frightening, and then it breaks out again from the darkness up ahead. One can see the muzzle flashes of weapons from which destruction is lashing out in its many forms. We charge forward, fall, pull ourselves up again, lie down behind the dead and wounded who provide the only cover, and fire into the night

156

in front of us. The fighting is hard and horrible. There is another loud bang behind us and the sound comes down the tunnel like a wave almost threatening to knock us over. A strong blast streaks past, shaking our helmets. Has the enemy blown up the stretch behind us? Is he going to blow it up in front? Then we would be lost, sitting hopelessly in a trap from which there would be no escape. We stumble forward with new uncertainty, firing, falling, picking ourselves up again. The fire up ahead dies down and it is suddenly light. The ventilation shaft above us has been torn open. One of the boys says that the Russians have been firing at the street with their tanks during the past few days and have ripped open the tunnel roof.

At last we have reached the Knie, the unlit station looming like a haven, even if it is not as clean as it used to be. The nearby Schiller Theatre, now only a heap of rubble, suddenly comes to mind. We stand around in the station and discuss what to do next. The enemy has pulled back deeper into the tunnel, but will surely come up against the German troops holding the Zoo U-Bahn station, in which case it will not be long before he returns.

We go farther down the tunnel. Berlin has now become a torn, flaming, uncoordinated object. The enemy is in the Tiergarten trying to get into the government quarter, but there are still German troops at the Zoo, like an island precariously hanging together in a mighty flood.

The firing does not stop. Our combat team spreads out even farther apart and partly holds back. The roof to the road has been torn open beyond the Zoo station and the tunnel has fallen in, so we have to make our way carefully over a maze of torn concrete and twisted rails, collapsed beams and electricity cables, constantly followed and driven on by the enemy fire, which seems to be coming from all directions. After the negotiation of each destroyed and demolished section, we vanish underground again. I have no idea how late it is, having lost all sense of time, and am surprised to be still alive. Our ranks have become thinner, but the Hitler Youths are fighting like the Devil, being driven on ceaselessly by their Waffen-SS leaders.

At last there is a big hole in the roof to the street above us, and heavy fire crashing down on the stones makes the traverse unthinkable. The boys come up from behind with shocked, white faces, charging forward. The enemy is firing Panzerfausts down through the ventilation shafts, blowing up the stretch behind us so that we are trapped and do not know how to get out. Then someone jumps over the maze of blown up roofing that half fills the shaft and vanishes unharmed into the half-shattered continuation of the tunnel, despite the hail of fire. Then I too suddenly jump up, ignoring the sound of shots striking all around me, falling and rolling forward, scrambling with bloody hands and clutching my weapon until it hurts, and then I am over. I roll into the passage and lie down on the rails, wanting to rest, only to rest.

One by one the others leap forward. Many remain lying, providing meagre cover for those following. Some are wounded and try to reach the shelter of the tunnel. We go on, leaving everything behind us like a nightmare. Suddenly voices call out ahead of us, awakening a many-voiced echo from the walls. We call back and go on faster. They are Germans and we have reached Wittenbergplatz station.

We sit down on the platform and take a rest as other soldiers come out of the darkness of the tunnels one by one and roll on to the platform, lying around as if dead. The soldiers holding the station are worried that the Russians might attack. The fighting in the city's U-Bahn tunnels is pitiless and cruel, one of them says. Whole combat teams of Germans and Russians have been cut off in various sections by demolition and then destroyed. Many of them were Hitler Youths trained as tank-hunting teams and then committed underground. I ask them about the situation at the Zoo, and someone tells me that both air raid shelters are forming the defence's strongest bulwarks[7], and that the enemy is closing up to these positions, having reached Nollendorfplatz on one side, and is pushing forward with the support of tanks.

A dark silent mass is sitting between the soldiers along the walls of the station, refugees from the city who have fled underground in search of shelter and are uncertain if they have made a cruel exchange now that the fighting has spread down here. They watch us with staring faces as we go past, the mothers holding their boys tightly to them or trying to conceal them. Do they think we would take their last children from them?

We climb up out of the U-Bahn station into the hallway, which is full of broken glass lying around like a carpet. Light sounds of combat are coming over an anti-tank barrier between the buildings on Tauentzien-strasse up toward Nollendorfplatz. The area around the Memorial Church is said to be still free of the enemy. We assemble in the ticket hall and count off. Not many of the original five hundred strong combat team are left, some having split off at Adolf-Hitler-Platz and a bigger group being left behind in the underground U-Bahn tunnels. Together with the boys of the Hitler Youth we now number just one hundred, and do not know what to do next.

Saturday 28 April 1945 (Evening)

A sergeant takes over command, and we go out into the street. Dusk is spreading its veil over the city, making the figures appear blurred. Shots are coming from the direction of Nollendorfplatz. We head towards the Memorial Church, once the symbol of Berlin's most prestigious street, but today only a burnt-out ruin with a dejected-looking tower. All around is a desert of stone, not a single building remaining intact, only some of the buildings on the Kurfürstendamm still appearing to be whole.

An armoured personnel carrier is standing at the junction of the Kurfürstendamm and Hardenbergstrasse. The sergeant inquires whether there is any accommodation around, and we are directed to the air raid bunker now serving the defence. We go along Budapester Strasse and turn left into the Zoological Gardens, where the colossal bulk of the Zoo-Bunker stands close to the S-Bahn. Sentries and tanks standing under the trees stop us, and we are then led to the bunker, which is one big field hospital. All the camp beds and the air raid shelter beds are filled with wounded. Soldiers, refugees and wounded are packed close together in the passages and the big shelter rooms. We are shown into a big room, in which every last place has been taken, and have to wait for further instructions. We split up, everyone looking for a place for himself in this already overfilled room. I am dead tired from the eternal to-ing and fro-ing, not having had a full night's sleep last night and having little chance of one tonight.

There is a sound of loud voices in the room. The air extractors are working, adding to the din with their monotonous whirring, which only makes one more tired. An unbearable heat presses on one's brain and makes one's head ache. Then a new group of soldiers enters the room and pushes inconsiderately through the mass of humanity, settling themselves down beside us. They say that the Russians have thrust forward to Nollendorfplatz, and that Savignyplatz has been occupied. The enemy is trying to drive a wedge between the Zoo and Wittenbergplatz from the corner of Augsburger Strasse and Passauer Strasse. It has been possible to clear Hardenbergstrasse only as far as the Knie. The ring around the Zoo is being drawn tighter.

The civilians say that Hanna Reitsch and Major Rudel are supposed to be in the bunker.[8] It is to be defended to the last man as the last strong point offering a focal point should the government quarter fall to the Bolshevists. Almost ten thousand people can be accommodated in the bunker, of which almost half are wounded and refugees.[9]

There is talk of a secret weapon that is about to be brought into action and that will change everything for the better. There are whispers about gas or a new kind of bomb that can be directed at America and has a destructive power never experienced before. In my opinion this is just another newspaper canard to whip up new resistance. A newspaper is being passed from hand to hand in which there is talk of a relief army that will shortly be engaging in the battle for Berlin.[10]

Sleeping in all this noise is unthinkable. We are lying here in a vast coffin with metre-thick walls, in which soldiers and civilians have been thrown together from all parts of Berlin. A woman from Weissensee is bemoaning the fact that she did not stay at home, and that the Russians were able to take that district without a fight. It is in this bunker that one first gets some idea of what the lunacy of fighting has caused, tearing the civilian population into this whirlpool of destruction. They sit around without hope, praying only that this misery will end.

Goebbels has ordered the bunker to be defended to the last man. There is talk of a breach between the Americans and the Russians. On the eve of Hitler's birthday, while we were standing on the Oder, Goebbels made a speech in a radio broadcast on these same lines. A leaflet is going the rounds after the newspaper. An elderly woman with a child, who tells me that she is its grandmother and that its mother has been killed, lets me read the leaflet: 'The perverse coalition between plutocracy and Bolshevism is at breaking point. The head of the enemy conspiracy has been crushed by fate. It was the same fate that enabled Hitler to stand upright and unwounded among the dead, severely wounded, and rubble on 20 July 1944. I never saw him waver or lose heart. He will follow his way until the end and there expect, not the downfall of his people, but rather a new happier beginning to an unparalleled blooming of Germanness.'

This appeal sounds like a voice from the grave. When we were on the East Front we were goaded into holding on once more with the miracles that would soon happen. We were told that the British and Americans had made peace and that the final enemy would be the Russians. Thousands had to give their lives because they believed this yet again, even though they had been lied to so many times before, and those who returned intact to Berlin in one piece, where the Western Powers should already have been, were deceived all over again.

The bunker seems to be teeming with prominenti brought together in this battle by its thick walls, and a few Knights' Cross holders and high ranking Party officials are walking around.

A soldier suddenly says that a Gauleiter[11] had set up his command post on a platform at Potsdamer Platz S-Bahn station. Wearing a brown leather overcoat and with a submachine gun under his arm, he would walk up and down the platform grinning. He and his staff were leading a merry life in the little railway staff offices on the platform with their stocks of wine and champagne, while the refugees on the platform opposite went hungry as they sought safety from the fury of destruction raging over the city. It seemed that this 'leader of the people' was out to enjoy the last dregs of his cup of plenty. What some of the civilians have to say is almost unbelievable. However, one only has to see their sorrowful faces to see things in a different light.

One soldier says that Hitler got married in the bunker under the Reichs Chancellery yesterday.[12] A latrine rumour? That would have been a jolly wedding night under the thunder of the guns! And we still have to go on fighting for this man, to whom Germany no longer belongs! Because of the oath we swore to him, soldiers and civilians have to go on dying. Someone says that Hitler has married an actress and that she will appear as a milkmaid on the new twenty mark note.

Depression has set in. Most people do not want to believe it, and even I find it unbelievable. I think that, as a result of the shock of the news of Hitler's marriage, many of them have started thinking for themselves. Someone says that, once the capital has fallen, he is to be flown out with the whole government from Ruhleben to Brazil to continue the fight from there, in any case as far as possible from the firing, so as to be out of immediate danger. A soldier claims to have seen Hitler climb into an armoured personnel carrier on the 27th, demanding to be taken to the scene of the fighting in the Tiergarten.[13] However, I think this just another fairy story, like so many others. A few years ago it was said that Hitler had been to the foremost trenches on the Russian front and personally led an attack, but this story has not lasted the course.

Some Red Cross nurses go along the rows. It is said that the bunker is going to be transformed into a defensive position and be cleared of civilians. The bunker is the place to which all kinds of people have swarmed to find shelter, coming from all sectors and districts of Berlin, fleeing here from the wrath of war and waiting for it to blow over them. They feel secure within these metre-thick walls and can wait for the end to come. How can the bunker possibly be cleared now? This big hospital, the Berliners' last refuge? Is there still a spot in this mortally wounded city bleeding from a thousand wounds where one can be safe?

The group that arrived after us is called out and disappears. A frightened nervousness suddenly spreads. The Russians are said to have made a surprise breakthrough. Where and when, nobody knows.

Suddenly our Ruhleben combat team leader enters the room and we have to get ourselves ready. The war goes on. Then he disappears again. The civilians become restless as we get up and make our way to the door, where we wait. Shortly afterwards the captain returns and we follow him in a long file through the passage, men joining us from other rooms as we pass. Then we go down the stairs and past some sentries to step out into the night.

The heavy armoured doors close behind us. Coming suddenly out of the light into the darkness blinds us. Shells are exploding quite near and there is the thundering of heavy artillery and tank guns. The S-Bahn embankment runs along on our right, and over there is the second flak bunker.[14] We carry on in long lines. The gigantic colossus of the bunker looms behind us like a threat.

Sunday 29 April 1945

We come to the S-Bahn line and head towards the station. The Zoological Gardens are on the left. We go along both sides of the street in long columns, almost 250 men. The combat team that split off at Adolf-Hitler-Platz and fought its way down the street suffered heavy losses, and arrived at the bunker soon after us, as the enemy had pulled back into the sidestreets when darkness fell.

The din of battle seems to be coming simultaneously from the direction of Wittenbergplatz and Nürnberger Platz, and appears to be increasing in volume and getting closer. The ring around the Zoo bunker is being closed within the course of a day. The territory east of Hofjägerallee via Lützowplatz to Wittenbergplatz has been occupied by the enemy, who is simultaneously thrusting towards the government quarter and the Brandenburg Gate via the Grosser Stern, says the staff sergeant as he comes along the ranks urging us to close up. If we are lucky, we should get to Ruhleben scot-free, which still seems likely at the moment, as the noise of battle is only coming from the south and east. I am surprised that we were allowed to leave the Zoo area when every man is needed there, but the staff sergeant says that they had no provisions for us, and that the fortress commandant at Ruhleben had insisted upon our return, as our combat team is an established part of the Ruhleben Fortress defence.

The S-Bahn station building looms out of the night. The street is strewn with glass shards and rubble. We pass under the bridge on Hardenbergstrasse toward the Knie. There is a big hole in the railway tracks above us through which one can see the starry heavens, apparently the result of a big shell or a demolition.

We go along pressed close to the buildings and ruins. The noise of battle comes from behind us like a dull thunder, and tank and artillery gun shots rip through the night. A few civilians hurry past us with their heavy burdens and disappear in the direction of the Zoo. A child is wandering about in the dark, crying and lost. In front of us is a half collapsed street barricade of toppled over trams, behind which some soldiers are patrolling.[15]

Another barricade grows out of the night. Trams, one with the route number 58 showing, have been driven into each other behind a barrier of stones and concrete. The soldiers defending it say that the enemy withdrew this evening, but they do not know to which street, nor whether he is in the buildings on the Kaiserdamm.

We climb over the barricade one by one, and once more find ourselves in a no-man's-land in the middle of Germany, in the middle of Berlin. We move cautiously along the walls, for the enemy could shower us with a hail of steel at any moment. All around is one unending desert of stone, and we feel lost in this frightful wasteland. We grope our way forward step by step, stopping still and listening to the night. Once a dog starts barking, making us draw together, the sound going plaintively through the darkness. Then it is quiet again and we go on. At last we reach the Knie, from where the Charlottenburger Chaussee[16] runs to the Grosser Stern on our right. There is a barricade across the street on our right, but it is dead and abandoned. A face appears briefly from the U-Bahn station and then vanishes again.

It is now two o'clock, another night without sleep, another night of fear in which we do not know if we will survive the day. Suddenly shots coming from Leibnitzstrasse bring us fully awake, as we had been going along the street half asleep. Things are happening up front. Bullets crack and hum past, hitting the walls. We reply, firing haphazardly into the darkness as we run across the street. Then we continue on our way with our senses heightenend, feeling our way forward, and leaving a few dead behind. The enemy seems to have cut some of us off, for the firing is increasing in volume behind us. But then come some hard footsteps and some figures appear from behind us. At first we think they are Russians, but they are our own people.

Bismarckstrasse seems endless. Then the Deutsches Opernhaus U-Bahn station appears. The grill at the station entrance has been torn off and riddled with bullets, the station sign broken off and lying in the gutter. We stop and some soldiers go cautiously down into the station to see if there are any enemy around. They return after a short while and bring with them a few soldiers who had stayed behind with the refugees, being too few to attempt a breakthrough to Ruhleben on their own. As we had already been told in the U-Bahn tunnels at midday, the enemy is supposed to be occupying Richard-Wagner-Platz and Charlottenburg S-Bahn station. Whether he is on this street, they cannot say. However, it is certain that he has occupied part of Bismarckstrasse and will also have blocked it.

We try to press on as quietly as possible, but it is hopeless. Our nailed boots do not allow us to tread quietly. They stop up ahead again, and we go forward to see what is happening. There is a barricade across the street about a hundred metres away with a dark object just in front of it, presumably a Russian tank. We dare not move. Someone calls quietly for a Panzerfaust, which comes up through the ranks. Then we advance slowly, every instant expecting the frightening silence to be broken by a gunshot that will send us to kingdom come. The first ones should have reached the barricade by now, and still there is no sound. We take heart and move faster, going past the dark colossus. It is a burnt-out 'Tiger' with its turret hatch standing open, its barrel slightly bent, and some dead lying around, both Germans and Russians with their distinctive helmets. There is even a Russian woman in a brown uniform, her hair in disarray, lying among the dead.

We breathe out. We carefully climb over the barricade and carry on with quick, light steps, our group moving forward like a long snake. We are already beginning to hope that everything will be alright and that we will reach the barracks without either fighting or casualties. We occasionally come across a dead man lying alone in the street, some from our group that set out from the barracks yesterday. There is a burnt out Waffen-SS armoured personnel carrier standing at the side of the street, and an anti-tank gun close to the buildings with its crew dead. Shot up Wehrmacht and civilian vehicles stand around, and a dead horse lies at the side of the street still harnessed to its wagon. Two men with bowls are cutting large chunks out of its body with knives, and are trying to separate a whole haunch, while a third man stands by keeping watch. They look up at us anxiously and yet defiantly as we go past. Are they afraid that we will take the meat off them or make them come with us?

Another U-Bahn station appears out of the night and we get another short break. It is Sophie-Charlotte-Platz that we are passing. Here too, as almost everywhere in Berlin, the U-Bahn station is overflowing with refugees, bits of baggage and even small pieces of furniture. We go down into the station to see if it is possible to continue underground. A few remain up on the street on guard until it is decided whether we continue above or below ground.

We are divided into two groups. One combat team will continue along the street to Adolf-Hitler-Platz, while the other will take the U-Bahn tunnel. I report to the group that will go by the street, for although it is safer underground, I could not bear being down there again, I would rather fight in the bright night than in underground tunnels that can so easily become burial chambers.

We leave the station as the other group disappears into the U-Bahn tunnel. One group will wait for the other at Adolf-Hitler-Platz until a certain time. If we do not meet up by then, each group will have to continue on its own.

Some of the soldiers who had at first gone with the combat team through the U-Bahn tunnel come rushing after us. Apparently it is much pleasanter for them too above ground than in the dark tunnels, where in the dark one can be killed any moment from round a corner. We carry on alongside the walls of the buildings, our footsteps hitting hard on the pavement, stopping from time to time to listen into the night. Then we march on again hesitantly. A shot rings out in some distant street, finding a loud echo in the night-dark streets. We stop and hold our breath, trying to see through the darkness. Once a dark figure slinks across the street, and we are about to open fire, but fortunately hold back, for it turns out to be a large dog that takes to its heels with huge bounds. Loud voices come from somewhere. Are they drunks brawling, the enemy, or our own troops? We go past a barricade behind which Hitler Youths are lying around dead, one with his Panzerfaust still uncocked, another with his head smashed to pulp. We go on, sniffing the air like animals, stopping and listening, going on again. Are we the only ones still alive in these dead streets? The barricades in the side-streets have been abandoned and the occasional undamaged building among the ruins gives no sign of life either. The sky is overshadowed by a straggly blanket of clouds that only seldom allow a glimpse of the shimmering stars above. A light breeze sweeps through the streets, sending scraps of paper and burnt rags whirling in the air.

We come to a dark cutting under the street, the S-Bahn line between Witzleben and Siemensstadt. On the bridge is a barricade made of vehicles driven into each other. We force our way through between the shot-up vehicles and come to the Kaiserdamm U-Bahn station, the last before Adolf-Hitler-Platz. In the station we ask whether the combat team has come through yet. They say not. We sit down on the platform with our weapons in our hands ready to fire, and wait. At last we can hear the distant clinking of boots in the dark shaft. The Berliners who have found shelter here have settled down for the night on boxes and chairs and have lit a few thin candles that throw out only a meagre glow, causing the big shadows of the people to dance like ghosts on the tiled walls. Half torn off cinema posters and theatre programmes speak of a world long gone. A poster with a smiling woman advertises Nivea.

I put my ear to the air and listen. I can hear the sound of hobnailed boots, just as one hears the rails rattle when a train approaches. Then the first man appears out of the shaft and climbs up on to the platform. Gradually they all assemble, and we wait a moment. The night is nearly over, yet another night without sleep. How many have there been over the past year from the nights of the bombing raids until now? The body has become accustomed to them, just as it has become accustomed to having little to eat.

The we move on again. The men of the underground combat team jump back down to the tracks and disappear one after another. A few of us that had previously preferred being above ground also go with them. We others climb the steps into the night.

It has become lighter. The night is beginning to fade, but only very slowly, almost unnoticeably, the stars emitting a faint shimmer and the clouds racing low over the sky as a new day signals its arrival. We carry on alongside the buildings now feeling confident that the last station will not prove an obstacle. I am almost asleep on my feet. Our combat team has become quite small, hardly fifty men, the others all having preferred the route under the street to over it.

There are some burnt-out ruins on the right of the street, and on the left is Broadcasting House.[17] We cannot see the radio tower in the Exhibition Grounds from where we are. And then Adolf-Hitler-Platz, the former Reichskanzlerplatz, appears in front of us.

The other combat team made it faster than we did and is already waiting at the U-Bahn station. Together we continue along the route of the U-Bahn, no longer needing to fear being stopped. Another barricade appears at the Neu-Westend U-Bahn station, from behind which the first German soldiers receive us with astonishment.

When we reach the S-Bahn, we climb down to the embankment and follow it on to the bridge over the Spandauer Chaussee, where we climb down again to the road. We then go past Ruhleben U-Bahn station, in front of which soldiers from the barracks have been posted as sentries, and follow the tramlines to the barracks, but turn off left before the barrack gates to go past the Mars Film Studios. I stop when we get to the supply bunker and let the others go on. Wegner, who is on sentry duty there, stuffs my pockets with a can of meat and one of chocolate. Then I go on wearily to the Convalescent Company building that we left yesterday at noon. The last stars are fading in the sky, and in the east the new day is slowly dawning.

When I report back, I am instructed to go to the room next door where the platoon commander, Sergeant Major Kaiser, is accommodated with his men. Blaczeck as company runner stays in the runners' room. I look for a free bed space and exhaustedly creep to a palliasse in the corner. I take off my greatcoat and lie down. It is dark in the room and there is a strong smell. The snoring of several men mingles with the deep breathing of the soldiers, but I hardly hear anything; I fall asleep.

NOTES

1. Lieutenant General Weidling, the Berlin Defence Area Commander, had planned to get Hitler out by this route, and so evacuate the garrison with him. He still had about 30,000 troops, but food and ammunition were fast running out, and he saw no point in continuing the defence of the capital. However, when he presented his plan to Hitler on the evening of the 28th, the latter refused to take the risk of falling alive into enemy hands, and ordered the fighting to continue in the vain hope of relief from the combined efforts of Wenck's 12th and Busse's 9th Armies, which he had ordered, but they had no intention of executing.
2. Now 'Olympia-Stadion'.
3. Colonel Dragunsky had set up his operational base at the northern end of the Grunewald, not far from Eichkamp.
4. See Appendix III.
5. Now 'Theodor-Heuss-Platz'.
6. Now 'Ernst-Reuter-Platz'.
7. The air raid shelters referred to were in fact the big flak bunker in the Zoological Gardens and the flak control tower immediately north of it in the Tiergarten, both of which provided air raid shelter facilities to the civilian population.
8. Neither of these two famous aviators was then in Berlin, although Hanna Reitsch had only just flown out that evening from the Tiergarten airstrip, and Lieutenant Colonel Hans Rudel, famous for his tank-busting exploits, had tried to land the previous night on Hitler's instructions but had found it impossible.
9. The Zoo flak bunker was forty metres high with five storeys above ground, the highest of which accommodated the 100-strong garrison manning the flak guns on the roof, consisting of four double 128mm mountings on the roof and twelve multiple-barrel 20mm or 37mm 'pompoms', manned mainly by Hitler Youth. The fourth storey housed a complete hospital intended primarily for prominenti, the third storey treasures from Berlin's many museums. The rest of the building contained kitchens, canteens and shelters for 15,000 people,

although probably twice that number sheltered there during the battle.

10. Wenck's 12th Army had been ordered to the relief of Berlin from the line of the Elbe, but had no intention of doing so and was instead engaged in rescuing the remains of the 9th Army.
11. Nazi Party leader-cum-governor of a province.
12. Hitler had married his mistress, Eva Braun, in the Führerbunker at about 0130 hours on the 28th.
13. Hitler only visited the front twice during the war. Once in Russia and then the Oder front on 3 March 1945, on both occasions no farther forward than a corps headquarters.
14. The flak command bunker of the 1st (Berlin) Flak Division, located across the Landwehr Canal in the Tiergarten.
15. This area was defended by troops of the 18th Panzergrenadier Division.
16. Today 'Strasse der 17. Juni'.
17. Haus des Rundfunks, then home of Sender Berlin, today of Sender Freies Berlin.

CHAPTER XI

Back in Barracks

Sunday 29 April 1945 (afternoon)

It is noon when I wake up. The lieutenant has ordered that I be excused guard duty, so I have been able to sleep without interruption. The new comrades, mainly older soldiers with a few years' experience in the Wehrmacht under their belts, are lying on their beds or eating the thin water soup that was issued at midday. I get up and still feel a leaden weight in all my limbs. I go and ask Blaczeck for a spoon and get myself a helping of the thin cabbage soup, in which one can only see water almost as green as washing-up water and a few indiscernible objects floating in it. Later I go and ask Blaczeck how the situation looks. He says that the enemy has already reoccupied the Reichssportfeld, but apparently has no further interest in the barracks, or is momentarily not strong enough to risk an attack. Some Russians were brought in yesterday afternoon as prisoners, including even a commissar. They were all shot after interrogation. One can hardly wonder if they do the same thing to us!

Later I am attached to a section under the command of Sergeant Major Kaiser with the task of searching a foreign labourers' camp near the S-Bahn. We set off twenty men strong, heavily armed as if going into battle. When I ask my neighbour why we should be taking such trouble, he says that I will soon find out.

We go alongside the S-Bahn and then turn left opposite the film studios and go under a bridge. The foreigners' camp we are looking for is just behind the embankment. As we pass through the camp gates, some men and women with shocked faces run into the huts. We have to surround the buildings while the sergeant major goes to see the camp guards, who have established themselves in the cookhouse. Then we have to search the huts. Apparently arms and equipment of foreign origin are hidden here.

Each one of us is detailed to a room. When I go into mine, some women cower in a corner and look at me fearfully. One of them speaks a little German and keeps repeating that they have no hidden weapons. I search the beds and lockers somewhat superficially and then sit down on a chair. The women become a bit more confident and venture out of their corner.

'No weapons, no weapons!' they murmur continuously with monotonous uniformity. The loud call of a woman's voice comes from the next room accompanied by the hard thump of a rifle butt on the floor. The girl who speaks German suddenly says that now a few more will be shot, just like yesterday. The other women start crying, two older ones, one already with silver-grey hair, and three younger ones, but not the interpreter. Judging by her childlike appearance, one of them cannot be more than 16 years old. The noise has become louder next door. Excited voices, above which a crying woman's voice can be heard, come from the room. They are mainly Belgian, Dutch and French accommodated here. In order to stop the crying, I ask the interpreter about the men. 'Shot', is all she says. 'Only those in the kitchen are left. The others were shot.'

It has gone quiet again next door. The sound of voices has disappeared into the yard. Suddenly a shot startles me. The women cross themselves and start crying again. One of them suddenly throws herself at me and tries to kiss my hands. Shocked and not knowing what to do to stop her, I rebuff her curtly. She then releases me and pulls back slowly. Now they watch every movement I make, their eyes bright with fear. When they see that I am calmly keeping back, their tension eases and they start crying again softly.

From outside comes a call for us to fall in. I get up and go outside. Sergeant Major Kaiser is standing in the yard as the men emerge from the huts one by one. The sergeant major is holding a Russian submachine gun in his hands that was found in one of the huts. 'I am slowly becoming disgusted', is all he says. Then we have to go round once more and look under the huts to see if there is any trace of weapons or secret stores. Behind one of the barracks is a pile of dead men whom the women presumably carried there, the men who were shot as a result of a secret radio transmitter and weapons being found in one of the huts. There are also some women who had been shot with the men lying underneath them. There is a fresh trace of blood in the sand, where a woman has just been shot for raising a Hitler Youth dagger that she had concealed in her locker.

The camp guards are sitting in the cookhouse, where all the cooking pots except one have been smashed. They are young Waffen-SS boys that have been given this cushy number as a reward for their 'good work' yesterday. A few civilians, the kitchen staff who survived the general butchery yesterday because they were not there when the search took place, are sitting in a corner. The Waffen-SS men are boasting how quickly they had shot the 'yobs'. I am horrified when I think that these youngsters could be set against not only the foreigners, but ourselves as well. I suddenly recall how they had tried to press us into joining the Waffen-SS while we were in Labour Service.[1] We had to run through the night in the pouring rain, dressed only in our track suits that we later had to take off.

We were soon soaked to the skin. It was February, and we froze like dogs. That worthy Bavarian, Captain Neuhoff, whom I had dubbed 'the Bavarian Dumpling', for which he especially 'loved' me, drove us on. Then we were suddenly stopped in the middle of a field that had been transformed into a single cold mush by melting snow and rain, and he asked: 'Who volunteers for the Waffen-SS?' But nobody did, just as nobody had volunteered when the Waffen-SS lieutenant had asked the same question at noon. 'What? You still don't want to?' and the dance went on. Lying down in the filthy melting snow, in the ice-cold puddles and streams, having to carry our track suits in our hands. Then we got again: 'Those who volunteer can go straight back to camp and have three days off duty.' Hauffe volunteered and could go, but he was the only one that night to give in. And we ran on through the wet fields, meadows and woods, stumbling over streams and tracks, all ice-cold and shivering bundles of nerves, having only one thought: 'This is not right!' We stopped when it gradually became light, 'So that those stupid villagers don't see it', as was cynically said. Then we could go back to camp, have a wash and put on our uniforms, and the night was over. There was breakfast and then the military training resumed, but nothing more was said about volunteering for the Waffen-SS

We set off back, marching through the camp gate, leaving the bloody place and the people to breathe out again behind us. They have survived once more, but who knows for how long?

We stop at the U-Bahn station, where some civilians come out of the cellars and beg for food. They have not eaten for three days, but we cannot help them, for we have had hardly anything to eat ourselves over the past few days.

We go back along the street to the barracks. One of the emergency companies, hastily thrown together and sent off to the fighting, comes towards us, old men with grey hair, young boys wearing items of Hitler Youth uniform, and a few soldiers among them. Today these are the combatants being recklessly sent into action. Practically all the civilians are wearing some worn-out item of uniform over their civilian clothing, mostly a grey jacket or a field cap. This tired mass has found its destiny as cannon fodder.

Back in barracks I lie down on my bed and try to forget the events of the last few hours, but without success. Later on I take a walk through the barracks and look at the buildings as if seeing them for the first time. The signs on the walls – 'March Company', 'Action Company' – have long since become illusory. They should now read: 'Hospital Block I', 'Hospital Block II', 'Refugee Block I', 'Refugee Block II' and 'Refugee Block III'. A sign should point to the Reichssportfeld, and on the barrack squares should be 'Cemetery I' and 'Cemetery II'. Then the graves should be signed: 'Mass Grave I', 'Mass Grave II' and '100 Dead' and '200 Dead'.

That is what the barracks have become, a vast cemetery for bodies and souls.

There are refugees with their children and babies lying in the straw and the sand of the stables. It is draughty as the windows are missing and there are shell holes in the walls that have been carefully covered with torn horse blankets and bits of cloth. The people are vegetating with their children and babies in this environment, having been without proper food for days and little water, trying to eke out their last provisions.

There is a big yellow BVG bus in front of the Quartermaster's Stores filled to the top with boots and uniforms, and some soldiers are emptying it as a clerk stands by and carefully records every item in a large register. These things are no longer being issued to the soldiers, the battalion commander having forbidden it, but are to be stacked neatly in the shelves until either a direct hit blows them to the winds, or the enemy takes them, although neither the battalion commander nor the quartermaster with his register will be there to check them out. There is nothing one can do; orders are orders, as the quartermasters say, and schnapps is schnapps, so everything will be neatly recorded in triplicate, of course. Military procedures must be maintained, even if death personally intervenes.

The bins are still standing behind the canteen where not so long ago the Hungarians used to scavenge through the slops from the Officers' Mess. Who knows where they are now?

I go back into the cellar. Blaczeck comes into the room and gives me some cigarettes. Later on the guard duties are allocated, but I am lucky, I do not have to get up until eight in the morning.

Evening comes slowly. Some Hindenburg Lights flicker on the table lighting up the faces of the soldiers sitting round it. The sergeant major's runner tries to get his hands on my pistol. A crafty old soldier, he tries to talk it off me, but it does not work and he goes away with a long face. Later on the sergeant major comes in and shares out the day's rations, one packet of long life bread among four men, when for days we have not had anything worthwhile in our stomachs. I open one of the cans that Wegner gave me and eat, then I stick piece after piece of chocolate into my mouth until I feel half way satisfied.

It is almost eight o'clock. The even tone of voices makes me sleepy and my eyes close. Someone tries to get a few tunes out of a mouth organ and others sing along quietly with it. There is a deep, even roaring around me like being at sea, powerful and yet peaceful, and I sink into the world of dreams.

Monday 30 April 1945

I am on sentry duty outside the cellar entrance. Although the world is falling apart, the normal procedures have to be followed under all circumstances for the ceremony of changing the guard. With a solemn face, the prescribed number of steps have to be paced out over the rubble and glass shards, and the guard commander assumes his new dignity for twenty-four hours.

Fortunately the Convalescent Company is not involved in the barrack guard duties. That is the responsibility of the March Company, which in its reconstituted state was not sent to the front, for the Russians had advanced so far that it was spared the journey, and now it is employed as the guard company and for the battalion commander's personal protection. It constitutes practically the only established personnel remaining in the barracks, which have become a real dove cote for the emergency companies.

We have to maintain a sentry on our building because the company sergeant major believes that we will forget obedience to orders without it. Sentry duty symbolises the responsibilities and duties of a soldier, and what has been laid down cannot be altered. However, whenever possible we shorten our spell of duty by smoking, for the time when we took everything lying down is past. We are no longer the innocents we were when we were called up.

I shorten my time on duty as much as possible by reading a novel that I have started behind the half open door. A small boy with a large shopping bag, his clothing in rags, comes up to me and asks me for some bread in a low voice, saying that he has not had anything to eat for days. As he stands in front of me, half starved and bleary eyed, hardly a child any longer with his old man's face, I would gladly give him everything, but unfortunately I have nothing left. Every evening we get some thin slices of long lasting bread that have to last us throughout the day. I follow him with my eyes when he leaves with his sad face.

The civilian population have had no rations issued to them since the Russians occupied the city's outskirts. Police and Waffen-SS troops have been guarding the various Wehrmacht supply depots and the vast cold-storage depots on the Spree until either the enemy came and captured them, or blew them up at the last minute. Although the city's inhabitants have had nothing to eat for days, supply depots are still being blown up in a senseless rage of destruction.

Hüsing comes to relieve me shortly after nine o'clock. I have been lying on my bed only a few minutes when the company sergeant major drives me off again, sending me up to the second floor, taking my weapon with me. The stairs are strewn with rubble and glass shards. Gerke is standing on the landing and tells me that we have to guard the things lying around in the rubble. Later on the company sergeant major comes along with some of the others and orders them to clean the rooms that are unoccupied. Most of the lockers and tables have been thrown over or broken and there are big holes in the walls from the tank gunfire. Dented steel helmets and bits of uniform and equipment are lying around in the rubble and glass shards, and the company sergeant major has mounted a sentry on these pathetic remains because he is afraid that the stragglers accommodated on the floor below might help themselves to them. Anyone who takes even a single item is to be shot immediately. It is laughable, indeed absurd to put a sentry on this, for the Wehrmacht would not be any the poorer. It seems to me that we are simply guarding rubble.

Schomberg relieves me shortly after ten o'clock. I only know his name from the list that the company sergeant major thrust into my hand and which I hand over to him. They are all new faces to Blaczeck and myself. It is just fortunate that we are now in an established unit and not back again with any old company to be thrown into the fighting in some other part of the city.

I go across to the supply bunker where the rest of the comrades who were called up with me and were wounded in the bombing attack of 23 April are to be found. They were lucky to have been wounded then, and so spared some hard times, for otherwise they would not be alive now. For their part in the defence of the barracks with Sergeant Rytn they have been given the guarding of the supply bunker as their reward, and so have a well-fed job and are spared the attentions of the company sergeant major and other superiors.

Wegner brings me some grease and I take my pistol apart to give it a good clean. Then we both fire a shot into the air, Wegner with his 98 and myself with my 76.5. In the past whenever a shot was fired on the barrack square without an order to do so, the old soldiers told us, the man firing it got three days in the 'cooler'. Those must have been happy times when there was still no war. I would much prefer to go into the 'cooler' if only shooting were totally forbidden.

Sergeant Major Kaiser's runner tries to take my pistol off me. He says that the company sergeant major would confiscate it for disturbing the peace at the front, especially as it had never been entered in my paybook. The runner, who comes from Berlin and is called Einsiedel, is one of the few among us who still believes in a miracle. He is always going to the lieutenant to report any of us who say anything against the war or about Hitler that he does not like. Fortunately, the sergeant major and the lieutenant seem to be of the same opinion as ourselves, and although they naturally give us a reprimand, it is only to observe form. And that is the odd thing about the company sergeant major. He does not believe in a good end himself, but is such a 'good soldier' that he would still go through Hell if ordered to, and would take us with him, even if he knew it was pointless.

Then I go to see Windhurst, who is guarding his Russians in the Medical Centre. He has pushed a table under the cellar window and is reading some newspapers with some other old men from his Landeswehr battalion[2]. He gives me one of the sheets. It is the *Panzerbär*, a combat newspaper for the defenders of Greater Berlin. Big headlines in red letters strike the eyes. 'We are holding on!', 'The hours of freedom are coming', 'Bulwark against Bolshevism', 'Berlin: mass grave for Soviet tanks', and 'Berlin fights for the Reich and Europe'. Reichs Defence Commissar Dr Goebbels has signed as editor. The newspaper's emblem is a Berlin bear holding two Panzerfausts in its claws.

One article reports that the Reichs Marshal Göring is ill. He has a chronic heart condition that has now reached an acute stage. As these times demand the full engagement of all forces, including healthy leaders, he has asked to be released from his command of the Luftwaffe. Hitler has agreed to his request and a completely unknown man has been appointed in his place, a Colonel General Ritter von Greim, simultaneously promoted to Field Marshal, is Göring's successor, a commander-in-chief without a command, for the Luftwaffe has ceased to exist.[3]

Another article speaks about the relief Wenck Army, which is marching on Berlin. 'Reserves marching in from all sides' is its title. This army is supposed to have already reached the Nikolassee from Potsdam and to be involved in hard fighting on its approach to the capital. A new army is said to have been formed in Pomerania under the direct command of Grand Admiral Dönitz and will be engaging in the battle for Berlin within the next few days. Also, in the Cottbus area, an army group consisting of troops from the Czech Protectorate is making rapid progress towards the city.[4] In the meantime Berlin women and those youths not yet in field grey should form a bulwark with the Wehrmacht against the Bolshevist onslaught.

The relief Wenck Army, which was already talked about at the Zoo, seems to me to have the best chance to get into the battle in time. Some wonderful things are said about this army, which is led by a very young general. According to the newspaper reports it should already be here, as the paper is already four days old.

There is also an extract from a speech broadcast on the radio by State Secretary Naumann on 28 April: 'The soldiers fighting under the eyes of the Supreme Commander-in-Chief are convinced that their steadfastness will rectify the situation, and that they will be able to defeat the enemy. The personal hand of the Führer can be felt on the whole conduct of this battle.'

Then Windhurst hands me another leaflet with an order of the day to the Wenck Army. 'Soldiers of the Wenck Army! An order of immense importance has removed you from your combat zone facing the enemy in the west and set you marching eastward. Your task is clear: Berlin remains German.'[5]

We calculate between us how long it can be before the Wenck Army can free us from the enemy's vice, and we come to 3 May. Until then we shall have to continue to hold out. The number of armies said to be coming to our relief almost cheers me up.

Then Windhorst gives me another article cut out of the *Panzerbär*.

'Major General Bärenfänger's reply: "Refused. Out!" The commander of the combat sector in the northeastern part of Berlin, Knights' Cross with Swords holder Major General Bärenfänger reports that his men have prepared a proper grave for Soviet tanks on the Frankfurter Allee battlefront. Soviet parliamentarians appeared in his command post to demand his surrender, but Bärenfänger replied in an angry voice: "Refused. Out!" Anything else said would have been superfluous.'

Even this article is already several days old and would have been long overtaken by events. According to the latest reports, the enemy is already at Pariser Platz and has taken the full length of Friedrichstrasse. This means that the city centre is virtually cut off and the government quarter lost. Even if the enemy cannot penetrate the Führerbunker under the Reichs Chancellery, one does not know what escape routes lead out of that maze of underground bunkers. Consequently, the battle has lost its last sense of purpose.

Together with Windhorst and his comrades we then discuss the Wenck Army, which for us is like an anchor that can still save us from the whirlpool of destruction. Windhorst's comrade is sceptical. He thinks that if the Wenck Army is so close, it would be child's play to liberate the outermost districts of Spandau and Ruhleben first, and then advance in a fan on the city centre, especially as this army is equipped with the latest weapons and is bringing several new war materiels with it. People have long talked about a gas that will change things.

It has gradually come up to noon, and my stomach is demanding its rights. Even if it is only thin watersoup with hardly any nourishment in it, it has the magic effect of giving satisfaction, if only for a few seconds. The company sergeant major reads out a list of names entitled to half a litre of soup each. We sit in the sun and spoon it down.

With the emergency companies that came into the barracks today were some Waffen-SS girls in uniform who had volunteered only a few days ago, and also among them a few female Flak Auxiliaries certainly not older than 15 or 16. Most of them were called up within the last few days to build barricades. Later they had simply been given uniforms and, since they had been cut off from their homes by the enemy, to avoid starving they had to join the emergency companies to be able to draw rations from the barracks. They, like ourselves, are the flotsam of this war.

In the afternoon Sergeant Major Kaiser comes and calls out a few of us by name. We have to get ready and smarten up our uniforms a bit. I give my boots a short brushing and knock the dust out of my tunic. Then we have to go outside and parade in front of the cellar entrance. Sergeant

Rytn comes along from the supply bunker with Wegner, Löffler and Bräuer, and joins us. Rytn says that I should try to get assigned to the supply bunker guard, then I would not have to stand guard day and night, and would have my rations to hand. The lieutenant would surely agree, as I had been a member of the Rytn combat team. But I no longer want to, although I often like to go over there and get something to eat.

The lieutenant arrives and takes the sergeant major's report. We are a colourful mix of soldiers and NCOs. We count off. Then the lieutenant reads out a list of names. One is missing – Sorgatz, who has stayed behind guarding the supply bunker. Then the lieutenant gives the words of command. We are just eighteen men altogether marching off to Battalion Headquarters, where we halt. We are sent to the canteen. The whole thing is baffling. None of us knows what is really happening. The lieutenant has stayed behind and the sergeant major leads us into the canteen, where we go into the hall. Shortly afterwards the lieutenant comes in with the battalion commander and makes his report. The latter stands us at ease, then announces that the Führer and Supreme Commander-in-Chief of the Armed Forces has awarded him the Oak Leaves to the Knights' Cross for the steadfast defence of the Ruhleben Fortress, and that he will continue to hold the position to the last man in this last bulwark against Bolshevism. He further announces that, in recognition of the brave conduct of the garrison, the city commandant has given him permission to issue honours and awards.

Sergeant Major Kaiser is called forward and awarded the Iron Cross First Class. He already holds the Iron Cross First Class from the First World War. Some of the men are generously promoted to lance corporal and also get the Iron Cross. There are a few among them who had fought to the last. Many are promoted for having come back to the fortress from Russian captivity. Then Sergeant Rytn and ourselves are left. The battalion commander calls us forward and praises us, as the youngest, for having held out so steadfastly. I suddenly recall the trench and the sergeant's threats about deserters. He had certainly played his part in preventing us from running back to the barracks when we thought all was lost. But the sergeant stands there with a calm face and does not seem to be thinking about it any more.

Later we go outside. The last thing I hear is that we are each to get half a litre of schnapps. That is all that sticks in my mind. I think I must be dreaming, for we have been given the title of 'Obergrenadier'. What a pompous title! Furthermore, we were even told that we might also get Iron Crosses, but the battalion commander has first to check back to find out whether he can award promotions and medals simultaneously. But I am not going to think about it. For me and just about all others of my age, a medal used to seem to be the greatest thing that one could achieve, but now I have come so far that I can only think about how many dead this fuss has cost, and I am not going to be whipped up into holding out just for a piece of tin.

The battalion commander's Oak Leaves have truly been dearly bought. Piles of dead, soldiers, Hitler Youths and Volkssturm have paid for his award while he sat in his bombproof cellar and chased the runners out into a hail of steel with his orders. And now he is trying to raise the fighting spirit of the troops with a shower of medals and promotions, when it is simply impossible, as it has long been buried with the unending, senseless demand for more sacrifices.

I go to see Windhorst for another talk. He is not there for the moment, nor are his colleagues. I climb through the window into the cellar, where the Russians are lying around peacefully chatting. I sit down and leaf through an illustrated magazine that has appeared from somewhere. Then Windhorst himself climbs though the window down the little ladder. When I ask him where he has been, he says only: 'In the canteen.' I already knew that. He has been promoted to corporal and has been awarded the War Service Cross First Class and the Iron Cross Second Class. The companies based on the barracks and those companies that happened to be in the barracks today have had a very fruitful harvest of medals, and it looks as if they want to dish out all the medals lying in the barracks in order to spur the men on to renewed fighting.

Windhorst complains about these laughable decorations. He thinks that now all sorts of things can be expected if they are being so free with their medals and promotions. I have to laugh. Calling us 16- and 17-year-olds 'Obergrenadier' after only five weeks of service is laughable when once it was only given to old sweats who had been shunted into dead ends. One cannot simply remove the pain of war or wipe out the number of dead with these extravagant gestures. I suddenly recall the staff sergeant in Lietzen with his brutal features, seeing the drunkard who slipped over to the enemy lines at night and strangled the enemy with his hammerlike hands, for which he had a chest covered in decorations as prizes and awards for all-round and continuous murder.

I go back to my accommodation and lie down on my bed. A confusing sound of voices reaches my ears and I fall asleep. It is evening when I wake up again. Two Hindenburg Lights are burning on the table, filling the room with a faint light, but this does not bother me: we have long been used to nothing else. Guard duties are allocated after supper and today I get the last one, from eleven o'clock to midnight, sharing it with Becker. This is the third time I will have had sentry duty today. Later we get some watersoup and a five-millimetre-thick slice of long-life bread, which only leaves you hungrier once you have eaten it.

Suddenly the sergeant major bursts into the room. 'Come with me immediately! Civilians are plundering a food supply train!' I quickly fasten my belt buckle and grab my pistol. Then we dash outside. It is already fully dark and we stumble over the rubble. The guard on the barrack gates points in the general direction of the railway embankment, where civilians are supposed to be at work. I would dearly like to turn back, but perhaps I can get something for my stomach. We climb over the fence that separates the embankment from the street, and scramble up the bank, crawl under several coupled-together wagons barring the way, and then see a white goods wagon, which some civilians are unloading. We encircle the wagon and the sergeant major asks them what they are doing. One of them says that they are unloading the wagon on the orders of the Volkssturm battalion commander in charge of the Volkssturm units at the Deutsche-Industrie-Werke. The sergeant major immediately forbids any further unloading and announces that they are to be shot for plundering. The civilians look shocked, and one of them suggests that the sergeant major should go to the battalion commander and shoot him if necessary, for he was the one who had given the order to unload the wagon. The sergeant major agrees and disappears into the night towards the Deutsche-Industrie-Werke.

We stand around not knowing what to do. The sergeant major has given us the order to wait for him, but we feel superfluous, laughably so, and we are sorry for the Volkssturm men, who are just as hungry as we are. It is slowly getting cold and we have not got our greatcoats. Several of us have already disappeared between the goods wagons. The civilians are talking quietly among themselves. Then the man who had been taking the big cartons out of the wagon gets up and comes across to us and tries to persuade us to leave. An old soldier asks him what is in the boxes. 'Tins of meat', he says, and rips open a box. The soldier takes two tins and disappears into the darkness.

There are now only four of us around the wagon. The civilians have got over their first shock and are laughing about the eagerness with which Sergeant Major Kaiser would have shot them out of hand. We feel a little uncomfortable and the butt of their laughter. I would like to disappear, as the sergeant major has already been gone half an hour. Perhaps the Volkssturm commander has offered him a glass of schnapps, something Kaiser could never refuse, and they have been drinking to brotherhood, while we have been forgotten. I go to the wagon and help myself to a tin, and then another, and stick them in my trouser pockets, which bulge like sacks, but I still dare not leave the scene. Of the four men still standing around, each waits for the first of the others to make a move, but none of us can decide, and so we all stay.

There are only three of the civilians left; the others have slipped away between the wagons, so our orders have already become irrelevant. I am gradually beginning to freeze, and I curse myself for not having gone with them. Nevertheless, it would have been difficult to leave earlier.

At last I have had enough. The sergeant major has been gone almost an hour, and there is still no sign of him. Apart from that, my guard duty starts soon. I go up to the line of wagons and slip through over the rails in the shadows beneath them.

I am hardly back in the accommodation when the others also return, complaining about the sergeant major leading us into such an escapade. I have to get myself ready. The sergeant major is still not back. Most of the others are lying on their beds asleep. I slip on my greatcoat and grab my rifle, then extinguish the light and relieve my predecessor.

The night is quiet, with a starry sky hanging clear over the city. The big trees rustle gently as if they are having a conversation. Once a dark shadow slinks across the earth and vanishes among the trees. The flash of a torch can be seen occasionally from the barrack gates, revealing people and their surroundings. I have lit a cigarette and am smoking it slowly behind my cupped hand. Torchlight flashes at the gates again illuminating a soldier who has come in from the street. His footsteps ring as if lost in the quiet night, which is undisturbed by any other sound. The soldier stops right in front of my entrance. I quickly stand to attention and stick the cigarette in my pocket, but he is already inside. It is Sergeant Major Kaiser, and apparently not quite sober. It seems that nothing has come of the 'shooting'.

As soon as he has disappeared into the cellar, I fish out the still burning cigarette from my pocket and quietly smoke on. There is also a tiny point of light in the air on my right that occasionally glows and goes out again.

Tuesday 1 May 1945

It is midnight and there is still no sign of the relief. The sentry who came on duty with me is also waiting at the other doorway. My eyes keep closing and my stomach is grumbling. The single thin slices of long life bread morning and evening are hardly enough to counter the overwhelming feeling that we have not eaten at all. Even the butter, which is issued generously and with which we can completely cover the bread, makes no difference. It would just be bad luck if one choked on it.

I look at the time. It is almost ten minutes past. I go across to the other cellar entrance, but the sentry has disappeared, so I go down the steps and into our sleeping room. The air is hardly bearable and has a bitter smell like a stable. Becker, who was on duty with me, is already lying on his bed asleep. The guard duty list is lying on the table. Gesche and Köpp have the duty from midnight until two o'clock, but I do not know them and do not know whom to wake. Staff Sergeant Köster, who is just turning over on his camp bed, blinks for a moment, so I shake him awake and ask where these two soldiers who should be on sentry duty are sleeping. He only knows that they are in the next room and then is away again.

I go into the next room where the 'prominenti' are accommodated.

Sergeant Major Kaiser, two sergeants and six corporals are lying around, as well as the SS girls who came into the barracks yesterday and could not get undressed fast enough. There appears to have been some sort of orgy here, for the girls are lying between the soldiers more or less clothed. They appear to feel better off here than when they ostentatiously swore to fight to the last man and to the last woman.

The light on the table has almost gone out. I shake one of the sleepers by the arm and he sits up with a start. I ask him his name. He looks at me blankly and murmurs that I already know him. 'Ditto', is all I can say. I shake the next man and tell him that he is on duty, and I have found the right man. It is Köpp. As he gets up, the blanket slips exposing the girl next to him lying stark naked, her firm breasts hitting me painfully in the eyes. Then she feels the cold and pulls the blanket back over her body. I turn round and go back to my sleeping room and crash down on my bed.

I am so hungry that my stomach is in cramp. I reach under the bed for the tin that I hid there from yesterday's alleged plundering of the railway wagon and open it with my bayonet. I am lucky, it is tinned meat. I fish it out of the tin with my spoon, but it is not all meat, only a thin layer with millet gruel underneath that tastes awful cold. I manage to get it down somehow, then throw the tin away under the bed and chew a sweet. Although I have not slept properly for days, I am not really tired. My body has got used to it and carries on functioning like a robot.

The guard reliefs are ready at last and come out of the next room. It is almost one o'clock and they have saved considerable time with their dawdling. The light on the table begins to flicker and finally goes out. It is now completely dark with just a thin shaft of light coming through a crack in the door to the next room. Several of the sleepers are loudly trying to saw down the Tiergarten.

There is a banging and noise in the room. I sit up half drunk with sleep. The sergeant major comes along the passage singing 'May has arrived'. Then I am properly awake. I get up and look for my mess tins that someone else has held on to. I find them at last in the next room, where one of the SS girls is eating out of them. If I am not mistaken, it is the one from last night.

There is a steaming food container standing outside that holy of holies, the lieutenant's command post. For breakfast on this holiday – I do not know what one can celebrate today when no one is working and the factories are in ruins – apart from the inevitable slice of long-life bread (only one as usual) we get a thin watersoup with a few cabbage leaves and some meat that one needs a magnifying glass to fish out. I could not stand eating in the room, where one could cut the air with a knife, and so go out into the square and sit on a fallen tree. It is real May weather. The sun is shining in the sky and peace reigns, and one yearns a bit for an excursion like in the old days.

Two dogs appear to have noticed that it is spring. The little one is behaving so badly that the big one bites his tail and sends him howling into a corner. A few men from the emergency companies are sitting around the square. As they are not in barracks for longer than twelve hours, they do not get any food. They will then be sent back into action in any old corner once more. They are nearly all Volkssturm men between 14 and 70 years old who look as if they will desert as soon as they can.

The company sergeant major comes up the steps and see me eating. He says that I must hurry as we have to clear away the rubble in the barracks and clean out the barrack-rooms. I make my getaway as soon as he disappears, not intending to be seen again this morning.

There are some big holes torn into the walls of the canteen building, and broken glass from its many windows is lying on the grass and paths. A dirty Red Cross flag is flying above the door of the East Block. The whole barracks seem to have become a field hospital. Some medical orderlies are carrying out the dead on stretchers to the square and casually tipping them out on the ground where the bushes around the war memorial have been chopped down to make room for the mass graves. A big rectangular grave is already half full of dead laid out like boards, one row lengthways and the next sideways.

The big door to the armoury is open and civilians are unscrewing the vices from the benches. Everything is topsy turvy. While on the one hand everything is being blown to the wind, on the other hand everything has to be kept in order. On my way to the supply bunker some shots come from the Reichssportfeld, where some clouds of smoke are rising. Wegner is sitting at the bunker entrance and is oiling a pistol that he has taken apart. He is armed like a robber baron. There is a captured Russian pistol, whose automatic action he is trying to master but resists all attempts to dismantle it, a German submachine gun, a Russian submachine gun with a drum magazine, and a Russian 9mm revolver. He is now trying to reassemble the Police 98mm pistol. Löffler's face appears in the bunker entrance, and he comes closer when he recognises me. He too is equipped in very warlike fashion. I look quite peace-loving in comparison with just my 76.5 Mauser pistol.

The we go into the bunker. The paymaster, who is responsible for the supplies, is making an inspection and carries a long list showing the number of boxes and sides of bacon. Sergeant Rytn is standing behind him, counting along with him. In the last room, where their beds are, whole boxes of tins of sausage and meat that they have been able to organise in the course of time are stacked and cardboard cartons of sweets and chocolate stand under their beds, so whenever they feel hungry they only have to feel under their beds. It is like fairy tale land, and only a few steps away we only get two slices of bread per day. However, they have nothing else, but with the sausage and meat and the other things they have, they can get along fine without bread.

Wegner suggests that we go along to Ruhleben U-Bahn station, where some more foreigners are said to have been shot today. We stuff our pockets full of sweets and set off. As we leave, we bump into Bräuer coming along the passage wearing the leather jacket of the Russian commissar who was captured and then killed. Wegner's trouser pockets are full of the colourful occupation money that the commissar had on him.

Just as we are leaving the bunker, a machine gun rakes the barracks again, and we quickly have to dive for cover. On the way to the U-Bahn station we pass the Hungarian huts behind the burnt-out film studios. None of the Hungarians are left. Most of the walls have collapsed, revealing their interiors with torn clothing and palliasses covered in piles of excrement, and dishes and glasses filled with urine. A few ripped apart pillows are lying on the tables, the floor, or the torn-apart double bunk beds. The lockers and stools are tipped over and smashed, as if the Vandals had been.

We step through the shot-up wooden fence on to the street and walk to the station. Left against the railway embankment lie some tipped over wagons that had been meant to block the street but were swept aside like toys by the Russian tanks. A concreted-in tank gun from the Deutsche-Industrie-Werke is aimed towards the barracks, but the Russians came from the opposite direction, so that the whole concreting-in work was pointless, like everything else done today.

Shortly before the station, which lies on the right-hand side of the street, and past which a street leads to the Reichssportfeld, the old trees have been blown up to lie across the roadway, their tree stumps looking like shaving brushes.

There are women and children sheltering in the U-Bahn station cellars with their worldly possessions, having come mainly from the houses around the Reichssportfeld when the Russians got near. They have also taken in some of the wounded, since the barracks were long overfull. The tired occupants have used up the last of their food reserves and have eaten nothing for hours, and since the water supply was cut off, they have had no water at all. The young women have to go as far as the barracks with their buckets to fetch water from the pumps, to be shared out drop by drop. We give the children all the sweets we have in our pockets and leave. We tell a girl to come to the bunker that evening to collect some food for the people there.

We climb up to the street again. The ticket offices and the kiosks at the barrier have been completely destroyed, as if attacked with axes. The valuable machine in the ticket office has been smashed out of all recognition and a few dead civilians are lying among the rubble. Wegner says that the foreigners from the camp near the station did this damage and so were shot.

Then we walk back to the barracks together. The sentry is surprised when we suddenly appear in front of him, as we had not gone out through the gates.

A horse and cart are standing in front of the bunker, and the paymaster is loading boxes with the comrades. Ostensibly they are intended for the combat team at the Deutsche-Industrie-Werke, but I think that he is going to hide them somewhere in order to be able to go into hiding should there be a retreat, and then remain under cover for a while. Once the wagon is fully loaded, he disappears, taking the keys to the rooms with him, not knowing that Sergeant Rytn has a spare set.

I stuff my pockets full again, stick a couple of tins of sausage and meat under my field blouse, and walk back to my accommodation. Some soldiers and commandeered Hitler Youths are cleaning the glass splinters and paper from the streets on the company sergeant major's orders, sweeping up the last corners with home-made brooms of twigs. I go past quickly and down into the cellar, hide the stuff under my bed, and then go out again. In front of the barrack blocks that used to accommodate the March Company and are now packed with refugees, stand the two pumps that have had to supply the whole barracks and the surrounding area since the waterworks ceased to function. A long queue is waiting with buckets, pots and cans, as two soldiers sweat over pumping water into a big cauldron that is clearly intended for the kitchens.

Windhorst is standing in front of a big cellar window at the medical centre, where a brick wall serves as a shield against splinters. He has to guard the Russians who used to work in the kitchens and quartermaster's stores and are now regarded as unreliable. Together with one other soldier, he has to stay day and night in the room where the Russians are lying around on palliasses. He has obtained a few improvements for them, including blankets. The relationship between guards and prisoners has become quite cordial, and some of the Russians withdraw from the table as we climb in through the window.

Windhorst pulls a newspaper from his pocket, an old *Völkischer Beobachter*. He opens it out and gives me a pamphlet. It is an Armed Services Report, no, an announcement that is supposed to be made as a special announcement on the radio next morning. I read: 'It is announced from Führer Headquarters that our Führer Adolf Hitler fell for Germany at this command post at the Reichs Chancellery this afternoon while fighting against Bolshevism to his last breath. On 30 April the Führer appointed Grand Admiral Dönitz as his successor. He assumes with that the position of Head of State and Reichs President. Reichs Minister Goebbels was appointed Reichs Chancellor.'

I feel as if I had been hit on the head. But then it is all the same to me, it hardly bothers me, for the time is over when I once thought that the heavens would collapse if that man no longer lived. Then we discuss it, and the news that is so meaningful begins to pale. Only the thought that I must really be free now, as the man to whom I swore an oath no longer lives, makes me happy. But Windhorst says that Hitler has declared that the oath applies to his successor.

The street in front of our building has been cleaned down to the finest speck, as if licked clean. They are already dishing out the food in the cellar, so I get my mess tins. This time it is thick pearl barley, which at least satisfies our hunger for once. The man serving it out says that this time the emergency companies were to have got some food, but as they have long been sent off into action, we are getting their share.

There is a heated debate in progress as I come into the cellar. Sergeant Major Kaiser has been spreading the news of Hitler's death, and everyone has got worked up. Silence falls when he says that Hitler could well have taken poison to avoid being beaten to death by the soldiers. Everyone is wondering to himself whether the death of Hitler will also mean the end of the war.

At three o'clock I go on sentry duty. Blaczeck stands at the other door. It is the company sergeant major's hobby horse to mount sentries whatever the circumstances, no matter how pointless, and he is constantly chasing the staff in the cellar to ensure they get no peace. Most of us hide to avoid being seen all day. Now he is going through the streets with that notorious slave-driver, Sergeant Richter, chasing people, and a few of their victims are picking up glass splinters carefully with their fingers and flattening the torn-up earth.

After guard duty we parade outside the building. Lieutenant Stichler marches us to the canteen building, where pay is being given out. There is a long line of soldiers in the cellars waiting to be paid, that is only moving forward slowly. At last we are in the room. A clerk takes our paybooks and records the receipt of the money. Then we have to sign for the receipt of RM 60. The paymaster is sitting at another table. He looks briefly at our paybooks and then hands out the banknotes with an elegant gesture. They are all brand new banknotes, fresh from the mint, all RM 20 notes of the 1939 issue. Some comrades have been given banknotes that look like photo paper and are signed by Himmler. We then return singly to the accommodation, some joking that: 'This new money is good enough to secure ourselves a window seat in the mass graves.'

I take off my jacket and lie down on my bed. The cellar is almost dark, and one only slowly readjusts to the light when someone comes in from the outside. Some new SS girls seem to have arrived meantime, for the faces sitting round the table and flirting with the soldiers are new. Most are still wearing items of uniform. I am only surprised that the company commander has not said anything about this state of affairs, but he too has one of these 'ladies' that he fancies in his command post. If the girls go on flirting like this, we should have a merry time here tonight, and those girls who were here yesterday or before will have to hang back until the new girls have been 'tried out.'

During the afternoon the company sergeant major's wife arrives in the barracks with their two boys. He does not seem all that happy that the soldiers will now have a hold on him should he find start finding fault with the presence of the 'ladies'. His wife is quite the opposite of him, being dainty and delicate. Of course, it is not every sergeant major who can choose the size of his wife, and no doubt he would have slipped home more than just a little of the supplies taken from our rations...

I go back up to the street. The barracks are now a vast field hospital and refugee asylum, soldiers being rare within these walls, women and children greatly outnumbering them.

An emergency company, consisting almost entirely of civilians, is coming through the gates. They halt in front of the battalion headquarters building and are allocated accommodation, but only for one night. Tomorrow they will be reassembled and sent off somewhere or other. Their young sergeant major, a small 19-year-old hardly bigger than a dwarf, walks past in highly polished boots. I have not cleaned my boots for days, nor changed the clothes that I have been wearing day and night. I have not changed my white vest for five weeks and have not even washed myself for days, but this sergeant major is going around with highly polished boots, treading carefully over the rubble that is still lying in the street over which he has no jurisdiction. He would dearly like to see it like the other streets that we have cleared of every last stone and piece of glass.

An armourers' workshop has been set up in the battalion headquarters building and old rifles and weapons of all sorts and from all countries are being made serviceable and pressed into the hands of the emergency and Volkssturm companies. Often the ammunition does not fit, so the men get weapons without bullets. Weapons and weapon parts are being brought in to be cleaned from every corner of the barracks and the roadside ditches, and are not held on to for long before being issued out again.

It is gradually becoming dark. The newly assembled combat teams are streaming out through the barrack gates to go back into the fire again as stragglers, refugees and women come in seeking shelter in the barracks. Many of those now returning have been here before, perhaps only hours ago, have been shot up in combat, or have turned round on their way out and have come back. The last is not easy, for a few soldiers or Waffen-SS men follow each group to prevent them breaking up before they reach their combat destination, if necessary with their weapons.

I have laid myself down on my bed and am trying to sleep. Suddenly there is a howling in the room that makes me jump off my bed. The lieutenant has ordered schnapps to be fetched from the canteen. Later the sergeant major comes in and gives us some of the details. On Grand

Admiral Dönitz's orders, the Berlin Army is to break out to the west to Wenck's relief army early tomorrow morning[6], and the supplies lying in the barracks are to distributed in order to avoid having to blow them up.

Some soldiers bring some large cardboard boxes into the room. We press round the table as they are opened, standing there as if dazzled. Whole packets of long-life bread, a case of dripping, boxes of quarter-hundredweights of sweets and butter, sausage in tins and tinned meat. Everyone helps himself to as much as he can grab, then we sit down on our beds and eat, cramming so much into our stomachs that we are soon like stuffed geese, hardly able to move. And the eating will continue the whole night long, as sleep is not to be thought of. The sergeant major has acquired a large can and sends me with it to fetch schnapps from the canteen. There are some big barrels of schnapps in the canteen cellar and boxes of tinned milk and fruit are being given out open-handedly to both soldiers and civilians. It seems that a state of euphoria has set in. Everyone seems to be afraid that this could only be a dream. The barracks are unrecognisable. The mass of previously held back provisions are pouring over us like a flood, and the refugees have brought suitcases to carry away their booty. Already some drunken soldiers are throwing their arms around each other. All the dams of discipline have been burst wide open and there is no holding back any more. Everyone is trying to take as much as he can. Who knows what tomorrow will bring, we are only living for today!

The barracks is like a disturbed anthill. Soldiers are hurrying across the square with big cans full of schnapps and disappearing into the buildings, while civilians stand in the shadows of the buildings waiting for their relatives to give them a hand to take the things they have obtained to their accommodation.

Here everyone is eagerly packing. Packs are only being filled with edible items. The sergeant major brings in some cigarettes, from which everyone gets five hundred. I do not know how I am going to carry all my stuff, as I only have my haversack and greatcoat pockets available. We pack and smoke away, drink more schnapps, then unpack and repack what to us seems the most valuable.

Then we sit down at the table and chat. Our tongues loosen up, the can having already been refilled several times. It is astonishing how much has been drunk. With the girls, who are also drinking a considerable amount, we are about thirty persons in all. I drink some schnapps and then chew a slice of long-life bread.

The time goes by slowly. The can is emptied yet again and a soldier gets up and takes it to be refilled. The atmosphere is lively, but I hold myself back a little. The slice of bread after every beaker of schnapps helps absorb the alcohol and I remain relatively sober. The sergeant major is drunk and makes a long speech about victory.

I go to the runners' room to see Blaczeck, who is still packing. Here too there is schnapps and the runners are attacking it liberally. Blaczeck shows me an appeal from Grand Admiral Dönitz that has just been broadcast to the troops. It is in the same tone as Hitler had used, so it seems that not much will change, even though he is dead.

The appeal 'To all Germans' goes as follows: 'German men and women! Soldiers of the German Armed Forces![7] Our Führer Adolf Hitler has fallen. Conscious of the responsibility, I assume leadership of the German people at this deeply fateful time. My first task is to save German people from destruction by the Bolshevist enemy. The fighting will continue only long enough for this. So far and so long as the achievement of this aim is hindered by the British and Americans, we must also continue to defend ourselves against them and fight on.'[8]

Another Order of the Day is entitled 'To the Armed Forces'

'German Armed Forces, my comrades! The Führer has fallen. True to his great idea of protecting the people of Europe from Bolshevism, he has given his life in selfless sacrifice and met a hero's death.[9] He has become one of the greatest German heroes. We dip our flags in deep respect and mourning. The Führer has named me Commander-in-Chief of the Armed Forces. I have taken it on to pursue the fight against Bolshevism, and to pursue it until the task is fulfilled. You have accomplished such great feats that today, as you now sense the end of the war, Germany can demand further efforts from you. I demand further unconditional commitment, discipline and obedience. The execution of my orders will prevent hatred and destruction. He who holds back from his duty is a coward. The oath of loyalty sworn to the Führer applies without repetition to me as the Führer's appointed Head of State and successor as Commander-in-Chief of the Armed Forces. Germany soldiers, do your duty! The lives of your people depend upon it!'

I am astonished. No word of peace. Only 'holding on'. Is the fighting to go on as hard as ever? Even when Hitler is dead? The Order of the Day resembles those that were coming out a short while ago bearing Hitler's name. The Western Powers are hardly mentioned, only the Bolshevist enemy. Should there be anything in what has been rumoured over the past few days, that Himmler has been negotiating peace with the British in Hamburg?[10] Even if only with the Western Powers. In any case he will have to hurry, as there is not much left of Germany still unoccupied, only a few linked positions in the north, the Czech Protectorate, and apparently to the south of Berlin, where Wenck's Army is supposed to be.

I go back across to the sleeping room. With the effects of the alcohol, everyone is merry and having a good time. Then somebody says what he is going to do when peace comes. The general feeling is that Dönitz will not continue the fight. Meanwhile the can is being refilled again and again. Everyone is drinking as much as possible, and the company sergeant major, the lieutenant and the other officers are looking quietly on. It soon occurs to me that they are letting us do this because not many of us will survive tomorrow.

Suddenly the company commander enters the room and waves those down who start to get up. He sits down with us and takes a beaker of schnapps with us. Then he suddenly speaks about the Order of the Day from the new Head of State and tries to explain to us why the fighting has to go on. 'We will have peace with the Western Powers within the next few days,' he says, 'then it will be only against the Bolshevists, and that will not go on much longer with them, only until the summer, and then you can all go home. And the oath to our glorious Führer is transferred to his successor. Whoever wants to desert will be shot. The war goes on!'

As he leaves, all becomes quiet. Nearly all have become thoughtful about what he has said, having already seen peace before them, and now it has been pushed back into the unreachable distance, and the fighting goes on, the dying goes on.

There are already a few asleep on their beds, but not for long, for they are woken up and come back to the table to join in as far as possible. The door stands open to the next room where the SS girls are sitting at the table or lying on the beds next to the soldiers. The waves of enthusiasm strike even higher, but do not break out into a wild ruckus, for it is more of a restrained enthusiasm and the voices are subdued. Everyone seems to be alone with their thoughts. Suddenly two girls come in draped in a blanket, which they suddenly throw aside and stand there stark naked, and everyone howls with laughter. Then it is quiet again and the girls disappear into the next room like sheepish poodles.

The sentry comes in bringing a blast of cold night air. Everything is scattered around. A few soldiers are sitting at the table, and the snores of those who have had too much come from the corners. Then two other girls come in and sit down beside the sergeant major. We carry on drinking, wanting to drive away the spectre of tomorrow, not wanting to see the vast misery that lies over us, because we want to live.

NOTES

1. The Waffen-SS did not come under the conscription laws applicable to the Wehrmacht, i.e. the Army, Navy and Air Force. Consequently enrolment was restricted to volunteers only.
2. The Landeswehr consisted of older reservists assigned to local defence.
3. A poorly worded signal from Göring, asking whether he was expected to take over the leadership in the event of Hitler's death, had been used by Martin Bormann, Hitler's secretary, as evidence of treachery, and Göring had been forced to resign all his offices or be shot as a traitor. Hitler's orders to von Greim to report to the Führerbunker had consumed some of the few remaining Luftwaffe resources and resulted in von Greim being badly

wounded in the leg, when the sole purpose had been to inform him of his new appointment, which could more easily have been done by wireless.

4. Wenck's 12th Army had stopped at Ferch on the Schwielowsee south of Potsdam with the intention of rescuing the remains of the 9th Army from the Spreewald 'cauldron' and also of offering an escape route for the Berlin garrison, but had no intention of proceeding any farther. The new formation in the north, the 21st Army, consisted of only two Regiments and was swept up in the retreat of the 3rd Panzer Army before it could do anything. Army Group 'Mitte' to the south had already lost most of the 4th Panzer Army in the opening battle and so stood no chance of breaking through to Berlin. The German title for the Czech Protectorate was *Protektorat Böhmen und Mähren*.

5. This pamphlet had been distributed in Berlin to encourage the Berliners and the defence.

6. This had nothing to do with Dönitz. Shortly before his suicide, Hitler gave General Weidling permission for a breakout, but Goebbels stopped it because he wanted to negotiate with the Soviets the formation of the new German government formulated in Hitler's will. When these negotiations failed, he and his wife committed suicide after murdering their six children. It was now too late for the planned breakout, and on the evening of 1 May General Weidling decided to surrender next morning, but gave permission for those who wished to do so to attempt a breakout before he surrendered.

7. In German the word 'soldier' applies equally to sailors and airmen.

8. Dönitz's priority at this time was the continued evacuation by sea of the millions of Germans fleeing the Soviets along the Baltic coast.

9. Bormann had not informed Dönitz of the true circumstances of Hitler's death. Hitler had committed suicide with his bride at 1530 hours on 30 April, i.e. the day before, in despair at the chances of Berlin being relieved.

10. Himmler's talks with the Swedish Ambassador to Germany, Count Bernadotte, concerning negotiations with the Western Powers, were revealed in a Reuters report broadcast by Radio Stockholm on the evening of 28 April.

CHAPTER XII

Breakout

Wednesday 2 May 1945 (Morning continued)

Two Hindenburg Lights are burning on the table, throwing out a flickering, weak light. We are sitting on stools and boxes, eating our rations, for although we have been given virtually nothing to eat for days, it is suddenly all there with more butter then we have seen in all our military experience. There are boxes of butter and dripping standing in the corner that already nobody looks at as we stick slices of bread thickly smeared with butter into our mouths. The big can of schnapps stands on the table, and we tip the sharp stuff down our throats, not knowing what tomorrow will bring. Sergeant Major Kaiser is no longer quite steady on his legs and is drinking to brotherhood with all of us, tears in his eyes, clasping us and kissing us on both cheeks. He has shaved badly and his bristles scratch like a yard broom. We enthusiastically call him 'Artur' and 'Du', never having dreamt of being on such intimate terms with a Prussian-smart staff sergeant or sergeant major.

There is a sergeant sitting across the table speaking to the SS girl in civilian clothes next to him, being affectionate and calling each other 'Schnucki' and 'Franzi'. He suddenly pulls out his pistol roaring out that he is going to shoot a rival lover he has just identified. I try to get the pistol off him before he does any damage, but he suddenly passes out and two men drag him off like a lump of wood into the next room, lay him down on a camp bed and come back again. Sergeant Major Kaiser is staring with glassy eyes into space and murmuring incomprehensibly, so we persuade him to lie down and put him on his camp bed, and a loud snoring concert soon indicates that he has fallen asleep.

Lieutenant Stichler enters the room and waves us down when 'Attention!' is called, then produces various bits of paper. He calls me over and gives me the commendations for the Iron Crosses. Sergeant Major Kaiser, who already has an Iron Cross from the First World War, gets another one. The sergeant sleeping drunk in the next room also gets an Iron Cross. We take our commendations and stick those of the sleepers in their pockets. The lieutenant gives me the commendations for Sergeant

191

Rytn and Wegner and the others, and orders me to give them to them at the bunker they are guarding.

I put on my greatcoat and go outside, where the night is bright and clear. Soldiers are hurrying across the square and disappearing into the shadows of the buildings. Ahead by the gates several soldiers are pushing aside the remains of the barricade to clear the street, and several flat carts are being hastily loaded outside the canteen building. A lamp burns over the entrance to the East Block with the Red Cross flag waving in the wind above it.

Wegner is sitting in front of the entrance to the bunker playing with his submachine gun, and we go into the bunker together. Against the walls are stacked cases of chocolate and sweets, butter and dripping, sausage and meat, all in tins. The individual rooms are now open since the paymaster, who had the keys, loaded up a wagon and disappeared with it, and one can see boxes stacked up to the ceiling. I hand out the commendations as Sergeant Rytn comes out of the sleeping room attracted by the noise. We squat down together on some boxes, slipping chocolate into our mouths, then some butter, and in between always a slug of schnapps. All are a bit shattered by the news and are boasting about what they will do when they get to Wenck's Army. I have to hurry, as the lieutenant has called. I stuff my pockets full again and walk back.

A few shots ring out from the Reichssportfeld and hit the buildings. Weak lights flicker in the windows of some of the individual blocks, and occasionally a figure rushes past like a shadow. The dead are stacked up in front of the war memorial, where the wind has partly torn away the tent-halves covering them. I go to the medical centre again where Windhorst is guarding his Russians in the cellar, sitting comfortably at the table reading some old letters. The Russians lying around the room look up at me as I climb in through the window. I quickly make my farewell with Windhorst, we exchange our civilian addresses, and then I go back.

I look in vain for the sentry as I go down the cellar steps. In the accommodation everyone is making a noise and singing, even the sentries have joined in. Sergeant Major Kaiser is sitting back at the table and is one of the loudest. Several soldiers are kneeling on their overfilled packs trying to get the straps to fasten. One is standing by the case of dripping filling his mess tins with a spoon. Several opened boxes are standing around forgotten.

It is two o'clock and I should really be going on guard duty. It has become quieter in the room and everyone is lying on their beds, except for one lying right across the table. The can of schnapps stands next to the quietly burning Hindenburg Light, so I get up and fill my water bottle. Then a sergeant comes in calling for the sentries. I look at my watch; it has just gone three, so I turn over on my other side and go back to sleep. Two men get up from their beds complaining and swearing, and leave the room.

I try hard to open my eyes, but they seem glued together. My skull aches as if a thousand devils were banging around inside, and at last I get my lids open. Soldiers are standing around the table finishing their packing and someone is trying to wake up Sergeant Major Kaiser. I carefully get out of my bed and go out into the dawn. The sentries have all been withdrawn and an oppressive silence has settled over the barracks. The fresh air gradually wakens me. My headache has diminished, leaving a tired, dull feeling. I go back down into the cellar, where the door to the command post is open and the company sergeant major is standing in the supply room trying to get us to move and stuff more food into our pockets. Blaczeck comes out of the runners' room, where the company sergeant major's wife is seeing to her boys. I quickly eat some slices of bread and empty a whole tin of sausage with them. Two of the SS girls, now wearing civilian clothes, are slapping Sergeant Major Kaiser's face, trying to bring him to his senses. The sergeant is barely sober and is reeling on his feet. The lieutenant suddenly enters, sees the girls with the sergeant major and the drunken sergeant, and begins screaming with rage. Then he slams the door shut.

The sergeant has become completely sober and even the sergeant major has got up. We put on our greatcoats, pick up our weapons and take a last look round. I go up into the barrack block and along the passages. Sandbags, steel helmets, bits of uniform and equipment are lying next to weapons and ammunition in the rubble, and big holes in the floors and walls show the damage caused by the night attack. The old Armed Forces Reports are still hanging outside the Duty NCO's room. Russians on the Oder, Americans and British in Bavaria and Hesse, Göttingen and Hannover occupied by the enemy. That is all that is left of 'German Livingspace.'

Vlassov Army posters and some with victory slogans hang torn on the walls. The tables and beds in the barrack-rooms have been thrown about and old newspapers are lying around. I go back down the stairs, whose bannisters are broken and some of the steps splintered. A Panzerfaust lies abandoned among the rubble and the wind comes in through the windows whipping up rags and paper into grotesque shapes.

Snores are coming from a dark cellar room. Curious, I push open the door and stop in surprise. It is the room next to the armoury where the armourer, Staff Sergeant Richter, is accommodated. Some light comes in from a half-open window. On the table stands a bottle of schnapps together with some other bottles, and butter and dripping, loaves and slices of bread lie scattered around. The base of a burnt out Hindenburg Light stands next to the bed on a chair, from which hangs a tunic with its shiny braid and pips. A dress is lying on the floor with a blouse, a pair of lace-up boots and a pair of ladies' shoes. The staff sergeant is lying snoring in his bed with a very young girl next to him whom I recognise as a waitress from the canteen who had volunteered for the SS only a few days ago. The notorious slave-driver, Staff Sergeant Richter, known among ourselves as 'The Bulldog', whom everyone would make a big detour to avoid whenever they saw him on the square, has discovered the pleasures of life.

A whistle blows somewhere. The snoring has turned to groans. I turn round, trip over a step and slam the door hard against the wall, then drum with both feet against the wood until the vaulted ceiling thunders. From inside comes a strangled cry as I go on down the passage.

Soldiers heavily laden with their packs and boxes, their weapons slung, are coming toward me and climbing up the steps to the square. I go to my bed to collect my weapon. Sergeant Major Kaiser is barely sober and fully apathetic. 'Leave me alone', he keeps on murmuring as the two girls and now some soldiers try to get him to move. Then they give up, and only one girl remains behind with him. There are some packets of pistol ammunition lying on the table, so I quickly stick them in my pocket, put on my cap, take my steel helmet and rifle, and go outside.

They are all standing around in front of the door, the whole complement of the Convalescent Company and the company commander, Lieutenant Stichler, who is walking up and down distractedly and looking at his watch. He is dragging his stiff leg more than usual and leaning on a stick, his face is tired and drawn, but his eyes sharp. There is a box of sweets in front of the doorway into which we dip from time to time, and a big box of cigarettes is quickly emptied. Most of us are loaded down like donkeys. Not only are our packs stuffed full until our shoulder straps seem ready to snap, but our pockets too, standing well out from our greatcoats, and many are also holding cardboard boxes in their hands.

The company sergeant major comes up the steps with his wife and two boys. His wife is carrying a heavy blue rucksack and has bags in her hands. The boys too are heavily laden. They live near the Knie U-Bahn station and fled to the barracks when the Russians got close, and now they are abandoning everything to go with their father on this last journey to the west. Staff Sergeant Richter appears sleepily in the doorway and behind him comes the girl with a crushed dress and creased blouse, a field cap at an angle on her head. She has dark rings under her eyes and looks dazed. Lieutenant Stichler sends a soldier to get Sergeant Major Kaiser. The boys from the bunker with Sergeant Rytn have still not arrived, so Blaczeck goes to get them.

The companies are coming out of the other barrack blocks and heading for the gates, and civilians are coming and going in the street. We fall in. The women and girls who want to join in the big flight with us wait alongside. Then we move off, slipping into the stream of humanity flooding relentlessly along the barrack streets, moving slowly forward. Civilians from the Volkssturm companies overtake us quickly, trying to

194

make their way home. At last we reach the gates. 'Stay together!' shouts the lieutenant back over the column, then we turn into the main stream swirling along the street outside and are quickly separated, for the street is blocked with vehicles of all kinds, big tractors pulling artillery pieces, tanks, horse-drawn artillery, motorcycles, officers' limousines fully loaded, many with a woman inside wearing an elegant fur coat, all jammed in an inextricable tangle. Horse-drawn carts are even trying to make their way forward along the tram tracks that line the sides of the street, and soldiers are pushing their way through between the vehicles. The bulk of the troops from all the strong points still engaged with the enemy are now pushing their way through to the west in the breakthrough to the Wenck Army, which should be somewhere near Potsdam.[1]

I let myself be driven along by the flood, while trying to keep in touch with the rest of the company among the vehicles and columns. On the right soldiers and civilians are hurrying forward along the railway embankment, and others are trying to climb up the bank in order to make better progress. On the left are allotment gardens with the inhabitants standing at their garden fences looking at the street. It has become even more difficult to move forward. Many cars appear with officers standing beside them, walking around excitedly and calming their wives or girlfriends sitting in the vehicles. Through their windows one can see elegant suitcases, carpets and clothing stacked up in the back. These gentlemen can see their hopes being dashed, for they thought it would be so easy, the soldiers would go ahead and clear the way, driving the enemy out of the buildings and off the streets, and then they would drive through comfortably in their limousines, stuffed full of their baggage and things under the protection of our weapons and tanks to 'break through' to the relief army and so escape the witches' cauldron in Berlin.

We pass under the S-Bahn bridge and then there are some burnt-out buildings and ruins alongside the street. In front of us is a mass of people unable to move, and I can hear sharp infantry fire. There are women among the soldiers carrying bags and rucksacks, some holding children by the hand. Most are people from outside the city who had fled in from the west or are afraid of the Russians. Some soldiers disappear into the buildings. Suddenly I see our company sergeant major with his wife behind him looking after the boys. The lieutenant's face also appears for a second and I make my way towards him, elbowing my way through, but the streets are fully blocked, so I press close to the buildings. The sea of people is dammed up behind a barricade. A mobile four-barrelled flak gun sends a burst to the Spandau town hall, from where shots are ripping into the barricade. A bridge across the Havel has been blown and lies in the water.[2]

On the right the S-Bahn tracks from Spandau main railway station pass between the buildings, and behind the barricade is an underpass. The enemy fire has eased off a bit as the flak gun sends its deafening salvoes across the river. I jump over the barricade and dive down the street. There are some dead lying on the pavement and in the roadway. machine gun bursts and rifle shots whip past and strike the walls.

At last I am standing in the underpass and can breathe out again. Behind me the street is almost empty, except that one can see soldiers' steel helmets showing above the barricade. The odd man jumps across successfully or stumbles, collapses and remains lying.

Shots ring out ahead again. Several soldiers have gathered under the bridge, their faces wet with sweat. Our company sergeant major and his wife have got through safely, and the boys too are standing there trembling. Suddenly a truck comes out of a side street and races over the dead and wounded. Its windscreen is splintered, the driver's face distorted and determined. He races past and we jump out of cover and run across to the pavement opposite. All hell has broken loose. machine gun salvoes hit the walls, grenades explode and walls collapse, then we are through and fall exhausted into a quieter pace.

There are ruins left and right. The flood of people has eased off, pressed tight under cover in a dead angle against the barricade. Only the odd soldier, woman, civilian or child is getting through alongside the buildings, and others are sitting down in the rubble resting. I have put on my steel helmet and stare at the street, listening to the sounds of combat. The buildings look as if they have been sawn off, mostly at the first storey and their cellars have collapsed and, amid their broken brickwork, people are struggling through to us, through the ruins and the streets with only one aim, one hope; to get to the west to the Wenck Army, away from Berlin's rubble waste, this vast cemetery. Everyone runs, racing through the fire. The dance of death has begun and the big reaper is mowing his broad swathes through the rows of women, children and soldiers.

The street ends and a big road junction appears with house facades and ruins, in which hundreds of people are crowding. On the left the street rises gradually up to the bridge. The street looks swept clean, but people are crouching on the steps leading up to the bridge, and soldiers are pressed behind the walls of the ruins leading to the Havel embankment. Occasionally a few people jump up out of the shelter of the steps and run across the bridge. The mass of people growing behind us in the dead angles begins to spill over. Beside me among the soldiers are women with babies in their arms, old women, children and young teenagers of both sexes. I look carefully over the top step. Shots are racing across the bridge, and the horror hits me for the bridge is swimming in blood.

They are calling from below and pressing forward. I take another deep breath and jump up and run into the tacking of the machine gun bursts, throwing myself into the death mill as the bullets strike all around. The road surface is slippery with blood and there are bodies lying around and hanging over the bridge railings. Vehicles and tanks race across grinding the bones with a crack. I dive forward, not seeing any more, just driven by the thought of finding over.

Then I throw myself down and slide behind a pillar. There is a dead man alongside me. A smashed truck has driven into the bridge superstructure and is stuck in the roadway, and a soldier and a woman are seeking cover between its wheels from the fire. Now shells are hitting the bridge. I jump up again. I can see figures ahead of me running and stumbling as if through a fog. I am without feeling and run, jumping over the dead and trampling on the wounded. Everyone is for himself and has no time to think of others. Then I reach the end of the bridge and crouch down behind the barricade, gasping for air. Shots wing over my head and hit the bodies. The number of figures on the bridge is increasing. Women with babies in their arms and holding children by the hand, Hitler Youths, girls, civilians, old men and women, fall to the ground, dragging down others with them, riddled with bullets and streaming with blood. Death plays his dance, mowing his bloody path. Tanks roll over the bridge, over people, squashing them to pulp, churning them up with their tracks and a wide street of death and blood, of bits of corpses and torn bodies spans the river murmuring beneath the bridge.

I run across to the shelter of the buildings, for only the bridge is under fire. A Luftwaffe General[3] is already gathering soldiers and flak auxiliaries to him. There is a sudden explosion on the bridge and an ammunition truck blazes red like a torch in the roadway. People run past it as it sparks and bangs. The bridge superstructure has been destroyed and people are falling into the river from the opposite bank of the Havel and swirling away. All Hell has opened up.

We creep along close to the buildings, still individually, one by one. The bridge now forms an almost insuperable barrier. Women go along holding crying children by the hand. Everything has been torn apart, but there is no stopping now. We come up to Spandau town hall, which is on fire. The tower soars above as if not having anything to do with it, surrounded by the flames. Shots come out of all the streets, driving us on. There are no pauses. Dead civilians wearing white armbands are lying in the street, and there are shot-up and burnt-out vehicles standing on the side. The S-Bahn underpass is under fire, and we have to go through it. I stop under the bridge. On the right the S-Bahn line goes to Spandau-West station, and on the left the blown bridge leads to Spandau main railway station.

We go along past the buildings with our weapons cocked ready for action. We shoot into the sidestreets and into the windows of the buildings whenever we suspect movement. A civilian comes across the street carrying a heavy bag and a soldier stops him. A shot rings out and the soldier sinks to the ground as the civilian vanishes into the nearest building, and some soldiers storm in after him. A German tank is burning on the street, its ammunition exploding, sending fragments howling into the air. Flashes come from its turret. We run past.

Machine guns are tacking up ahead. Occasionally the face of an occupant appears in a building and pulls back in terror. Ground-attack aircraft are combing the streets with the fire of their machine guns and cannon, chasing us into the buildings.[4] Then we dash out again and carry on. We are also under increasingly heavy mortar fire and jump into a slit trench that runs alongside the road against the fence between the buildings, duck down and stick our heads in the sand.[5] The trench gradually fills and a Waffen-SS officer tries to drive us out again with his weapon to clear a garden path on our left, but he threatens in vain, for we are not obeying orders any more.

The firing has eased off a bit and familiar faces appear on the street. Lieutenant Stichler, Staff Sergeant Richter and his girlfriend, Blaczeck and other soldiers of the Convalescent Company, and soldiers and civilians, women and children who have escaped from the Hell so far, are coming up from behind one by one. The dance of death continues, the curtain sinking slowly on the big tragedy of Berlin, and we keep going towards the Wenck Army, in which we see our last hope, but still do not know what will happen when we get to it.

The ground-attack aircraft have gone. We go on slowly past the buildings. On the street to the right is the red brick wall of a factory, then the buildings come to an end. We have gone into the hallway of an apartment block. There is a Waffen-SS armoured personnel carrier standing at the crossroads, and some soldiers are trying to set up a machine gun in the street, but do not come back, lying there dead, and a combat team has been shot up while crossing the field. The soldiers have gone into the surrounding buildings, waiting for the fire to lift. I spot the face of the lieutenant for a second behind the factory gate across the street and run across to safety. A Waffen-SS officer says that they are only enemy supply troops in the gardens. Does he think that we are going to fall for that? Part of our crowd from the barracks have gathered behind the gate. Suddenly mortar fire starts up. We go on, passing through a large workshop filled with lathes and milling machines. The ceiling has holes in it from the earlier fighting. Then we go through a sawmill. The wall of one of the sheds is broken and cut planks are lying around and some dead are lying next to fresh craters. We clatter over the planks, cross some grass and climb over a low fence. In the distance on the right is a railway line and there are little houses and summerhouses in the gardens in front of us. We have reached Staaken Garden City.[6]

The artillery fire increases, hitting the shed behind us and sending the planks whirling into the air. Now it is hitting the gardens, the houses and the paths. A little air raid shelter in the sand in front of us is packed with people. We go inside the house and climb down into the cellar. A few wounded come in behind us and are bandaged. The windows are shaking in their frames, the cellar and steps tightly packed, the smell of blood and sweat filling the room, and some children are crying. The shells are exploding outside. I go up into the house, not being able to bear it any longer in the cellar, where a direct hit would turn us all into mush. There are fresh traces of blood in the hall and on the door, and I go into the living room, where the decoration shows good taste. The windows are broken and glass splinters are lying on the floor. From the kitchen one can see the railway line, behind which are supposed to be the Russians, according to the civilians, and one can make out dark spots moving about on the tracks. A man hurries up the garden path and vanishes into the house opposite. I go into the bedroom and look out into the garden. Where once was the small air raid shelter is now a big hole in the ground with dead and torn bodies scattered around. A wounded man is brought into the house by two soldiers. He has a splinter in his abdomen and his scrotum has been torn off. He will not last out much longer, as there are no doctors or nurses to help him.

When it quietens down, the comrades emerge from the cellar. The lieutenant says that we must stick close to his heels. Then we slip out of the house and go on to the garden path. The man from the house opposite shows us the way, and we move off, climbing over garden fences, along little open drains full of water, and across paths that are under fire. We go over more fences and at last reach a garden, go into the house and down into the cellar.

We are now twenty men from Ruhleben. The occupants, two elderly people, bring us chairs and stools. They appear to be frightened of us, for the white flag is still hanging over their front door. They say that the attack came as a complete surprise for the Russians, and that the officer living with them had warned them to leave everything as it was when he left them this morning. He should be coming back again today. I sit on my steel helmet and doze. Lieutenant Stichler pulls a map out of his pocket and explains to us what we are going to do. We have to get through Staaken to the Döberitz Training Area. The Wenck Army is behind Döberitz village, where they have taken up positions to wait for us. We will then get several weeks' rest and be accommodated in huts that the Wenck Army has set up for us. Reichs President Dönitz himself with his staff will explain the situation to us in the hutted camp. The towns of Potsdam and Nauen should already have been retaken by the Relief Army.

There are not many young faces left in the room. Of those that were enlisted with me five whole weeks ago, only Blaczeck is here. Wegner and the others have disappeared without trace. We were 150 young men then,

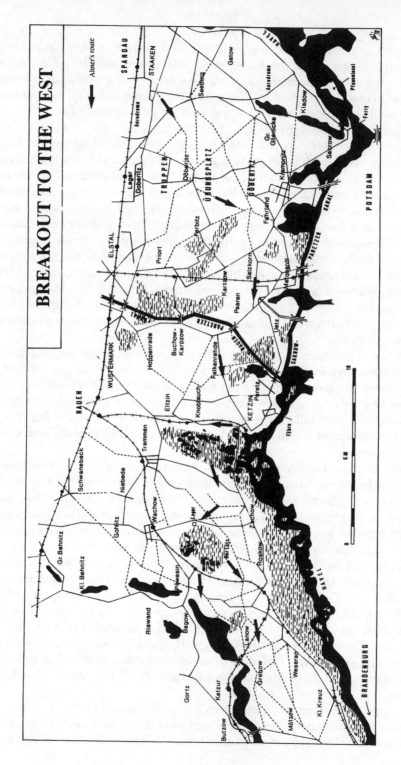

and now only eight are still alive, of which two of us are here. Who knows, perhaps the others are also now dead?

It has quietened down on the street. From somewhere or other comes the howling of tank engines, and we leave the cellar. Some officers and soldiers are standing at the street corner with some tanks, vehicles and assault guns parked under the trees. A Luftwaffe general is leaning against a tank talking to a Waffen-SS major. Soldiers are standing around in the gardens of the houses, in the cellars and on the street. Then we start moving. Women and civilians are sitting on the tanks with big pieces of baggage, holding on to the turrets and guns. The tanks roll forward and turn right into the street, passing close to the parked trucks and cars. The engines roar into life and they race past through the streets with rattling tracks, turn round the corner and vanish from our sight. Tank after tank races past, fully laden with women, soldiers and civilians. Then it happens. There is some hesitant firing, then the roaring becomes one big din. The enemy are firing from the houses at the vehicles going past. All hell has broken loose again.

The trucks are stormed by the troops. Although according to the orders only the wounded should climb aboard, nobody cares about that any more, for no one is prepared to give up the place he has fought for. Those who cannot get on try to get out of the place by making a big detour. Everyone is pressed tight together on the trucks with women, children, soldiers and civilians piled up on top of one another in the back. I sit on the left front wing of a truck, having no proper hold, my fingers having to press into the slits of the bonnet. A young girl is sitting on the right front wing holding on tight, and people are clinging like burrs to the cab, the running boards and the sides of the truck. Then the truck moves off, the engine roaring into life and we shoot along the street, a strong slipstream hitting me in the face, making my eyes water. I clutch on tightly, bracing my feet against the thin front bumper. The truck swings round a corner and I nearly fall off. Shots ring out from the houses. The enemy is standing at the fences and lampposts, shooting at the passing vehicles.

A wounded man is sitting half upright in the street. He looks at us rushing towards him and vanishes as the truck goes over him without even a bump. There is a scream, and the right hand wing is empty. Two slender hands clutch the metal of the bonnet and slip away. Trees and houses fly towards us. We take the bends with the truck skidding, driving over dead and wounded, threatening to tip over as we take the curves at top speed, taking off and slamming down hard again. My steel helmet has slipped down over my face and I cannot see anything. I can only hear the slipstream whistling around my ears.

We stop suddenly and I get down off the truck with stiff legs. Troops are fighting across the fields beyond the village and from behind us come the sounds of the Hell we have just been through. A few dead who were killed on the way are thrown off the truck, then an ambulance goes ahead of us with blood dripping down to the earth from it, and we climb back on our truck as the ambulance turns round the corner. The engine roars into life again and we race into another dance of Hell. The trees, houses, the dead, and the enemy shooting at us openly as we race by. A machine gun fires bursts at us from one corner and is soon passed, and we still drive on. The way has no end to it and the firing does not stop. Is this going to go on all day long?

At last things quieten down, the din of battle is behind us and the truck slows to walking pace. We have left the village and are driving along a track churned up by tank tracks. Shots come from a slit trench in the field on the left, a few hand grenades are thrown across and the firing stops. Several vehicles are stuck in the sand with their tyres shot through, while others are trying to move on again, and eight horses are struggling to extricate a gun that has slipped into a roadside ditch. Soldiers and civilians are taking the same route, even some women among them, and it is a wonder that they have got through unscathed.

There is a hold-up just in front of us. The road turns right at a farm and a truck has got stuck on the bend. Suddenly shells explode close to the road and a truck in front of us bursts into flames. The passengers jump off and run into the field with their clothes on fire. Another truck is hit and torn bodies with their limbs ripped off are hurled into the air and fall around, blood spurting about. The car in front us cannot move as a mangled corpse is stuck between its wheels. Then the explosions occur all around us, striking into the tangle of vehicles that have run into each other, throwing metal and bits of bodies around. The next shell could hit our truck, so I jump off the wing and go over to the right, where a trench runs under the fence into the field. Suddenly something hits me, throwing me down. I look at it in horror. It is a bloody something without either head, hands or feet, just a bloody, smashed torso. I run along the trench as if whipped by demons. My uniform is red with the blood that seems to be raining from the sky. I jump out of the trench, which is full of civilians and women, and run on in the open. Ground-attack aircraft are racing low over the ground and fountains of steel and muck are erupting, and shrapnel is bursting overhead, showering us with splinters. The cries of those hit shrill through the air. On the bend in the road is a jumble of burning, overturned, shot-up vehicles and people. Figures are running across the fields through the hail of steel, falling and lying still. The trench runs under the broken fence and two girls are trying to get a bicycle through the hole, but then give up. Dead and wounded are lying around as crater after crater appears in the earth. A herd of cattle that were grazing nearby, and have been driven crazy with shock, stampede among the explosions, knocking people over, and tanks are rolling over the fields with howling engines, crushing the dead and living under their tracks. I

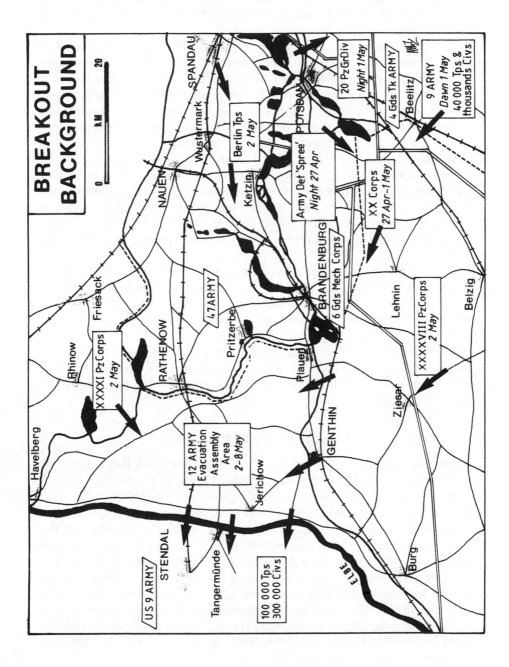

BREAKOUT BACKGROUND

0   20
kM

US 9 ARMY

STENDAL

Tangermünde

100 000 Tps
300 000 Civs

ELBE

Burg

GENTHIN

Jerichow

12 ARMY
Evacuation
Assembly
Area
2-8 May

RATHENOW

4 7 ARMY

Havelberg

Rhinow

XXXXI PzCorps
2 May

Friesack

NAUEN

Pritzerbe

Plaue

BRANDENBURG

6 Gds Mech Corps

Ziesar

Lehnin

XXXXVIII PzCorps
2 May

Belzig

XX Corps
27 Apr–1 May

Army Det 'Spree'
Night 27 Apr

Ketzin

Berlin Tps
2 May

Westermark

SPANDAU

POTSDAM

20 PzGrDiv
Night 1 May

4 Gds Tk ARMY

Beelitz

9 ARMY
Dawn 1 May
40 000 Tps &
thousands Civs

run across the fields as shrapnel bursts high above us, showering us with splinters, as shells howl past and explode, and low-flying aircraft roar over the field knocking the people down.

I am no longer running. I have given it up. Death is faster, and takes those it wants. The earth down here seems to be nothing but Hell. I stagger into a small dugout of the hutted camp that lined the road and has now been torn into a thousand pieces. Outside people are running past and falling. Sometimes a big tank goes by along on the road like a spectre, and one tries not to hear the crunch of bones. The firing seems to have got even worse. I pull myself up again and plunge forward.

Suddenly a fountain of muck shoots up near me and I am thrown to the ground. I can feel a raging pain in my foot. Is this the end? It is dark in front of my eyes and there is a searing pain in my foot as if a burning stick has been bored into the skin. I pull myself up, ignoring the pain. A riderless horse comes racing through the fire with whirling hooves and nearly knocks me over, but I hurry on, not looking. I just want to live, only to live.

Another few metres and the wood begins. The shelling is less and the big concert is behind me. I go faster, determined not to fail just before my goal, for the wood means safety, and then I am inside the wood and throw myself down, pressing my glowing face into the moss, and gradually the roaring in my head dies down.

I examine my foot. There is a splinter sticking out of my right boot that has bored its way into my foot, and now the pain comes in earnest. I pull myself up so as not to think about it, and continue along the road of the big flight, the great retreat.

Wednesday 2 May 1945, noon

My body gradually begins to relax. The noise of the firing that lies behind me has not lessened, and drums on without a break. People stumble out of the Hell and throw themselves on the ground in the shelter of the trees. Behind them, like ghosts, the people stumble between the fountains of dirt and steel erupting from the earth. Occasionally a vehicle races through the fire over the dead and the craters that threaten to engulf it, or a big tank breaks through with a racing engine and clanking tracks, the people clinging to the armour plating and letting the storm rage over them. They are the luckiest in that they come through the hellish fire more quickly than the soldiers who have to do it on foot. The tank stops at the edge of the wood and the turret hatch opens. The tank commander throws off the dead who have been riddled with splinters on the way, then the tank rolls on, disappearing among the trees.

I get up and walk on, not wanting to lose contact. In the wood to the left and right of the track lie rucksacks, packs, weapons and ammunition, food and articles of clothing, all unnecessary ballast in this dance with death. Nevertheless, some soldiers and civilians are still carrying almost biblical loads, apparently unable to part with possessions that hold so little value in comparison with the loss of one's life.

A tank rolls slowly alongside me with a wounded man lying on it. One of his legs is almost off, hanging on by a few shreds of flesh just above the knee and swinging slowly to and fro whenever the tank bumps over a crater or a fallen tree. A broad stream of blood is flowing down the steel plates and dripping into the sand of the track. A woman sitting next to him has put her rucksack on the turret and is nursing her arm in which a splinter has torn a hole, the blood dripping between her fingers. Some wounded who have staggered here with their last strength are lying in the wood next to the road, slowly bleeding to death. Fully conscious, they watch the army flee past and receive no help. There are no doctors or nurses or, if there are, they go past unseeing and uncaring.

I bite back the pain that races through my body every time I put my foot down. When an ambulance comes past, I hang on to the door and walk along with it. The vehicle is overflowing and is driving along without any air in its tyres. There are even wounded clinging on to the roof, severely wounded. Less severe cases do not count when one considers the pain of these mangled bodies. I let go of the door and continue walking slowly along the track.

A big truck goes by towing a trailer. One of the rear wheels has been shot through and the whole vehicle is swinging from side to side across the track, threatening to get caught up in the trees. The sounds of battle are gradually diminishing behind us. Occasionally shrapnel bursts in the treetops above us, the splinters showering down like rain, then everyone speeds up, almost automatically, but only for a few steps and then they fall back to a slower pace. A wounded man is lying on the track, having fallen off a tank, and is calling for help. The next vehicle that comes along could crush him under its wheels. I go past him impassively. Dead are lying about and are walked round. I suddenly realise that I do not have a weapon any more. I must have dropped it when I jumped into the trench, so I take the pistol out of my pocket and it lies cool and reassuring in my hot hands, then I stick it into my belt. From time to time I sit down in the wood and pause for a few breaths. Some soldiers and civilians with dulled eyes are lying down resting in the wood. There are even some women who have got through the artillery fire.

Then fear of the enemy bringing his barrage forward and resuming the dance with death quickens our pace again. We are chased and driven on whenever the gunfire sounds louder in the distance, or the humming of an aircraft engine comes from overhead. Even when it is really quiet, we are still afraid. A creeping, awful, silent fear pricks at our heels and gives us no peace. The words 'heroic life' and 'heroic death' ring maliciously in my ears.

People are moving along well spread out, some of them in pairs. The wood is like a vast maze and we do not know where we will end up. Everyone watches the man in front of him and does what he does, climbing over trees when he does. Tank tracks have dug deep into the sand of the track on the right, and we follow these spurs like the thread that will bring us to safety.

We have been walking for hours, a tired mass of humanity. The wood is endless. Occasionally a bird flutters up or a hare scuttles away with its ears laid back. Everything has gone quiet. The silence of nature lies over us and lets us breathe more easily. The distances between the figures get greater and greater, so that one hardly can make out the figure in front among the trees. At last the wood ends.

On the left the wood goes on beyond a field where there are some thick bushes. On the right is a low plantation of pines, the trees barely man height. An occasional shot comes from the edge of the wood or the bushes. I go across to the other side of the track and fight my way through the pines. The needles hit me in the face and my fingers become sticky and resinous. A wounded man with a bandaged foot is lying on a path calling for help. Another shot rings out and I hurry past him. 'Help me, comrade, please help!' I cannot help him and have to cover my ears not to hear.

A gentle whinnying comes from behind. I turn around. A paymaster is leading a foal by a rope and has tied his pack to its back. Then the plantation comes to an end. The land rises a little on the right and is divided by some collapsed fences. There are some big deciduous trees that stretch their crowns high above the track and thick bushes along the roadside ditches provide cover. Suddenly some ruined houses appear, overgrown with moss and looking as if they have been empty for years. On one hangs a sign half washed out by the rain with the word 'Döberitz' on it. The houses and their half wrecked barns are lonely and quiet and I hurry past, for it is uncomfortable in this village, where the enemy could be sitting behind the blind windows. At last the houses are behind and the wood begins again. A colourful sign with a zeppelin painted on it points the way to Staaken Airfield, and a cut-out cannon to the Döberitz Training Area, where the Relief Army should be in position waiting for us. I find it odd that it has not pushed forward to Staaken, for the wood was unoccupied, but then think no more of it, believing only that it will soon be over and at last I will find rest.

The tank tracks show the way like railway lines, you only have to follow them. The countryside has become hilly with tall, arid pines standing out of the poor, bright, sandy soil. My boots sink deep into the sand, which is unmistakeably that of the Brandenburg heathland. There are some prominent wooden buildings on some of the hilltops, gaily painted and half covered by bushes, most completely destroyed. Concrete pillboxes with bright loopholes grow out of the ground, half-rusted bits of shells are lying around, and craters have been ripped out of the earth. I am passing through the training area's target village, where once soldiers were trained and shells ploughed into the wooden buildings.

A burning tank bars the route, the Balkan Cross bright against the speckled green camouflage sides. Its ammunition is exploding with a banging and whistling like a firework display and I have to make a big detour to get through. Then I suddenly lose sight of the man in front of me. He seems to have sunk into the ground. I go all over the place looking for the tank tracks and at last find a few lost bits of baggage and stumble back on the route with relief.

The wood is getting thicker again. Once an aircraft crosses over the treetops. Then the training area comes to an end. Behind us is a sign saying 'Entry forbidden!' But there is still no sign of the Relief Army, nor of the huts that should be waiting for us.

Moving along I can hardly feel my wounded foot any more, only a dull pain. A hundred metres in front of me is a civilian. The man behind me is some distance back. The land climbs on either side and I am going along a sunken road with a tank standing on the track right in front of me. People are going around it and resting in the woods on either side, lying stretched out on the ground and eating or smoking. Everyone is all mixed up together – officers and soldiers, civilians, Volkssturm, flak auxiliaries, girls of the Labour Service and a few female signals auxiliaries in uniform, even some children. The tank driver is going round with a blackened face on which the sweat has made broad furrows, examining the hot armoured plates over the engine with a worried look, for the engine has been running without a break since early this morning.

There are some other vehicles in front of the tank. The wounded are being unloaded from an ambulance and laid out on the edge of the wood. 'Those that cannot be helped any more', says someone suddenly close to me. 'They are only taking up the places of the healthy ones.'

Two Waffen-SS officers with majors' insignia are standing with the general by a tank looking at a map. It is the general from the bridge, who has come through in one piece. I stop near the tank and lie down, fish a cigarette out of my tunic pocket and ask a major lying near me for a light. Then I stretch out and look up into the trees. The pain in my foot has lessened considerably. The officers are joking with the 'ladies', some of whom are doubling up with laughter. The sound of the many voices comes to me gently, indistinguishable and confused. Empty chocolate boxes, sweet wrappers and silver paper from long life bread packets lie strewn around on the ground.

The general goes up to the Waffen-SS officers and points at his watch. Then they slowly gather up their things and stand up. They lift the women up on to the tanks, where they disappear down the turret hatches, then they put their baggage into the ambulance. We have all stood up and are waiting for the march to continue.

Two Russian airmen with shaven heads and wearing thickly padded overalls are sitting on a tree. One of them has been wounded in the shoulder. They sit there not taking part, only their eyes taking a lively interest. A Waffen-SS man with a submachine gun stands beside them and does not let them out of his sight. They had to make an emergency landing when their petrol tank was hit, a soldier says, and have been interrogated and will be shot afterwards. I dare not get worked up about it, for I have seen too many dead today to concern myself with these two, but I am ashamed of those who gave the order for this. If the Russians should treat us in the same way, we will have no cause to wonder why.

The tanks and the other vehicles are fully loaded with people. The tank engines roar into life together and one colossus after another rolls with rattling tracks close past the waiting vehicles. The wounded who had been unloaded from the ambulance are left behind, watching the departure with sad eyes. They are finished with life, having already half bled to death, if not already unconscious.

We have got moving again and trot along like an impassive mass. It is comforting not to have to go on alone, not knowing if one is going to lose sight of the man in front at any moment. Close in front of us the track splits half left and half right. The tanks roll into the right-hand track and move a little faster so that we can no longer keep up with them and gradually fall behind. When the tanks in which the Waffen-SS officers are sitting are out of sight, a few soldiers stop the ambulance and remove the baggage. The locks are burst open and a flood of colourful clothing, material and shoes cascades out, and we go across to pick up the foodstuffs. In one of the suitcases are thick bundles of new, unused banknotes, fresh from the mint, and a soldier rips open the bundles and gives out a few notes to everyone passing. The ambulance driver is being held back by other soldiers and is only released when the suitcases are empty. Then he tries to stuff the remains of the shoes and clothing back into the suitcases. A soldier sits down behind the steering wheel, switches on the engine, sending the vehicle forward with a jerk, and drives off. The driver stands there aghast at this audacity, and looks bewildered after his vehicle as it goes out of sight round a bend.

We are no longer an unrestrained mob, but have formed a long, single column. One stumbles along behind the other, watching the heels of the man in front. This way one can fall asleep. We move along all mixed up in any old order, with women and children among the soldiers, a few paymasters and administrative officials in immaculate uniforms in between contrasting sharply with the dirty, tired soldiers. Some men ahead have put the old general into the ranks and are moving along slowly with him. He has lost his cap, and his silvery hair flutters round his head.

Some slit trenches and air raid shelter trenches have been dug on the right, where the remains of some collapsed huts are lying around. Some abandoned vehicles have been stripped of everything that was not firmly attached, and there are boxes of Panzerfausts, stacks of artillery shells and a toppled-over gun without its breechblock, altogether a sad sight.

An administrative official in the rank of major suddenly announces that the Wenck Army was here. I look carefully but can see no evidence to support this. It strikes me as strange that we have been marching since five this morning to meet the Wenck Army, which should first have been at Döberitz, then in the woods of the training area, but have been through both without seeing the least sign of it. In a report the day before yesterday, it was said that the army stood before Berlin, was engaged in hard fighting in Potsdam, and was driving forward steadily on the capital. It was presented to us as the safety anchor that would snatch us out of the turmoil of destruction, and we excitedly followed the directions for the advance of this army that was to relieve and liberate Berlin. Now we have gone through death and destruction, women and children who did not want to be taken by the Russians too, and there is still nothing to be seen of Wenck and his men.

Suddenly some women and children come hastening toward us. 'The Russians are coming!' is all they say and rush past with frightened faces. We are shocked and do not know what to do. We ask those women nearest to us, who say that the wood ends shortly and that the chaussee passes not so far off, and that the Russians are coming across the fields to the left of the chaussee.

We go carefully along through the trees until the wood suddenly ends and the track goes on between the fields. On the left, still some distance away, figures are going across the field, and one of our tanks is on the road firing at the enemy. There is a village at some distance away on the right. The first of us are already going along the road behind the slow moving column of tanks and vehicles. Some of us continue along the track, but I turn off and go straight across the fields. The ground is boggy and my feet sink almost to my ankles, the cold water running through the holes in my boots and swilling between my toes with every step. I walk carefully, as if on eggs. Apart from the splinter in my foot, I have no pain at the moment, although I have blisters between my toes and under my feet, as my boots are too tight. It is a tiresome business having to pull one's feet out of the wet holes with every step, but I am happy to be off the road at last.

The tanks have driven off ahead to guard against surprises, only the heavy tank remaining firing on the roadside where the chaussee leads into the wood. Later it too comes racing past with a thunderous din. I have an unbearable thirst, but my waterbottle is empty, the schnapps from last night long since gone. I go a little faster to get closer to the lead and win a little time in case there is a pump somewhere. There are only a few weapons left in our ranks. There are still at least twelve hundred of us, soldiers and civilians together, scarcely half of whom are carrying weapons, and only a few have handguns.

We cross over a railway line.[7] A clamouring crowd press round the pump in front of the railway crossing keeper's house. On the left is a house on its own, hidden behind a wooden fence. I push against the gate, which to my surprise gives way, and go up to the house where an elderly woman sitting on a bench gets up when I ask her for water. She then fills my waterbottle with coffee and brings me yet another pot that I quickly drink down. Then I go back out again, anxious not to lose contact, for the dog always bites the one who is last.

There is a solitary farm on our left from where some women come up to the roadside wearing colourful headscarves, bringing us buckets of milk. (There seem to be no men left here.) Some of the girls, as one can see clearly from their blue-green stockings, are signals auxiliaries. On the right-hand side of the road stands a tracked tractor with two large trailers loaded with petrol drums, and sitting in the cab is a Russian in a light uniform, his face smashed beyond recognition by bullets. A little farther on stands another tractor with two trailers, whose driver and his escort are also dead. I feel uncomfortable about this, as we are in Russian territory and could easily be dealt with as snipers if we were caught. The women tell us that they were startled when shots rang out on the roadway as the tanks knocked out these drivers. The engine of one of the tractors is still ticking over, sending blue exhaust smoke billowing into the air above the bonnet. A soldier tries to get the other tractor going, but is unable to do so. Then we climb on to the trailers and shoot holes into the petrol drums so that the petrol runs down into the road.

The first tractor has been unhooked from its trailers and moves off with much puffing and snorting, the cab looking like one from an old steam engine. The driver cannot get the hang of it, and almost hits the trees on either side of the road. The soldiers hang on to the radiator, the cab roof and every conceivable projection, or let themselves be pulled along. Some cows running around in the fields on our left look on in astonishment at our progress. On the right is a wide ditch and behind it a leafy wood.

Some youngsters from the next village come towards us bringing us several boxes of rifle ammunition that we badly need, as hardly anyone who still has a rifle has enough bullets. We pack the boxes into the cab and the tractor continues on its way, reeling like a drunk.

A village lies ahead of us, its church tower standing brightly above the roofs. Dark smoke is rising from the centre of the village, where some buildings seem to be on fire as the tanks drive through. The tractor makes a sudden sharp turn to the right and runs into the ditch. The soldiers jump off grumbling and walk on, leaving the tractor where it is.

We approach the village and pass the sign at the entrance. It is Falkenrehde.[8] The people are standing in front of their houses watching us, and have brought out some large dishes with bread and coffee for us. We sit down on the doorsteps and eat in peace while a team goes through the houses and stalls to prevent any hidden Russians becoming a danger to us. One man says that in Priort at noon today eleven tanks that had broken through from Berlin were shot up one after another by the Russians as if they had been on the ranges, and that only a few of the crews and the women sitting on the tanks got away safely.

We go through the streets of the tidy village stretching our legs. Nearly everyone who came through the Döberitz woods is here. The general says that the Russians have blocked the route behind us and that we have only been able to slip through so far because the tanks have been able to keep the enemy at a distance. A few have split off on the way, so that we are now down to about a thousand people. Those that have split off are mainly women who stayed behind in the farms to wait until we were far enough away and then turned back, having lost all hope of getting through Russian territory to the west.

The tank has returned and is standing in the village square, where the children are dancing delightedly around it. They have not seen German tanks for a long time and want to climb aboard, but the commander curtly waves them away. The other three light tanks are in the villages that we will have to pass through before dark. I look at my watch. It is almost six o'clock.

We set off again. The children accompany us part of the way as far as the end of the village, and then are called back by their anxious mothers. A few women and civilians have remained in the village to wait until the Russians come, which cannot be all that long, as we are practically alone wandering about in enemy territory. The trucks have nearly all been abandoned on the roadside for lack of fuel or because their tyres are completely ruined, so that driving on is no longer possible. But here too everything that was not securely fastened down has already been removed; even the ripped out seats are being carried off by some soldiers.

We have long since left the village behind. There are some leafy woods on our right, and fields run off to distant woods on our left, with some prominent towers that are either part of a radio transmitting station or the derricks of a coalmine. There is also the line of a railway embankment in the distance.

It is gradually becoming dark, almost completely so. The sun has gone down and the first shadows of the night are spreading and hanging in the trees.

The heavy tank drives past us often, checking the villages in front and behind us. Occasionally one hears distant dull discharges and then sees dark smoke and flashes of light. An occasional shot comes from the woods, causing us to fire back madly, although it certainly has no result, but we dare not enter the woods ourselves. Most villages are free of Russians, who withdrew into the woods when the first tanks appeared, as their only heavy weapons and anti-tank guns are up at Wustermark.

Once a biplane flies over the fields not far off and then turns towards the road. The tanks sends several machine gun bursts after it, and the aircraft disappears behind the wood. I start thinking about what will happen to us if we do not reach the Elbe. Will the Russians deal with us as our troops did with their prisoners, even if it was done mainly by the Waffen-SS? Will we be shot after a short interrogation, or straight away? They will find the dead men on the tractors and will then have reason enough to do it, and once they knock out the tanks, we will be as good as defenceless and there would then be no reason to go on fighting just so as not to fall into Russian hands. We know only one goal, have only one thought, to the west, to the Wenck Army, which finally must be somewhere, perhaps not so far away.

Some dead horses are lying in the ditch, all swollen and giving off a bestial stink, and we have to hold our noses as we go past. The gun they were towing lies tipped up in the ditch, and a soldier seems to have been crushed beneath it, for a pair of issue boots are sticking out.

Another yellow place sign appears with the name 'Ketzin' on it and one of the light tanks is waiting at the village entrance.[9] It drives past us and rattles through the village to the exit at the far end. Everything is well organised and, if only the enemy would leave us in peace, we would have a chance of reaching our goal, but only then.

The inhabitants are also standing in front of their doors here, but do not appear to be especially pleased to see us. Nor can we blame them, for they have already had several days of peace in the village when our tanks arrived today. A house that the Russians had fortified is shot into flames and the blazing fire can be seen bright and clear in front of the other buildings through the darkness sinking around us.

We march through the village. An emergency bridge has been thrown across the Havel. Despite its primitive construction, it can carry a considerable weight, as tanks have been crossing it without a problem.[10] On the right the chaussee branches off to the right along the Havel, and the road on the left leads to Potsdam. We ask the inhabitants if they know where the Wenck Army is, but they have not even heard of it. There is no German army or army group in this area. The fighting has been over in Potsdam for days, and only on Pfaueninsel (Peacock Island) has the defence lasted longer. Perhaps the army is in Brandenburg, which has been holding out for ten days.[11]

As we are going past a house, a young flak auxiliary rushes out of the gate and says that some German prisoners are locked up in there and we should go with him and blow down the door, as the Russians have gone off with the keys. Being curious, I go into the yard to find out at first hand how the Russians have been treating them. Some soldiers knock at the door, then remain silent with only the footsteps of those going past the yard to be heard. We knock again and call out. This time someone can be heard behind the door and a German voice tells us to go away.

It is now completely dark. The cool of night descends and makes us shiver and we all have a gnawing hunger, despite having been given bread and coffee in Falkenrehde. Then we turn left into a road. On the right a track leads to a barn where a few figures are running across the fields and disappearing among the trees – presumably the Russians occupying the village and who have been waiting for us to leave. Two Russian trucks are standing close to the houses with red flags on their bonnets, and a heavy anti-tank gun is coupled to one of them. The farmers from the village have rendered its breechblock unserviceable with heavy blacksmiths' hammers. We climb aboard the trucks looking for food. Someone throws the heavy cases off to smash on the street and a host of Russian medals spills out on to the cobbles. The whole truck is loaded with Russian medals of all kinds and sizes. On the other truck are cases of black bread, tins of sardines in oil, packets of butter and tins of meat. The villagers eagerly assist with the unloading and soon there is nothing left. When I climb down, I find myself standing on a carpet of medals strewn all over the ground, stars of all colours and sizes, of silver, gold and red enamel.

We sit down under the trees and eat. Behind us the barn to which the Russians fled has been set on fire by the German tanks, and some of the villagers are trying to put out the fire with stirrup pumps, but they stand no chance for the flames are consuming more and more, and leaping up high.

Suddenly shots ring out from the edge of the woods. A tank drives up and fires some shots into the plantation, making the trees look like plucked chickens, and then turns back. We are going to try and reach Genthin via Pritzherbe, north of Brandenburg, and then thrust forward to Jerichow, which is only a few steps from the Elbe. The enemy has pushed forward as far as Pritzherbe, the villagers tell us, but they do not know what lies between the Elbe and the line that the Russians have occupied. In any case, the Russians will have blocked all the routes open to us, and will have prepared some special surprises for us. We go on. The main roads will have to be avoided if we are not to fall into the hands of the enemy. We turn into a track leading toward Eltzin. It has become quite dark. The column is seriously reduced and we are now down to about eight hundred men. A burning tank stands on the track with its crew standing beside it. It had track damage and the crew have blown it up. We pass it to the left and right.

Suddenly fountains of earth shoot up in the field. The explosions and the gurgling of the mortars rips us out of the complacency into which we had sunk. We run out into the field and press ourselves down in the furrows. Two Waffen-SS officers go on, ducking down to size up the situation. The earth is damp and cold, and the cold seems to be climbing out of every crevice, turning the body into a numbed mass. The explosions have moved off a little and are falling at regular intervals, so we duck down instinctively whenever the roaring comes. Some of the soldiers have thrown their weapons away and are hiding in the field. It is dark and the heavens hover like a bell over us. I am suddenly tired and I fall asleep.

Something rolls against my head. I open my eyes and take some time to get used to the darkness. Then I see that my comrades have long since disappeared, and that the last stragglers are already going past. I get up quickly and try to get back forward again as quickly as possible. My body is ice cold and I am shivering uncontrollably. Occasionally I stumble half asleep into the man in front of me, and only come to my senses after an angry word has been said.

It is now so dark that one can hardly make out the man in front. Somewhere in the night a searchlight is sweeping to and fro as if it was waving. It is due west and that is where I want to be, for I think that the Russians cannot be there yet, and all the others seem to be thinking the same thing, but on a pitch black night like this, even the smallest light looks really close and yet is so far away.

I have now almost reached the head of the column. The Waffen-SS officers are moving just ahead of us and talking quietly. They seem to be the only officers left, for the general has disappeared. Then we suddenly stop while one of the officers examines a map with a shaded torch and makes movements as if he were looking for something. We continue forward a little, and then turn right into a narrow path.

It is becoming misty and the waving searchlight is no longer visible, a serious blow for us as the point to steer by is now missing. We suddenly find ourselves in a plantation again, stumbling over asparagus beds. We go around for a long time looking for the path, which we fortunately find again and then go back along the path to where we turned into it. Our column has become very small. Apparently the tail did not notice that we had turned off and have gone straight on. The Waffen-SS officers have disappeared and we stand around not knowing what to do. The mist is slowly descending around us like a blanket so that we cannot see anything. We go on walking as if through a steaming laundry without either map or compass to help us find our way, simply following the direction that we think must be to the west, and the whole crowd tags along behind.

Soon we have left the track and are walking across meadows and fields. Two civilians are pushing their bicycles along regardless of whether we are crossing streams or going across the fields. Our feet are soon cold and heavy from the wet soil that sticks to our soles like lead. Whenever we cross a field our trousers get wet up to the calves from the dew, and the cold seeps through our bodies. It is still like being in a laundry, one can just see the man in front and on the flank like disappearing ghosts. The cursing from the men as they stumble over furrows and ditches hangs in the air like the voices of ghosts.

Suddenly we come to a stop. We can hear mortar firing from quite close and scraps of words in Russian floating toward us. We quietly move across to the opposite side. A metalled road lies in front of us, where the mist ends abruptly as if it had been cut off. We lie in the roadside ditch and dare each other to be the first across, then all cross the road together. We later come across the tracks of a railway and again hear voices that cause us to lie still and tense, listening in the night.

Then we hasten back, going across the railway tracks, the ballast rattling against the rails under our feet. As I am crossing the signal wire, I get caught and it gives out a ringing tone. Then we go back over fields and meadows, climbing across streams and cattle enclosures. Once a tall wire fence blocks our route and we have difficulty getting our tired bodies over it. We are becoming more careless and seem to be going round in circles. Fields and fences look familiar, as if we have already been here. Then we look at the ground and see our tracks going across the fields.

Some of us go our own ways and others break off. We suddenly plunge back into the mist and are lost again. We decide on a new direction and note that other people have already gone this way, but we do not know whether it was ourselves or another group.

The mist gradually begins to lift. The various groups have merged together again and are plodding wearily across the fields. We can hardly lift our feet, our legs are so tired. Sometimes we confer and everyone looks in another direction and says that he is sure it is the right way. Then we go on in whatever direction the first one to move off takes. Eventually we break into a heated debate over the route, which has to be decided now so that we can at least be under cover by the morning and not run into the hands of the Russians in the open fields. Everyone has his own opinion about the best route to take, and sometimes the voices get so excited that someone has to call for silence. Somebody proposes that the command should be given to an officer, who can then lead the whole crowd wherever seems right to him.

We look around to see if we have an officer among us, and eventually find one, the old administrative official of major's rank with crossed batons on his epaulets. However, he does not seem to know much about compasses and heavenly bodies as guides, and would like to decline the responsibility on account of his age. But when one of the crowd shouts 'Coward!', he agrees to take the matter in hand and abruptly points in one direction, and we move off.

Later one group splits off to go in the direction they think more likely, and vanish in the darkness. We are tired and are stumbling half asleep across the fields. Hunger starts to bore into my stomach, evoking the desire for a piece of bread. Suddenly I fall flat on my face. I had been walking in my sleep.

I look at my watch and am surprised. Midnight is long gone. I have now been on my feet for twenty-four hours, almost without a break, and there is still no end in sight.

NOTES

1. With Lieutenant General Weidling's permission, Major General Otto Sydow commanding the 1st (Berlin) Flak Division, had organised a breakout from the Zoo position during the night for those who wished to go. The infantry and accompanying civilians had made their way up the tunnels under the enemy lines, and the armour and vehicles had driven up Kantstrasse, joining up with the troops being forced out of the Kurfürstendamm area outside the Exhibition Halls on Masurenallee. The Soviets, and the Polish infantry that had reinforced the 2nd Guards Tank Army on 1 May in the area through which the Germans had come, had made no effort to stop them, presumably being exhausted by the previous day's fighting and impromptu May Day celebrations, and Dragunsky's 55th Guards Tank Brigade, that were supposed to be blocking such an escape route, had similarly failed to exert themselves.
2. The main railway bridge close to the town hall. Only the Charlotten and Schulenburg Bridges survived over the Havel, and these had to be repeatedly fought over. The Frey Bridge farther south carrying the Heerstrasse had been destroyed the previous evening when a chance Soviet shell hit the prepared demolition chamber. The breakout across the Charlotten Bridge was led by Major Horst Zobel of the 1st Battalion, 'Müncheberg' Panzer Regiment, who used an armoured personnel carrier instead of his usual tank, in order to have better visibility.
3. Presumably Major General Otto Sydow.
4. Now on Brunsbüttler Damm.
5. With the 125th Rifle Corps of the 47th Army in this sector was the 5th Mortar Regiment of the 1st Polish Mortar Brigade.
6. *Gartenstadt Staaken.*
7. Near Salzkorn.
8. The Russians must have already repaired the bridge across the canal here, for it had been blown on 23 April by the local Volkssturm.
9. Ketzin was the place where on 25 April where elements of the 4th Guards Tank Army of Marshal Koniev's 1st Ukrainian Front met elements of 47th Army of Marshal Zhukov's 1st Byelorussian Front to complete the encirclement of Berlin.
10. The Russians built their bridges of wood in the Roman style.
11. Most of the Potsdam garrison had escaped south to join the 12th Army on the night of the 27th/28th, and the town had then been occupied by elements of the Soviet 47th Army penetrating from the north on the 28th. However, the 20th Panzergrenadier Division, down to about ninety men, had been trapped on Wannsee 'island' and Pfaueninsel (Peacock Island) since 24 April by the

10th Guards Tank Corps of the 4th Guards Tank Army, and when they tried to break out through Wannsee on the night of 1/2 May they were almost completely wiped out. Most of the survivors of this action were accounted for in a battle around the Headquarters of the 4th Guards Tank Army at Schenkenhorst on the 2nd, and only a very few individuals from this formation eventually escaped to the west.

CHAPTER XIII
Flight

Thursday 3 May 1945

The night slowly begins to recede. The mist hanging over the fields is beginning to thin out, the stars are fading and the shadows of the trees stand out more distinctly. The fields are wet and the clods of earth sticking to our boots seem heavier than ever. We plod along like sleepwalkers through the landscape as the night slowly pulls back its cover. We have no goal and no direction any more, having lost all orientation. All we seek is a corner to creep into before the day breaks.

We are still almost five hundred men, several determinedly carrying heavy packs. Despite all their misery and fatigue, they would rather fall down under the weight of them than lose them. It is uncanny how, at the moment when the curtain is beginning to fall on the biggest tragedy of all, these people can hang on to their wretched possessions and will not let them go.

It has become lighter. Visibility is still limited and we are looking for a piece of woodland or a bushy patch. The wet earth clings like chains, making the going arduous and difficult. The water swills round in our sodden boots at every step and drives the cold through our bodies making our teeth chatter. We are dead tired and empty. We pull up a few turnips to chew them raw, but our bodies have had enough of this abuse and more and more are falling behind. Sometimes the uniform stumping on the field becomes muffled as we come to meadows or fields in which the young corn is trampled under by our column. Our trousers brush against grass wet with the dew and our legs get even colder.

First of all we have find cover as soon as possible and a bright streak in the eastern sky warns us to hurry. We stop and gather round the only officer still in our ranks, and those coming up from behind ask indignantly why we have stopped. The two civilians are still pushing their bicycles, even though they look ready to collapse from exhaustion. We stand in front of the adminstrative official with major's rank, who is suddenly being pressed into making a decision in his task of finding us somewhere safe. He looks almost as helpless as we are when he pulls his cap from his

219

head and runs his fingers through his hair as if he is lost. He is certainly already in his 50s. They are getting impatient behind. Then he pulls himself together and points to where on the horizon a dark wall stands that could perhaps be a wood. Then we plod off, completely unconvinced, but still going along with him. Only a few continue in the old direction and are soon swallowed up in the darkness, their voices humming through the mist. We go along with the officer in the lead towards the dark something, going over fields, over meadows, staggering over streams and sending the water splashing up high to make our bodies even colder. The dark wall slowly grows taller, and we are all hoping that it will turn out to be a wood.

We stop again and let ourselves slip down into the murky clay that sticks to our uniforms like a crust. The cold that seems to creep out of the ground stifles any thinking. The thin strip in the east is brighter, heralding the new day. We prise our abused bodies from the ground and stumble on like ghosts, half asleep, but several stay behind and the column is growing thinner and thinner. The wall in front of us grows with every step. For us it means cover, safety and rest for the next few hours. Gradually we see that it really is a wood and not just a figment of the imagination brought on by our overtired senses. It is getting closer with every laborious and difficult step. The body gathers together its resources and pumps out its last efforts, driving one forward like an engine. Finally, it is almost like the end of a race as we feel firm grass under our feet. But then, as if to remind us that even here we are not safe, that we will not be safe anywhere, a tank engine suddenly roars into life close by, making our hearts miss a beat. We stand still, as if rooted to the spot, until the sound gradually dies away, then we go in among the widely spaced trees and let ourselves sink exhausted to the ground.

I lean against a tree and rummage in my haversack with numbed fingers and pull out the last tin from my greatcoat pocket, where it has burst the stitching. The trees are rustling peacefully above our heads. All the soldiers have fallen silent and have spread out in the wood. Occasionally a figure emerges from the mist, struggles up to the trees and throws itself panting on the ground. I take my pocket knife from the cover my mother crocheted for me and gave me with the knife that last day. I go round the tin with my knife to open it, and the knife suddenly snaps, remaining stuck in the tin. The major silently hands me his knife and I open the tin. I spread a few slices of bread that I have been saving thickly with sausage and eat reasonably in peace for the first time in a long while.

Strength returns to my body with renewed courage to face life. Dawn comes quickly, the sky turning red in the east and mist hangs in the air. We are as if on an island in this high woodland. We do not know how big it is, nor whether it is safe enough to conceal us for the day, for the wood is not very thick. There are some bushes and some tall grass in places, but

220

bright sand in others, typical of the Mark Brandenburg. We pull back from the edge of the wood, from where we can look out back over the fields that we plodded across during the night and see the tracks that we trampled on a broad front and that could easily give us away to the enemy. I lie down in the grass for the fatigue that lies like lead in my limbs is making me stagger. Soldiers are lying asleep between the bushes, in which the drops of dew hang like diamonds, hardly discernible in their grey-green greatcoats and uniforms. Others are lying on the ground on tent-halves, hoping to keep out the cold. I stand up again, as it is unbearable on the wet ground. The wound in my foot has started hurting again and I dare not remove my boot in case I reopen the wound, which is clogged with clotted blood and dirt. When I touch it, I can feel the tip of the splinter that pierced my boot and is now fastening the foot and leather together. I am wounded, but have held out so far, although it seems that an eternity lies between today and yesterday.

I move around a little, looking for a place that will shelter me for the day. In the direction from which we came, the first rays of sunshine are streaming through the mist as if through a milky windowpane. To the right of us, that is to the north, the wood goes on for a few hundred metres and then drops into the fields, the land also falling away to the west. A track runs between the wood and the fields from south to north, and one can see the marks of tank tracks sunk deep into its sand. The wood is about a hundred metres wide from east to west, and the whole thing resembles a narrow hand towel. What lies to the south cannot be seen, as the mist still whirling over the ground obstructs the view.

I go to and fro, trying to warm up. It is almost unbearable in this cool morning air with wet clothes on one's body. Then I stop. What day is it today? Sunday? Monday? I try and work it out, but without success. It really does not matter what day it is.

It has become lighter and some birds are flitting from tree to tree and twittering. A hen cackles somewhere and must be quite close. If one could only draw aside the mist that is obscuring our surroundings behind its veil. Most of the soldiers have stood up and are walking around. There are even some female flak auxiliaries and girls from the Labour Service here standing talking to the flak auxiliaries, discussing what best to do.

I think about the fact that we are already in May. Spring has been here for nearly a month but we have not benefitted from it. We are standing here, not knowing what will become of us. To my astonishment, I discover that we have a prisoner among us, a small, shaven-headed Russian. A youngster in Labour Service uniform, no older than 17, has given him his pack to carry, calls him simply 'Ivan' and, as he speaks Russian, can converse with him easily. Our column is a complete mixture. There are soldiers from all branches of the service, Volkssturm and civilians, flak auxiliaries, and women and girls in both uniform and civilian clothes. This

221

is the crew that is left. We now also have an officer of the Waffen-SS with us, as well as the administrative official and a paymaster. Some of the NCOs have removed their epaulettes and are mixing in with the crowd. The Waffen-SS lieutenant has gathered some Waffen-SS men around him. Everyone is standing about waiting for something to happen, but a few soldiers have gone off independently, disappearing into the bushes.

The Waffen-SS lieutenant and the administrative official are studying a large map, trying to determine our exact location. Then we are divided up into sections. The NCOs have put their epaulettes back on, if mainly only on one shoulder. Every thirty men form a platoon, and together we form two companies of one hundred men each. But barely a third of us have rifles, and there are no automatic weapons at all. There are only ten rounds available per rifle, but we do not intend to fight any more. We just want to get away from here as far as possible to the west.

We are waiting until the mist lifts. It slowly drifts away and a farm appears not too far off. One of the Waffen-SS men gets on a civilian's bicycle and rides off. The mist rises higher and hangs in the trees. Then the blood pounds in our veins, for there is a road barely two hundred metres away beyond a gentle slope and tanks with infantry sitting on them fill the road from the first houses in the village on the right to a bend in the road on the left.

We pull back shocked deeper into the wood, for it would provide us with no cover if the enemy decided to comb this area, and when a twig snaps underfoot we are scared that the enemy will hear it, and hardly dare breathe. Our prisoner stands leaning against a tree, calmly chewing a piece of bread that his escort has given him. The Labour Servicemen hand out tins of sardines in oil from a wooden box that they took from the Russian truck yesterday, and the soldiers crowd in from all round, not bothering whether they make a noise or not, like hungry animals. The Waffen-SS man comes back quickly on his bicycle up the track from the farm to our group. The enemy on the road have still not noticed us, wisps of mist still lying around providing us with a scanty cover. We then look for the village on the map to find out where we are. It is called Zachow and is occupied by the Russians.

The Waffen-SS lieutenant tells us that it is only a short distance to Roskow, and that there is a gap between Päwesin and Weseran through which we can get to the west. Päwesin is the farthest place occupied by the Russians, and then we will come to German territory and to the Elbe, where the Americans are and we have made peace with them. We will try and get through there. Then he gives us the order to wait and disappears with his Waffen-SS men between the trees. We walk excitedly around. Can it be true? Is there only a short distance separating us from the German troops? Hopefully we will come through, and without a fight.

We have gone deeper into the wood so as not to be seen by the Russians, and I sit on the ground. The cold has receded and the sun is high in the sky, promising a fine spring day. The Waffen-SS lieutenant comes back with his men, speaks with the major, and then disappears again among the trees. The section leaders run to the major when he calls quietly, and then come back and whisper their orders.

Some soldiers have slipped away, and I would dearly like to do the same myself, but then we move out in a long column with wide gaps between the sections and individuals. There are not many of the older ones left, we are nearly all youngsters. The flak auxiliaries make their section leaders angry, as they pay no attention to their orders and walk along whispering with the girls. The paymaster is walking alongside us in a huff because he has not been given a section. His blue rucksack and big briefcase are stuffed full and the neck of a bottle sticks out promisingly through the opening, showing that it has been consulted several times by its owner.

We go deeper into the wood, then turn left toward the west and drop down into the fields. Then we go north along the track where the tank tracks gradually disappear into the sandy soil. The head of the column turns left and we go along a narrow strip of grass between two ploughed fields. Behind us the sun is climbing above the trees and throwing its golden light over the countryside.

We go across the fields in a long single file in the sunshine and with a wide view as if there was no war, as if the countryside we were passing was not occupied by the enemy. The ploughed earth next to the grass strip steams as if alive as our eyes wander across the countryside in the sunlight. The head of the column has stopped and we close up. Figures are coming along the track in grey-green uniforms with camouflage nets over their helmets. At first we think they are Russians, but it is the Waffen-SS lieutenant with his men in their camouflage uniforms. He gives the direction for us to follow.

We set off again, and the Waffen-SS men disappear among the bushes on the chaussee. We come to a crossroads and cross a stream on a swaying footbridge. Some of the civilians go off to the right on their own towards a village that we can see in the distance. They are lucky as they are in civilian clothes and no one will stop them. We sit down beside the path and smoke. The path is very narrow, only wide enough for one man. The soil is heavy and damp, and steams gently in the morning sunshine. Some beetles are playing in the grass, and once a lizard looks out curiously from its hiding place and blinks at us. Then it rustles and vanishes. A colourful butterfly flutters by.

We go on again. The wood lies far behind us and what lies before us, we do not know. Suddenly whistles shrill and the sound is taken up on all sides, a trilling and whistling that assaults our ears. We look ahead and move on. A broad stream lies in front of the path with thick shrubs and swamp bushes, the ground wet and damp, and there are ashes, broken dishes, empty tins and other rubbish strewn among the bushes.[1] Right up ahead among the bushes one can see some dark vehicles that could be tanks. The whistling goes on and on, spreading wide across the country-side as if all Hell had broken loose. Many are calling for help, and there is a figure standing on a tank waving a white cloth to and fro. Shots ring out and splash into the small pools between the reeds and the wet, acidic meadows. We have disintegrated, with everyone running off in different directions. Nobody knows what is happening. The whistling and trilling does not stop. Shots whip past and now shells are falling in the area, sending fountains of water and muck into the air to rain down on us. They are still calling from the tanks, but we do not know what to make of it.

The major is running around in the bushes trying to restore some sort of order, but it is useless, that was the last blow. Everyone is now thinking for themselves and will only do what they think is right. A wounded man is wading through the water in the shelter of the bushes, and I have lain down on the ground, ignoring the storm around me, just looking at the sun. The paymaster comes back with a horrified face, having gone forward by mistake, and throws himself panting to the ground. He removes his cap to reveal a completely bald head. With the thick pouches under his eyes and his thick fingers, he is a typical example of an 'indispensible' who has sat out the war in barracks eating himself thick and fat off the land, and now, the first time that he finds himself in a mess, he has to do it in his pants.

Suddenly the Waffen-SS lieutenant reappears, looks at the paymaster and chases him forward with his pistol. For the very first time I share the same thoughts as a Waffen-SS officer. There is no one to be seen on the tanks any more, and the firing has died down. From somewhere come cries of 'Hurrah!' and then no more, but there is still that whistling in the distance that is driving us crazy. Figures near the tanks are waving long cloths and the first of our group have already reached them.

Some soldiers have helped themselves to the paymaster's rucksack and are passing round cigarettes and food. A bottle of schnapps makes the rounds, then is thrown in the water. We go back to the bridge. Individual soldiers are making their way across the fields to try and break through on their own. Shots come from up front again and there is some shouting.

I go past the swampy area on my right toward the west. A destroyed hutted camp with a high barbed wire fence, apparently a prisoner of war camp, lies in the fields, and scraps of paper and material litter the path. The wind is blowing the feathers from slashed feather bedding about through the air like little aircraft, and in the kitchen, a whole wall of which has been broken down, rubbish and excreta lie between the dirty cauldrons. A white towel hangs over the entrance gate, blowing in the wind.

Here and there a soldier emerges from the bushes and reeds and tags on. At last I draw level with the tanks that had been giving us such headaches. They are German, the tanks and vehicles that left us in the lurch yesterday. Now only three light and one heavy tank are sunk deep in the swamp, together with some trucks up to their axles in the mud. The tanks are full of wounded. The unwounded cleared off yesterday, leaving the wounded to their fate. There are also women in the tanks. One has been shot in the stomach but is still alive. A youngster from the flak has a big splinter in his arm and is groaning softly. A Luftwaffe clerk has several splinters in his leg. The shaft of his elegant boots is riddled through with splinters, and a dirty blue piece of flesh is showing through a hole in the sole of the boot. They had taken us for Russians and wanted to surrender. There are also some dead in the reeds who bled to death during the night.

A small crowd has formed round the tanks. The major says that we should attack the village on the road to the right and drive off the Russians, then we can march to the west and, once we have crossed the road and have the Russians behind us, we will have made it.

We move one by one across the fields towards the west, and a few of the lightly wounded join us from the tanks. Some farmers come out of a barn and look at us as if we were ghosts. One takes a spade, starts to dig and pulls out schnapps and wine that he had buried, pressing the bottles into our hands. We go out through the yard gate. On the right, not so far off, is the village. It should be Tremmen the major says, but the farmer says it is Päwesin. The whistling starts up again in the village and shots whip over the fields.

We gather on the chaussee, being perhaps one hundred men now. Even the prisoner with the Labour Serviceman is still there. Beyond the road the land sinks a little into woods several hundred metres away and we will have to thrust forward across the road towards the woods, then we will have crossed the enemy line and will get through alright, the major says. We load our weapons and I take my pistol in my hands. The major shouts 'Go!' and we thrust forward on a broad front across the road. We run over the field, heading for the woods as machine gun bursts whip out from the village and hit us in the flank. Suddenly fountains of steel and muck erupt and rain down on us and Russians can be seen coming from the village, also heading for the woods. The fountains from the artillery fire are increasing, and the machine gun bursts have found their first victims, people falling as if mown down. We turn round, give up and go back to the road.

Many dead are lying on the fine green field. The paymaster is in front of me. He suddenly throws up a hand, turns round and collapses on his back, dead.

We stop on the far side of the road, barely fifty of us now, flak auxiliaries, soldiers and a few civilians. Machine gun bursts are still whipping

225

across the field and shells are hitting the ground. We throw ourselves down in the roadside ditch and wait for what is to come. The sky has clouded over and a light rain has begun to fall. A farm close to the road is burning sky high from a direct hit and an excited horse races from it into the village. Suddenly a truck moves forward along the road with a machine gun mounted on its cab and saws through the silence with its bursts as we shoot madly at the engine to bring the vehicle to a halt. The enemy is firing at us from the ditches on both sides of the road. At last the truck stops and tries to reverse and disappear into the village, but stops again and also stops firing. Figures jump off into the roadside ditches and disappear in the direction of the village.

From somewhere comes the howling of a tank engine, like the roar of an aroused tiger. Then a tank slowly moves across the fields and rolls on to the road, its shells smashing into the trees. Now there is no stopping us, we all run off in different directions. I go through the farm, where a fence provides cover from view from the road, and hasten on down to the swamp, where the tank cannot follow. Shells strike in the hutted camp, sending bits of wood hurling high into the air. The shots howl into the swamp thickets, sending up fountains of water and mud. A Russian biplane streaks low overhead, the crew leaning wide over the side to look around, and I can see their big goggles. They swing round and come clattering over me again, but I do not bother to throw myself down, for it has all become so pointless.

My boots are sinking up to my ankles in the mire, the water spilling over the top. The swamp is like a maze of ponds and wet meadows, and a fine rain is falling from the sky, soaking me to the skin. The tanks are in front of me. The women and girls who came here with us this morning are sitting on the tanks looking into space, and shriek in unison when I suddenly step out from behind the bushes. A Waffen-SS man is apparently trying to get one of the trucks packed with wounded to go. We first have to unload it to push it on to firm ground. In the meantime still more have bled to death. The others sit on the tanks and trucks with blanched faces, already half gone, unconcerned with what is happening, but once the Waffen-SS man has refilled his truck with wounded laid any old how, they become more lively. We give the truck a push and it drives off towards the village with a white flag fluttering in front.

The women and girls disappear towards the farm to find civilian clothing and conceal themselves. I head off to the south. Right in front of me is a small strip of woodland that perhaps can shelter me until evening. A dead straight stream runs alongside the path and steel helmets, bits of equipment and broken weapons lie in the clear water. I throw my steel helmet in, causing a big splash in the water, put on my field cap and carry on.

The rain has eased off, and one can see some torn clouds of smoke rising

226

in the sky behind the reeds and bushes. The trilling and whistling is still continuing quite far off. There are some soldiers sitting on the path next to the stream up ahead among the trees, so I run up and sit down with them. The Labour Service man and his Russian are also there. There is a big farm in the wood with smoke coming from its chimney, but exactly how big it is cannot be determined, as the trees prevent a clear view, nor do we know whether it is occupied. A few men are coming towards us from the swamp, slowly and wide apart, and a Volkssturm man wearing a soldier's cap, on which four pips are shining, sits down beside us. Then come two policemen in green uniforms, a tall sergeant, whose steel helmet sits like a bag on his head, and a smaller one without any headdress. One by one come a civilian, the flak youngster with the smashed arm and the Luftwaffe clerk with the riddled foot. Then we get up and go on. We turn right and cross the stream. Some children are playing in the wood near the farm, a dog comes towards us barking and the children disappear into the farm. We approach cautiously. Then a woman comes out bringing us bread. She cuts off big slices and presses them into our hands and some girls appear with hot coffee that refreshes our frozen bodies.

The woman says that we will have to hurry, the Poles who used to work here are now with the Russians in the village and come back to sleep at night. In any case they are free from four o'clock and could easily be back within half an hour. The sun has come out again and we can see a village between the fields to the south of our position with figures going past the houses, but we cannot make out who they are. Once a rider gallops across fields and disappears between the houses. I dig into my pocket and pull out a cigarette.

The Volkssturm man with the silver pips hands out cigars with bands round them from a box that he has found somewhere and suddenly announces that he is now going to take over the command, as he has the highest rank and is the oldest among us. Those who want to go with him should say so, but in any case he requires absolute obedience and those who do not obey his orders will be shot. We laugh, but humour him. We get together and discuss the matter. Eight men decide to go with him, the flak youngster, the clerk, the two policemen, a civilian, two soldiers and myself.

The woman then tries to explain the situation as well as she can. She says that we will come to the road within several hundred metres. The village on the left is called Roskow, and south of there is Brandenburg on the Havel. If we head due west we will cross the road from Brandenburg to Rathenow between Plaue and Pritzerbe and eventually come to the Elbe. She says that the Russians have not pushed forward as far as there yet.[2]

We move on again, keeping close to the edge of the wood, where there are some slit trenches and slots for tanks. Weapons and pieces of equipment fill the trenches and in one of the foxholes are cuff-bands inscribed *Leibstandarte Adolf Hitler* and Waffen-SS collar patches.[3] We advance cautiously, for Russian armoured cars are flashing past on the road. Once a horse-drawn convoy goes past with the wheels rumbling loudly on the cobbles and the whinnying of the horse ringing out widely over the countryside. Women in brown uniforms and brightly coloured headscarves are sitting on the highly loaded wagons singing and chatting. A solitary Russian soldier rides behind the column with a submachine gun slung across his back. The wheels rumble into the distance taking their singing and laughing with them.

On the right a woman is digging in a garden. She stands there bent over and turns her back on us as we go past quietly, close to the road. On the left is a plantation with a camouflaged bunker next to the road. Two German soldiers who must have been dead for days are lying in a foxhole. Between the trees are some shot up cars from which everything removable has been stripped, an ambulance whose wheels have been removed is spattered with blood, and has a thick coating of blood on its floor. A completely smashed motorcycle lies between some bits of uniform and a dead man. Broken rifles, ammunition, egg hand grenades and steel helmets make a desolate picture. The broad band of the road goes ahead of us and there is no one to be seen. We run quickly across to the other side and drop into the ditch. There are thick bushes over the ditch to left and right whose branches form a tunnel. The bottom of the ditch is a little damp. Two soldiers are sitting up ahead on the sides waiting for nightfall.

We carry on, look carefully through the bushes and step out into the path. The countryside lies peaceful and quiet in the sun, and below in the village the railway lines that cut through the fields glisten, the fields and meadows laid out like a chessboard. We duck down and advance. Two men have stayed behind and two others have joined us. The Volkssturm man keeps urging us to go faster. My foot begins to hurt again. The wood starts about two thousand metres in front of us. We throw aside all caution and focus on our goal. Whenever a vehicle goes past on the road we throw ourselves down for a short while, and then immediately get up again. Then the path rises a little and we run over the railway line that cuts through the fields like a silver ribbon. We stop in some thick bushes and take a break.

The sun shines again over the world, which has put on its spring jewellery. No more shooting, no more dull thunder of a distant storm like we have heard for days vibrates in the air, no tacking of a machine gun, no clatter of an aircraft engine or roaring of a giant tank serve to remind one of war. The world lies at peace.

The flak youngster is beside me holding his arm and looking with lacklustre eyes into space. The pain that he must be suffering has drawn deep lines into his face, which no longer looks that of a child.

An enemy armoured car goes past on the road and we throw ourselves down on the edge of the path, pressing our heads into the ground. A cross path appears ahead of us, going in a wide curve over the fields to the right, and on the left it runs into the village. A thick hedge separates us from the fields that lead up to the woods.

We push through the hedge and go across the soft ground towards the point of the wood. It is no longer a walk, only a staggering along. The Volkssturm man is well in front with the policemen. Then they stop. The wood that will end the misery and stress, the fear and haste, lies within reach. We grit our teeth and hurry directly towards the wood that gets nearer with every step.

Suddenly shouts come from behind us. We turn round and see that they are Russians. We start to run across the field to the wood that means salvation to us. Suddenly shots ring out and plough into the field. The tall police sergeant hurries to the right and vanishes behind some bushes. We keep going, unable to grasp that it is all over now, that the dance of death of the last few days has all been futile – the pain, the hunger, the misery. Our lungs are panting. Then we stop and look back. I throw my pistol far away into the field, and soon they are standing in front of us. The flight has ended, the hunt is over. Then we turn back to the road.

I see the field in the sunshine as if through a veil. I see the spring. Somewhere a lark rises singing, but I do not see it. I am dead beat and empty. We have been through Hell. And the sun shines over the spring countryside as we go across the fields with pounding hearts, an aircraft engine in the distance sounding like a big bumble-bee. Everything was so pointless, the dead, the flowing blood, the horror.

We head for the chaussee, which runs like a light band across the fields and meadows, moving wide apart with sunken heads. I have fallen behind a little, as the pain in my foot has become unbearable. The Russians are walking scattered among us. We all have the same question inside us: 'What now? Will we be killed as we were told? Or do we have a short time before execution?' Suddenly one of the Russians stops and waits for me, as I am the last. 'This is the end!' I slowly go up to him. Then he takes my arm. I am afraid that he will take me aside somewhere where no one will see us, and put an end to me, but then I notice that he is supporting me, walking in step with me and guiding me. He gives me a cigarette and lights one for himself. 'War over! All go home!' he says to me. I am astonished. The immense tension of the last few days gives way inside me, and I am suddenly unable to hold back the tears, tears of relief that the enemy is human after all, and that I could ever have believed otherwise.

Then we are standing on the edge of the road. An officer makes us stand together and sorts out the wounded. The healthy ones walk off slowly while we sit on the roadside and wait for a truck to take us away as Russian supply convoys go past. I suddenly realise that I am saved now, that the time of misery and death lies behind us like a bad dream, and that the future, which had laid before me threatening and dark, has lost all its fears.

A truck stops at the roadside and some Russian soldiers help us to get into it. We are going to Brandenburg, to a hospital. Then we sit in the truck and look out at the countryside. The engine comes to life and we move off, driving into the unknown, but full of confidence. We are driving into a life that has been given back to us. The evening sunshine glows over the fields. It is over.

NOTES

1. This swampy area is known as 'Der Lötz'.
2. The farthest west line occupied by the 47th Army at this stage was based on the chain of lakes running north-east of Brandenburg toward Päwesin.
3. The *Leibstandarte Adolf Hitler*, Hitler's Waffen-SS Lifeguards, fielded a Panzergrenadier Division at the Front whose members rotated with the Berlin-based Regiment. The Division was in Hungary at this time but the Regiment had taken an active part in the defence of the city, particularly around the Reichs Chancellery, under which lay Hitler's Führerbunker. A tank company, however, fought in Wilmersdorf and, it would seem, had taken part in the breakout over the Spandau bridges and reached at least as far as here independently of the others.

Execution Place No. 5 – The Murellenschlucht

Senior Wehrmacht Officer
Spandau Garrison

AZ: 14p   Most Urgent!

Berlin-Spandau, 17 Feb 45

Re: Order passed today by telephone from Maj Fritze at Wehrmacht
     Kommandatura Berlin
Subject: Execution of death sentence at 1000 hrs on Sunday, 18 Feb 45
To: Gren.Rft.& Trg.Bn.67 via Gren.Rft.& Trg.Regt.523

   The flying court martial of the GOC Wehrkreis III[1] has today
apparently sentenced six soldiers to death by shooting.
   In accordance with the instruction to the Wehrmacht Garrison
Commander No. 391/44 (Secret) of 8 Nov 44, the battalion is tasked
with the conduct of the execution at the Execution Place in the
Murellenschlucht at 1000 hrs on 18 Feb 45.
   To this end the battalion will detail 1 officer in charge, a firing
squad of 1 NCO and 8 men, and 2 men to bind the condemned to the
stakes.
   The battalion will supply the coffins and receive the death certi-
ficates from the certifying officials at the execution.
   The bodies are to be taken immediately to the special cemetery at
the Hahneberg and be handed over individually with the death
certificates to the garrison commander's representative there.
   Report on completion to the garrison commander.

                                                         (Signed)

It was upon orders such as this that Altner's Grenadier Reinforcement &
Training Battalion 309 was tasked with carrying out executions.
   Retired Pastor Manfred Engelbrecht wrote:

231

From the daughter of the since deceased Pastor Joahnnes Theile, who lived in Staaken Parish and was responsible for the Military Prison[2], we have meanwhile learned that already in 1943 he had accompanied condemned officers and soldiers in the last hours before the execution of their death sentances in the Murellenschlucht in order to be close to them. They were condemned to death by 'proper' war courts martial. The Catholic priest came from Gatow and was called Jurytkow.

There were also those condemned in connection with the 20 July 1944 plot among them. Of the war sentences only one is known to us so far. That was the sentence to death of Lieutenant General Gustav Heisterberg von Zielberg. According to the report we have, only one, very thick, stake was used for the 1943/44 shootings.

Then, however, after 13 February 1945, the day that the court martial was empowered to give death sentences by hanging, three stakes were rammed in at the execution places for the condemned to be fastened to. Sometimes, it appears, they were escorted by a padre. The prisoners and their coffins were brought along in two vehicles.

We know of two eye witnesses who as recruits had to watch shootings after they had completed their rifle training. One of them has written us a report, and three others are known from their books describing the battle of Berlin.

In the meantime the present pastor of Staaken village church, Norbert Rauer, has found in a 'Provisional Register of Deaths' the names of twenty soldiers killed in the Murellenschlucht. On a list in the Wehrmacht Personnel Archives he found eighty-five names of persons executed by shooting who are buried at the special cemetery near Seeburg/Engelfelde, where they lie in five double rows. Eighty of these were shot in the Murellenschlucht. Likewise, in the period 15 February to 14 or 15 April 1945, 104 soldiers were shot there by German firing squads and buried at the 'In den Kisseln' cemetery in Spandau.

A stone identifies these dead in both Seeburg and Spandau. On the Seeburg stone it says: 'To the Anti-Fascist Resistance Fighters'. At 'In den Kisseln' 'To the Victims of Fascism'. In Seeburg there is no path in and no information and only a name on the fenced-in but maintained area between the fields. In the Spandau cemetery there are name tablets distributed among other dead, about whom one would also like to know to which shots they fell victim.[3]

The Charlottenburg Working Group that is seeking to have a memorial set up in the Murellenschluct to commemorate those executed there, have established that between January and April 1945 at least 235 Germans, soldiers, were executed there after being condemned by 'proper' courts martial.

NOTES

1. Wehrkreis III comprised the Berlin Military District.
2. The Spandau garrison prison which became Spandau Allied Prison from 1947 to 1988, when it was demolished after the death of Rudolf Hess.
3. The inscriptions reflect the different attitudes of the East Germans and the West Berliners before Unification.

APPENDIX II

The Underground Factory

The factory had been built as the result of a decision made by the Wehrmacht's Heereswaffenamt (Army Weapons Adminstration) back in 1938 to go in for the manufacture of Chlortrifloride for the recently discovered nerve-gas TABUN. Chlortrifloride, or N-Stuff, as it was called, is an aggressive, highly inflammable substance that needs very special handling. In order to remain perfectly dry, the factory needed a shell five metres thick to prevent any intrusion from the water table. It was envisaged that the whole production process would take place underground as far as loading the finished product in steel containers on railway wagons. However, it would take time to complete the construction of the bunker, for which it was stipulated that only German-born nationals could be employed, so some above-ground laboratories and plants were erected to enable the preliminary development of the manufacturing process from laboratory to factory-scale production. In fact the construction of the bunker was to take until 1943, a full five years to complete, one delaying factor being the difficulty of meeting the manpower requirements at the height of the war.

When Albert Speer became the Minister for Armaments and Munitions in 1943, he decided to implement the production of SARIN II, a later generation of nerve-gas, at the same site. The two products and those concerned with them were kept completely separate. A small satelite camp of the Sachsenhausen Concentration Camp was set up that year in the woods north of the site, but whether the inmates were employed in the construction of the SARIN II installations, or used in the assembly of V-Weapons in part of the underground factory remains uncertain.

Considerable effort was given by the Germans to camouflaging the site from aerial observation. Transportation was by a special narrow-gauge track connecting with the main lines at Briesen. These tracks followed the contour of a new concrete road through the forest built to detour local traffic away from the site and were countersunk in the road surface to conceal their profile. Production also required a heavy consumption of electrical power, and immediate post-war maps show a line of overhead pylons stopping abruptly a considerable distance from the site. This clue to something unusual in the vicinity that would merit such a supply was later removed. During the war the Germans continued to rely on camouflage for the protection of the site and no anti-aircraft guns were deployed that might have attracted attention to it.

The upper level of the five-storey factory was concealed under a natural hill in such a way that a railway line ran right through it in a tunnel. Three ventilation towers projected above the hill below the height of the tops of the trees that covered it.

During the brief period the factory was operational between October 1944 and February 1945 between twenty-two and thirty tons of Chlortrifloride were finally produced. By this time the site was under SS control and it seems that V-Weapons were also assembled here. When the Red Army established bridgeheads across the Oder river at the beginning of February 1945, production was hastily abandoned and the satellite concentration camp disbanded.

Clearly the factory and site would have been stripped by the Soviets of everything removable in 1945 as part of their reparations scheme. Having no further interest in the site at that time, the Soviets handed it back to the local authorities and it was not until the 1950s that the Soviet Army returned to establish a unit there that had regular contact with the local residents. In this connection, it is believed that the principal communications facility for the Headquarters of the Group of Soviet Forces in Germany at Zossen-Wunsdorf was moved here following the Anglo-American spy tunnel intercept from the south-east corner of the American Sector of Berlin being discovered in April 1956.

Then in the 1970s work was begun on converting the factory into the GSFG command bunker. One of the ventilation towers was filled with filters for use in case of a biological attack, when the other two could be cut off. The railway tunnel was blocked off at either end and airproof personnel entrances installed incorporating a series of three massive steel doors about a metre wide, two metres high and half a metre thick. Between these doors were built decontamination facilities overlooked by control cubicles, and a hospital installed close behind.

Down below the various production chambers were converted into the control bunker role with raised floors under the communications rooms allowing easy access for the technicians, a special wall-papered, self-contained suite for the C-in-C, and other facilities for the senior officers. The soldiers appear to have been allocated collapsible bunks hinged to the corridor walls denoted by painted numbers. The main operations room had a false ceiling reducing its orginal height.

From interpreters who took part, it is known that Warsaw Pact exercises were conducted here, and from 1988 onwards helicopters were heard landing at the site.

The Soviets left the original production structures alone, apart from two

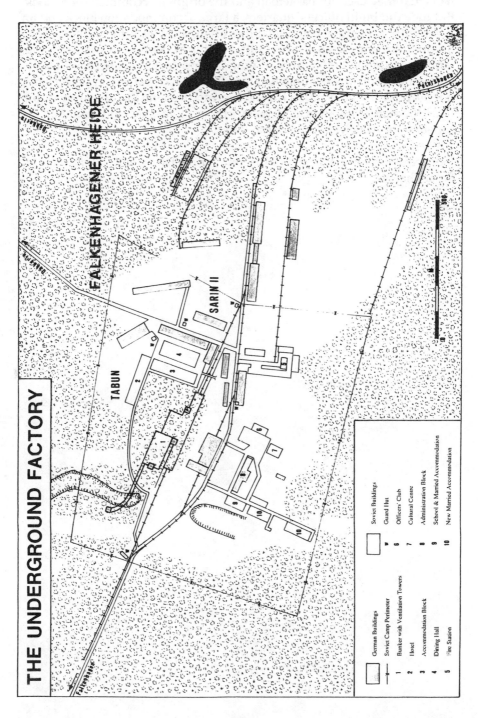

THE UNDERGROUND FACTORY

FALKENHAGENER HEIDE

TABUN

SARIN II

German Buildings
Soviet Camp Perimeter
1   Bunker with Ventilation Towers
2   Hotel
3   Accommodation Block
4   Dining Hall
5   Fire Station

Soviet Buildings
w   Guard Hut
6   Officers' Club
7   Cultural Centre
8   Administration Block
9   School & Married Accommodation
10   New Married Accommodation

halls that they used for basketball and the original accommodation block. But they did build officers' quarters, a large accommodation block and an hotel with a separate, communal mess hall, all within the outline of the original structures. They also built a cultural centre, an officers' club, family accommodation and a school, and even some new family accommodation blocks immediately before their departure in 1992. Had it not been for the Four plus Two Agreement, it seems that the army of the new Russian Federation had been prepared to stay and maintain its capacity for a nuclear or biological strike.

[Sources: Seelow Heights Museum and Dr Heini Hofmann of Falkenhagen]

APPENDIX III

The Situation in West Berlin – 27/28 April 1945

The Soviet advance through Siemensstadt by elements of the 2nd Guards Tank Army of the 1st Byelorussian Front and penetration as far as Ruhleben Racecourse had taken place on the 27th as described, but this involved a crossing of the inter-front boundary, and when Colonel Dragunsky's strongly reinforced 55th Guards Tank Brigade of the 1st Ukrainian Front advancing along the Reichsstrasse made contact that day, the former were obliged to withdraw back across the Spree again.

The attack on Ruhleben Barracks on the 28th was conducted by elements of Colonel Dragunsky's brigade, the main body of which had been ordered to launch an attack eastwards along Kantstrasse at dawn that day in support of Marshal Koniev's attempt with the 3rd Guards Tank Army to reach the Reichstag ahead of his rival, Marshal Zhukov. Colonel Dragunsky therefore decided to secure his rear with this attack on the Olympic Stadium, Reichssportfeld and Ruhleben positions by part of his force.

It was mid-morning when Koniev discovered that his route was already blocked by some of Zhukov's troops. He quit Berlin, leaving the 3rd Guards Tank Army to change course towards the Kurfürstendamm. Meanwhile Dragunsky's main force had become heavily involved in the area around Karl-August-Platz. Orders for them to return to a blocking position in the Westend took another day or so to implement, and then it seems they holed up in the barracks and tramsheds located off Königin-Elisabeth-Strasse in the Westend and let the battle finish without them.

BERLIN SURROUNDED

R Reichtag (Soviet goal)

F Führerbunker

✳ Flak-towers

Soviet moves and positions on 23 April

Soviet moves and positions on 28 April

55 Gds Tk Bde's operations

City boundary

5 Shock Army

MARZAHN

32 Corps

8 Gds Army & 1 Gds Tk Army

KÖPENICK

26 Gds Corps

9 Corps

Karlshorst

4 Gds Corps

29 Gds Corps

Adlershof

Grünau

Rudow

3 Shock Army

WEISSENSEE

Evening 21 April First Soviet troops Enter Berlin

26 Gds Corps

7 Corps

LICHTENBERG

TREPTOW

Britz

Buckow

12 Gds Corps

79 Corps

Niederschönhausen

PRENZLAUER BERG

HORST WESSEL

Friedrichshain

KREUZBERG

NEUKÖLLN

Evening 22 April Canal reached

Marienfelde

PANKOW

Humboldthain

MITTE

Evening 22 April Canal reached

9 Mech Corps

Mariendorf

3 Gds Tk Army

2 Gds Tk Army

1 Mech Corps

12 Gds Tk Corps

REINICKENDORF

Wittenau

R

TIERGARTEN

F

Moabit

SCHÖNEBERG

STEGLITZ

6 Gds Tk Corps

7 Gds Tk Corps

WEDDING

Zoo

Dahlem

ZEHLENDORF

Tegel

Siemensstadt

CHARLOTTENBURG

WILMERSDORF

Grunewald

Heiligensee

Ruhleben

GRUNEWALD FOREST

Night of 22/23 April. Havel crossed

47 Army

125 Corps

SPANDAU

Staaken

Gatow

Kladow

Wannsee

Henningsdorf

25 April Encirclement completed at Paretz

APPENDIX IV
The Hitler Youth in Combat

The Hitler Youth organisation under the leadership of Reichs Youth Leader Artur Axmann was actively engaged in combat operations in 1945. In an interview with Chronos-Film, Axmann stated:

The effects of the 20th July on the youth were such that seventy percent of the next age group [due for conscription] volunteered [for active service]...

The tank-crackers first came into play during the final weeks. This began at the time when the Russians stood on the East Prussian border. Besides the many combat roles, too numerous to go into detail about now, there was also the digging of trenches and anti-tank ditches on our borders. And once the Russians had penetrated our home territory, the crucial question was how to deal with the tanks that broke through.

My guide line for this was: first, the enemy is in our homeland; second, the Youth must be adequately trained in combatting tanks at close range; third, there must be no infantry commitment of the Youth. So in mid February the first close tank engagement unit of the Hitler Youth was established by my deputy and chief-of-staff, Helmut Möckel... The first close tank engagement brigade was nominally under me, but was actually led by Hitler Youth Leader Oberbannführer Kern. Such a close tank engagement unit was set up in every area against tanks that broke through, that is tanks that had broken through the lines of our fighting troops.

For me the most crucial question in the establishment of close tank engagement units was that of motivation. And here we have to put ourselves back to the time of the last weeks of the war. What did these close tank engagement units consist of?

They included many 16- and 17-year-olds who had not been absorbed by the emergency organisation of the army in the retreat from the east. There were also youngsters who had lost their parents in the flight through death, or had become separated from them in the

241

flight. A considerably large number of these eastern youngsters were in the close tank engagement units.

There were many youngsters who had been in the bombing attack on Dresden, and many who had experienced the rape of their mothers and sisters. So I can say that these youngsters were motivated. We did not have to motivate them.

And thus they fought very bravely and destroyed many tanks.

Armin Lehmann, who as a 16-year-old was a member of the Combat Team 'Gutschke' fighting near Frankfurt on the Oder, was sent to Berlin to attend Hitler's birthday parade in the Reichs Chancellery garden on 20 April, where he was awarded the Iron Cross Second Class for his earlier exploits with the unit when fighting near Breslau. After the parade Axmann retained him as one of his runners, in which capacity he remained until severely wounded in the breakout attempt from the city centre on 2 May. Until Axmann moved his headquarters from the Kaiserdamm to the Party Chancellery in Wilhelmstrasse on the night of 23/24 April, Lehmann was delivering despatches to Hitler Youth combat groups in Spandau (HJ-Kampfgruppe Heissmeyer), at the Pichelsdorf bridges over the Havel (HJ-Regiment), and at the Olympic Stadium to the 5,000-strong HJ-Kampfgruppe Hamann among others, including mixed Volkssturm/Hitler Youth units in various parts of the city. He also reports one Hitler Youth combat group in the Propaganda Ministry off Wilhelmstrasse. In all he reckons there must have been at least twenty Hitler Youth combat teams engaged in the city and elsewhere.

It seems that, because Lieutenant General Weidling had shown his opposition to using Hitler Youth units in combat, Axmann was bypassing the military command and issuing orders directly to these units either in his own name or Hitler's. On 26 April Hitler awarded Axmann the Golden Cross of the German Order in recognition of the role played by the Hitler Youth.

Only the month before, Axmann had exhorted the children of the Reich with:

> There is only victory or annihilation. Know no bounds in your love of your people; equally know no bounds in your hatred of the enemy. It is your duty to watch when others tire, to stand when others weaken. Your greatest honour is your unshakeable fidelity to Adolf Hitler.

Another prominent person to have exhorted the Hitler Youth was Carl Diem, the Secretary of the German Olympic Committee, who had staged the 1936 Games, ending the opening day with a dramatic presentation of heroic combat as an ideal of sacrifice for one's country. Then in February 1945 he addressed a mixed group of Hitler Youth and Volkssturm at the Reichs Sport School in a manner described by a witness as being similar to Goebbels' appeal for total war at the Sportpalast two years earlier.

Index